JEAN MACÉ

THÉÂTRE
DU
PETIT CHATEAU

J. HETZEL
LIBRAIRIE CLAYE
18 RUE JACOB

Eug. FROMENT.

The Gymnasium of the Imagination

A COLLECTION OF CHILDREN'S PLAYS IN ENGLISH, 1780–1860

Jonathan Levy

CONTRIBUTIONS IN DRAMA AND THEATRE STUDIES
NUMBER 40

GREENWOOD PRESS
New York • Westport, Connecticut • London

Library of Congress Cataloging-in-Publication Data

The Gymnasium of the Imagination : a collection of children's
  plays in English, 1780–1860 / [compiled by] Jonathan Levy.
      p.   cm. — (Contributions in drama and theatre studies,
  ISSN 0163-3821 ; no. 40)
    Includes bibliographical references (p.   ) and index.
    ISBN 0-313-26697-2 (alk. paper)
    1. English drama—19th century. 2. English drama—18th
  century. 3. Children's plays, English. I. Levy, Jonathan.
  II. Series.
  PR1271.G96 1992
  822.008'09282–dc20   91-16448

British Library Cataloguing in Publication Data is available.

Library of Congress Catalog Card Number: 91-16448
ISBN: 0-313-26697-2
ISSN: 0163-3821

First published in 1992

Greenwood Press, 88 Post Road West, Westport, CT 06881
An imprint of Greenwood Publishing Group, Inc.

Printed in the United States of America

The paper used in this book complies with the
Permanent Paper Standard issued by the National
Information Standards Organization (Z39.48–1984).

10 9 8 7 6 5 4 3 2 1

CONTENTS

PREFACE

Plays written for children between 1780 and 1860, the period this anthology covers, are now virtually unknown. The section on Children's Theatre in *The Reader's Encyclopedia of World Drama*, a standard reference work on the theatre, mentions *no* play for children written between *Jack Juggler* (1558) and *Peter Pan* (1903). Yet there was, in fact, a substantial body of plays for children written during that period, many of them by writers of note and some of them very good plays. As the general introduction to this book and the prefatory material to each play will suggest, a great deal of speculation took place then on how and why participation in live theatre could do children good, both as actors and as audience. These rationales, as well as the plays themselves, are worth serious reconsideration today.

The chief problem in putting together this anthology has been deciding what good plays to leave out. There are enough plays for children from this period to fill several anthologies. Given this embarrassment of riches, I asked several questions of the plays I chose to include in this book. They are, roughly in order of importance, as follows:

1. Is the play *as a play* still worth reading and perhaps producing?
2. Was the play important in its time, and/or did it have a significant influence?

3. Does the play so fully embody the style, technique, point of view, or sensibility of a certain kind of play that it can stand as a representative of a class?
4. Does the play give an especially vivid and particular picture of a certain time, place, or circumstance?

If I could answer "yes" to any of these questions, I considered including the play. If I could answer "yes" to more than one question, I did include the play.

In addition, I determined to include at least one play from each of the five major genres I describe in my introduction. But I must admit that, as will become increasingly clear to the reader who reads this anthology through, I am partial to plays of any genre that present scenes of vanished real life and am particularly attracted to dialogue that sounds like the real speech of boys and girls of a hundred and fifty or two hundred years ago.

In my biographical notes preceding each play, I have given more space to the less-known playwrights. In my critical notes, I have suggested what drew me to select the play.

Other anthologists may use other criteria. They might, for example, choose to collect exclusively American or English plays, as documents in the history of education in this or that country. Or they might choose to collect plays on a common theme — school life, for example — or plays that are adaptations of the same story, like *Beauty and the Beast*, either as a mirror of changing taste and sensibility or as a primer for playwrights. Of course, they also might choose plays by author or by genre. My point is that I hope this book will be the first of many, for the surface has barely been scratched.

I wish to express my thanks to the following people for the invaluable help they gave me in writing this book: Rose C. Brown; Deborah Brudno; Rodney Dennis; Kathleen Donovan; Claire Gabriel; Christlieb Haller, M.D.; Joseph Keller; Eloise Lawrence; Virginia Lawrence; George Medaus; Leslie Morris; Jeanne Newlin; Wendy Thomas; and Ellen Winner.

A NOTE ON THE TEXT

For the convenience of the reader, the format of the plays has been standardized as much as possible. However, the punctuation of the plays has been left as it was. Punctuation for a playwright can be what dynamic markings, particularly rests, can be for a composer: an indication to the play's performers of how the playwright hears the piece in his or her mind's ear. A playwright, like a composer, hears silences as well as sounds. Dialogue is a judicious combination of both, and creative punctuation is the only way a playwright has to indicate where the silences belong. Other typographical oddities, like italics or capitals in odd places, have been used by playwrights to indicate emphasis or volume. I have left all these as I found them in the original texts, on the assumption that the reader would welcome any hint as to how the playwrights heard their plays in their heads.

Charles Stearns, for example — Master of Arts and candidate for the presidency of Harvard — punctuates with dashes. His *Dramatic Dialogues* are as full of dashes as Jane Austen's letter. I have left them in place as the best clue to the modern reader as to what Stearns heard in his mind's ear. Stearns could, had he wanted to, have "corrected" his text when he came to print it. He chose not to, and so have I.

I have also retained the original stage directions, although they are occasionally typographically cumbersome and more than occasionally inappropriate for modern performance. I have done so first, because they indicate to the modern reader how authors imagined their plays and second, because they so often indicate vividly how the plays were performed in their own time.

I have dated each play with the date of its publication rather than the date of its composition. Because this is a collection of plays in English, I have dated the two foreign plays I include with the dates of their English translations. In both cases, this date is close enough to the date of original publication to maintain my chronology.

Whenever possible, I have used my own copy of the text. When I have not, I have found the best version I could and cited its source.

THE GYMNASIUM
OF THE
IMAGINATION

INTRODUCTION

Children have acted in England at least since the twelfth century and in English at least since the sixteenth. Originally, the actors were boy choristers in dramatic intervals in Church ritual. As these intervals developed into the Mystery and Miracle cycles, the choristers became actors. By the time the Mystery and Miracle cycles had run their course, professional companies of boy actors had been formed and, as we learn from *Hamlet*, became the fashion. Between 1558 and 1576, forty-six companies of boy actors performed at Court before Queen Elizabeth compared with thirty-two performances by men. Only after 1576, when James Burbage built his theatre, did companies of adults begin to achieve the same degree of public favor as companies of boys.

Plays were performed in schools in England very soon after there were schools. They were performed first at Winchester in the last third of the fifteenth century and soon after that at Eton and Westminster. A Shrewsbury school ordinance of 1577–78 decreed that "every Thursday the scholars of the highest form ... shall for exercise declaim and play one act of a comedy."[1] These comedies were in Latin, but the first regular comedies written in English, *Ralph Roister Doister* and *Gammer Gurton's Needle* (also sixteenth century) were performed first at Eton and Cambridge, respectively.[2]

The schoolboy actors who performed these plays were beautifully trained. Expert rhetoricians and musicians taught them, and the best writers of the day wrote for them. In fact, theatre was so central a part of education at the great schools that Ben Jonson was prompted to rail against schoolmasters "who make all their scholars play-boys."

Until the middle of the eighteenth century, theatre was a part of education only for boys. Then, from France, came "a species of dramatick composition hitherto unknown,"[3] which not only made theatre a part of the education of girls but also changed the nature and the premise of what theatre for children of both sexes was to be.

In 1779–80, the first of the four volumes of Mme de Genlis's *Théâtre à l'Usage des Jeunes Personnes* was published in Switzerland.[4] The plays in these four volumes, along with the plays of Mme de Genlis's fellow countryman and contemporary, Arnaud Berquin, had a deep influence on their contemporaries and perhaps an even deeper influence on the children's playwrights who followed them. For the plays were both novel and modern.

Nothing, of course, comes from nothing. French children had performed plays as part of their education ever since Mme de Maintenon produced plays, including Racine's *Athalie* and *Esther*, with her pupils at St. Cyr, and Mme Le Prince de Beaumont wrote dialogues for her pupils to recite.[5] But Mme de Genlis's plays were different from those of her predecessors. Because of the nature of the composition she undertook, she imposed constraints on herself that forced her to develop new strategies to make her plays both playable and interesting. These strategies became the basis of a new dramaturgy for playwriting for children.

Essentially, the premises of this new dramaturgy are threefold: first, that children's plays should be based not on the struggle between good and evil, but rather on the struggle between good and not-yet-good; second (a corollary), that in children's plays real evil will not be shown and that, when wickedness of any kind is shown, unless it is clearly reformed and repentant by the final curtain, it will be shown to be inept or else will be so outrageously overwritten as to be unbelievable; and third, that the sensibility that suffuses plays for children should be one of triumphant sweetness and light.

Mme de Genlis made her plan clear in the preface to the first volume of her plays. Her intention, she wrote, was to write plays that would be "moral treatises put into action." They would contain no intrigue or violent passions, no irreversibly wicked characters, and "no sentence which . . . should not be a precept."[6]

The novelty of this apparently simple plan is still striking. Since Aristotle, playwrights had depended on "intrigue" of one kind or another to advance plots. Even Diderot, whose plays those of Mme de Genlis resemble, took "intrigue" for granted,[7] for what kind of dramatic interest could exist without the conflict between good and evil, the struggle between powerful wills, or the exhibition of strong passions?

Mme de Genlis's answer was this: the dramatic interest aroused by plays of progressive understanding and/or redemption; plays whose moving force is gradual enlightenment, a moving toward the light, rather than contention. In this new kind of play, real evil need never be shown.

The principle that children should be kept in innocence, kept from the spectacle of real evil, is so modern as to seem self-evident. But it is not self-evident, and it was once the exception rather than the rule.

A hundred years before *The Theatre of Education* appeared, a poem frequently reprinted in English and American school books, *A Dialogue between Christ, Youth and the Devil*, had as its educational premise that the way to keep children from being bad is to terrify them into being good. Therefore, the more vividly horrific evil can be depicted, the more *present* it can be made to seem, the more effective the lesson. The poem concludes:

> Thus end the days of woeful youth,
> Who won't obey nor mind the truth

Nor hearken to what preachers say
But do their parents disobey.
They in their youth go down to hell,
Under eternal wrath to dwell.
Many don't live out half their days,
For cleaving unto sinful ways.[8]

Mme de Genlis's plays operate on an entirely different principle, the principle of empathy. She believed that instilling in her audience an aura of intense feeling, rising from a push toward goodness, would naturally "improve the heart and inculcate morals."[9]

Servants are traditionally dressed in the cast-off clothes of their masters, in knee-britches and wigs in the nineteenth century and in morning coats and wing collars in the twentieth. In much the same way, children are clothed in the discarded emotions of their elders. The sensibility of the eighteenth-century *comédie larmoyante* and the *drame bourgeois*, which, at its worst, degenerated into holy-card kitsch in the nineteenth century, is still very much with us in the twentieth. We exhibit it on stage for our children, when we would not for a moment think of sitting through it ourselves. It may therefore be damning Mme de Genlis's plays with faint praise to say that, in their palpable aura of good-will, their easy tears, their impulsive exchanges of fine sentiment bordering on (and sometimes crossing the border into) sentimentality, they are still very much with us. Yet, for good or ill, they are.

Mme de Genlis's plays became enormously popular in England. They were published and republished, translated and retranslated. They were played regularly in schools and in private homes and, according to Fanny Kemble, when played by young French emigrés, they "became the fashionable frenzy of the day."[10]

Mme de Genlis was widely imitated, first and most notably by Arnaud Berquin, who in turn was widely translated and imitated himself. Between them, de Genlis and Berquin, for good or ill, influenced most of the writers of plays for children in both England and America who followed them. Their plays became so well known as to become traditional. When Eliza Follen published her collection of *Home Dramas* in Boston in 1859, she inlcuded two of Berquin's plays, which, she wrote, "will, I think, be gladly welcomed for Auld Lang Syne, by the parents, and I hope by the children for ther own sake."[11]

Despite the popularity of de Genlis, Berquin, and other continental and English writers, there was a feeling in America that foreign plays simply did not sufficiently reflect American life, that they were not, in short, American enough. As the "American Lady" wrote in 1824 in the preface to *Evenings in New England*, a collection of stories and plays:

To write books for children, after Miss Edgeworth and Mrs. Barbauld have written, is indeed presumptuous. Excellent as those books are, they are emphatically *English*; and I indulged the hope that American scenes, and American characters, would give a delightful locality to the following stories.[12]

Very few of the American writers who wrote for children were professional playwrights. For the most part, they were either publishers of school texts, particularly texts of elocution and rhetoric, who could not find American plays to include in their texts or schoolmasters and mistresses who wanted American scenes, written in American English on American subjects, for their pupils to act. And so, slowly and haphazardly, from the end of the eighteenth century, a body of plays, playlets, and dialogues developed, written ad hoc by amateur playwrights, with no thought of professional production, much less of posterity, that document and reflect the daily life and language of ordinary Americans for three-quarters of a century, most particularly and perhaps most valuably reflecting the daily life and speech of American children.

In the same period, both in France and in England, a passion for amateur theatricals developed, and a body of plays written to be performed at home grew parallel to the body of plays written to be performed in school. Sometimes, such plays were quite elaborately rehearsed and mounted in private theatres. Sometimes, like the elaborate production of Mrs. Inchbald's *Lovers' Vows* described in *Mansfield Park*, they were performed by and for adults. Sometimes they were acted exclusively by children, either in plays like Anna Jameson's, written to order for particular children, or in adult plays adapted for children, like the *Othello* in French in which, at five, Anna Cora Mowatt made her stage debut.[13] But often and most naturally, the plays were performed by mixed casts of adults and children, with everyone old enough to stand still and speak included. Indeed, the fact that these Home Entertainments were occasions in which a whole family could participate was one of their greatest appeals. As an early American translator of Berquin wrote:

The parents, by performing a part in them, will enjoy the delightful satisfaction of participating in the gayety of their young family; and it may be considered a new band to unite them still more tenderly to each other, from an interchange of gratitude and pleasure.[14]

Arguably, the greatest writer of home entertainments was Maria Edgeworth, who originally wrote her *Little Plays* for her large family and tailored the roles she wrote for them to their talents. She wrote expansive, bravura parts for her extrovert father, small parts for small children, and walk-on (or carry-on) parts for children who could not yet speak. For herself she wrote comic turns: "Miss Edgeworth," she wrote, "as the Widow Ross, 'a cursed scold,' was quite at home."[15]

Plays written to be performed at home had several distinct advantages over plays written to be performed at school. The first was that they were less limited in the subjects they could treat. School plays tended to be about school subjects. The serious plays were often pseudoclassical dramas, patriotic tableaux, or plays with copybook morals so clearly pointed that no student or parent could miss them. The comedies were often watered-down versions of literary comedy, rustic turns, or skits about school itself. There are several exceptions — the *Dramatic Dialogues* of Charles Stearns is one — but, in general, home entertainments could simply be freer in their range of subject matter than school plays.

The second advantage was that school plays were more limited in their tone. Although some schoolmasters and mistresses gave their pupil-actors considerable latitude — a latitude the more remarkable compared with what is typically thought suitable for school today — there was nonetheless a *school tone*, a circumference of decorum, that was not to be stepped out of in a classroom, even though the classroom was for the moment being used as a theatre. Moreover, there was always the sense that the theatre that took place in school should be part of a school subject, a branch of Elocution or Rhetoric, and thus must not only *be* improving but also *feel* improving.

Third and last, there were in school built-in practical limitations that did not exist at home. Plays written for school usually had to be short enough to be done in one class period. They had to be rehearsed in time stolen from arithmetic or Latin composition. In single-sex schools, there was the vexing question of whether to limit the cast of plays to one sex or else to deal with boys in skirts or girls in beards.

Of course, home entertainments had their own drawbacks. They could be filled with private jokes, incomprehensible to anyone outside the family, much less to a general reader 200 years later. They could sometimes be carelessly made, depending on the goodwill of the partisan audience and on a complicity between family members on both sides of the footlights to exuse sloppy or self-indulgent dramaturgy.

Plays written for children to act, both at home and in school, were of many kinds. In fact, the only major genre that seems not to be represented is full-length tragedy. Nevertheless, the great majority of the plays seem to fall chiefly into five main categories: dramatic proverbs and other moral tales; history plays, including sacred history; sentimental comedies; fairy tales and Eastern tales; and familiar dialogues. Some writers, like Julia Corner, excelled in one genre — in her case, fairy tales — and for the most part stuck to it. Others, like Mme de Genlis, wrote in virtually every genre, including fairy tales, which she claimed to mistrust. Because the divisions among these five major genres are clear and because I have included at least one example of each genre in this anthology, it is perhaps useful to discuss each genre separately.

DRAMATIC PROVERBS

A dramatic proverb is a short play, usually in one act, in which the title is illustrated or proven by the plot. It was originally a French form that had its origin in the *jeu des proverbes*, a parlor game fashionable during the reign of Louis XIII, the point of which was to keep a conversation composed entirely of proverbs going as long as possible. The game was soon adapted for the amateur theatricals that became popular in the salons of the late seventeenth century.

Originally, these *proverbes dramatiques* took the form of loose scenarios, with the dialogue and the details of the plot left up to the actors. They were played like games of charades, with the audience invited to guess the proverb the play had illustrated. As the genre developed, it became more fixed in its form. Louis Carrogis, known as Carmontelle, developed the possibilities of the form; Théodore Leclercq embellished it; and Alfred de Musset perfected it, turning what began as a parlor game into high dramatic art.[16]

Although the *proverbe dramatique* began as an adult form, acted by adults for adults, it was soon seen to be a dramatic form easily adaptable for children, and from the end of the seventeenth century it was used as such. Mme de Maintenon wrote *proverbes* to be acted by her pupils at St. Cyr, as did Moissy, Garnier, and Mme de Laisse.[17] Mme de Genlis herself included several *proverbes dramatiques* in her *Théâtre d'Education*.

In the 25 years before the Revolution, the dramatic proverb flourished as a form for children. It flourished because it was seen to be potentially educational, and educational in several ways. First, dramatic proverbs did what all performing was thought to do for children: improve their memories, pronunciation, and carriage and give them a sense of self-possession. Second, dramatic proverbs taught manners and public behavior, as the title of Alexendre Moissy's 1769 collection of dramatic proverbs reflects: *Petits drames dialogués sur les proverbes propres à former les moeurs des enfants et des jeunes personnes.* They also, as Carmontelle observed, forced young people to observe other people and to get out of themselves.[18]

Of course, other forms of theatre for children did all this as well. What the dramatic proverb did uniquely was to focus on a single principle, expressed in an aphorism or a maxim, and to prove that principle *in action.*

As a cross between a *jeu d'esprit* and a syllogism, the *proverbe dramatique* was particularly suited to the French sensibility. As a Moral Tale on its feet, it was particularly suited to the English. Because the lesson the *proverbe* taught was clearly stated in its title and because a *proverbe dramatique* incorporated both the proof and the conclusion of a moral lesson, it gave parents and teachers an excuse to permit the children in their charge to enjoy the fun of the theatre under the unexceptionable guise of Moral Education.

Surely, no adult's mind was ever changed by a *proverbe dramatique,* nor could anyone expect that it would be. But children were different, or at least were thought to be different. Simple, memorable formulations of moral principles had been used in the moral education of children at least since Seneca,[19] because children, unlike adults, had had little experience of life that might contradict the lessons they were being taught. Acting a lesson, that is, *as if living it,* could only embed it more deeply.[20]

Whether this perception is true or not is still not clear. What is clear is that the belief that it was true freed the playwrights who wrote *proverbes* from the obligation of being moral and instructive scene by scene and line by line. The lesson of the play was taken care of by the form itself. The moral was in the plot, stated in the play's title and usually reiterated in the play's last line. Thus, the playwright was free to concentrate on letting as much real life into his play as he could. Indeed, the *realer* the action of the play was, the closer it came to the actual, recognizable life of the children on stage and in the audience, the closer it came (in Moissy's words) to "des choses qui les regardent, qui les amusent, and qui les intéressent,"[21] the deeper and more permanent the moral lesson of the play was thought likely to be.

The dramatic proverb influenced English and American playwrights for children deeply, although not all the writers it influenced wrote specifically in the form. Charles Stearns, for example, gave each of his dramatic dialogues a subtitle that, slightly rephrased, could have been the title of a dramatic proverb, for example, *The Wooden Boy: The Folly of Local Prejudice.* But several writers did write true dramatic proverbs. Anna Jameson, whose *Much Coin, Much Care* is included in this colleciton, did so, as did Henry Wadsworth Longfellow, who published a collection of dramatic proverbs for his students at Bowdoin. Longfellow's rationale for publishing his book is worth quoting in full.

The more I see the life of an instructer [*sic*] the more I wonder at the course generally pursued by teachers. They seem to forget, that the youthful mind is to be *interested* in order to be instructed: or at least they overlook the means, by which they may best lead on the mental faculties, at an age when amusement is a more powerful incitement than improvement. . . .The little collection of dramas, which I now proposed to publish, unites all the simplicity, and ease of conversation, with the interest of a short comedy, whose point turns on some humorous situation in com[m]on life, and whose plot illustrates some familiar proverb, which stands at its head by way of motto. . . . The work from which I make the selection is a collection of Dramatic Proverbs, or small plays, such as are performed in Paris by ladies and gentlemen in private society. The book is so exactly what we stand in need of, that I am only surprised that something of the kind has not appeared before.[22]

HISTORY PLAYS

History, if it is nothing else, is plots, as playwrights from Aeschylus on have known. A quarter of Shakespeare's plays are histories. History plays were a staple of the eighteenth and nineteenth centuries and were common well into the middle of the twentieth century. There are, today, fewer history plays on our stages than there have been in past times. Perhaps private lives have replaced our public lives as our central interest. Or perhaps, first because of newsreels and now because of television news, when we imagine history now we imagine it as film.

For whatever reason, the great history plays of the late twentieth century are yet to be written. When they are, they will almost certainly not be the neat textbook pageants or the great patriotic spectacles of the past. They are more likely to treat history reflectively, as an analogy, because history always offers us analogies to our present condition. And analogies, when we are allowed to draw them for ourselves, can be more powerful and more memorable than direct statements. The biggest mistake made by those who would use the theatre to teach is that they cannot resist drawing our morals for us. As Sir Walter Scott warned Maria Edgeworth, chiding her for her tendency to moralize openly, "The rats would not go into the trap if they could smell the hand of the rat-catcher."[23]

SACRED HISTORY

Biblical history draws its own morals. Gospel means "God's Word," and God's Word is meant to be spread. In times when most of the laity could not read, the Word had to be told and shown. Sermons could tell it and sacred pictures could show it, but only theatre could do both, and do both simultaneously.

Religious drama, in one form or another, has been a staple of the theatre in England since the Mystery and Miracle plays in the Middle Ages. It was, as Strindberg notes scathingly in the preface to *Miss Julie*, a Biblium Pauperum, a pauper's Bible. In 1805, a reviewer of the uninspired sacred dramas of John Collet, an imitator of Hannah More, suggested that religious plays be performed on the Sabbath, as the poor man's equivalent of sacred music.

Sacred dramas would be more useful for the amusement of the people on the sabbath-day, than sacred music is for that of the higher classes; and if there be no objection to the one, there surely can be none to the other. . . . Open a Sunday-theatre: a good Samson among the Philistines would be the best champion against the united calvinists: and the itinerants might preach about fire and brimstone to empty benches, while their former congregations crowded to see it raining down upon Sodom.[24]

The Jesuits had performed sacred drama in their schools since the sixteenth century. They extended it to include post-biblical religious history and certain subjects from secular history as well. Moreover, with their usual clarity, the Jesuits articulated their reasons for making the acting of history part of their students' curriculum. Acting taught Latin, it taught elocution, and it taught them "a genteel way of behaving, and carriage [which would] brake them of that bashfullness so natural to the English."[25] What is more, there was a chance that it might teach them heroism, or even virtue.

Perhaps one day, when they shall have grown up, these young people will be fired with the desire of equalling these virtues and will be, in their turn, ambitious for a good death. They would like perhaps actually to imitate those whose actions they represent to-day, and carry off similar victories.[26]

It was Hannah More who wrote the first sacred dramas exclusively for English children. Her *Sacred Dramas* were printed in 1782 and were widely performed and widely imitated in her own time and well into the following century. T. S. Eliot said that the Mass is the greatest show on earth. The sacred dramas written for children in England and America in the 75 years after the French Revolution are not that. They often seem stiff and lifeless today, like the libretti of Handel's sacred oratorios without the saving grace of the music. Nevertheless, even at their most awkward and most wooden, they are touching and have a certain dignity. For, like the Passion Play and the purimspiel, they are an expression of a deep desire: the desire to reenact our most central and essential history in order to transmit it to our young and, in the most vivid way possible beside actually reliving it, to repossess it ourselves.

SECULAR HISTORY

Plays about history, especially national history, have long been a staple of school theatre for at least two reasons: they teach facts and they arouse patriotism. They are also the only genre of school play with the exception of sacred history that is a natural outgrowth of, and hence a natural adjunct to, a school subject. As Barbara Hofland (Wreaks) Hoole wrote in 1810, in the preface to her *Little Dramas for Young People*, taken from subjects in English history:

The little dramatic sketches of history now offered to the rising generation were written for the use of a seminary of young ladies, many of whom were particularly desirous of impressing on their minds the leading facts of English history; and the writer, anxious to facilitate their progress, conceiving that a series of little tragedies, taken from such periods of time as appeared most likely to link by association the most intersting characters and incidents of our history, might conduce to this end, as calculated to awaken reflection and invigorate memory, she devoted the leisure of a vacation to these imperfect (but she trusts not useless or improper) compositions.[27]

First in England and later, enthusiastically, in America, plays on subjects of national history were written and performed extensively. Indeed, there is a certain kind of history play that has come to be the paradigm of the bad school play, for history plays have their own pieties. Still, the pieties are different from those of plays based on sacred history.

Plays on secular history are not obliged to retain the same quality of hushed sanctity that plays on sacred history do. They can be rousing. They can be partisan. They can be funny. The playwright may, if he likes, add characters and change the language. He can even improve the plot. Hannah More said that, when she came to write her sacred dramas, she felt she stood on holy ground. Writers of plays based on secular history felt under no such contraint. Although they might for pedagogic purposes adhere strictly to historical truth (as Mrs. Hoole did "except in the use of a little music"), they could also take liberties and often did, usually in favor of the playwright's native land.

Finally, a playwright could use a historical subject to make a contemporary point or as a point of departure for political satire. This is apparently what R. S. Storrs did in 1806 in *A Dialogue, exhibiting some of the principles and practical consequences of Modern Infidelity.* As he notes in his straight-faced introductory note:

The public are now presented with the Dialogue that was prepared for the Exhibition in Clinton Academy, on the 2d day of April. My object in selecting it was solely to expose the folly and immoral tendency of modern Infidelity. It has, by some, been supposed to implicate the character of Mr. Jefferson — I can only observe, that I myself had no such apprehension; and whether it does or does not, I leave to the decision of a candid public.[28]

SENTIMENTAL COMEDY

SENSIBI'LITY, sèn-sè-bil-è-tè. n.s. [*sensibilité*, Fr.]
2 Quickness of perception; delicacy.
  Modesty is a kind of quick and delicate feeling in the soul; it
  is such an exquisite *sensibility*, as warns a woman to shun
  the first appearance of every thing hurtful.   *Addison.*
                                    Johnson's *Dictionary*, 1755

Sweet Sensibility! thou soothing pow'r
Who shedd'st thy blessing on the natal hour,
Like fairy favors! Art can never seize,
Nor Affectation catch thy pow'r to please:
Thy subtile essence still eludes the chains
Of Definition, and defeats her pains.
                            Hannah More, *Sensibility*, 1782

Northrop Frye has called the last half of the eighteenth
century "The Age of Sensiibility" to distinguish it, on the one
hand, from "the reptilian Classicism" of the first half of
that century, "all cold and dry reason," and, on the other,
from the "mammalian Romanticism" of the early nineteenth century, "all warm and wet feeling."[29] In the theatre,
sensibility found its form in a new genre, originally imported
from France, that was neither comedy nor tragedy, but
a blending of both, suffused with a "conscious and almost
stylized   sentimentality."[30] This form, called *comédie
larmoyante* in France, became known in England as sentimental
comedy.

The origin, nature, and progress of sentimental comedy in
the adult theatre has been documented and discussed at
length, particularly as a theatrical form that reflected the
values and interests of an increasingly powerful middle class.[31]
What has not been sufficiently considered is why this new form
soon came to be considered the ideal theatrical form for
children, so much so that it is still clearly recognizable in much
of the theatre and most of the television made for children
today.

One possibility is this: that the idea of what theatre might be and the idea of what a child was were both changing and, in sentimental comedy, the two new ideas coalesced.

By the last third of the eighteenth century, children were no longer seen as "diminutive adult[s], passive and unremarkable" but as representatives "not figuratively, but in flesh and blood [of] man's potential for immediate and future freedom and fulfillment."[32] They were now thought to be innately good and, given instruction and guidance, perfectible. Alongside this belief in the perfectibility of the human spirit grew a sense of pleasure in the observation of the human spirit perfecting itself.

At the same time, the theatre was coming to be seen as a place of education and instruction for human faculties that could not be so well educated and instructed elsewhere, as a kind of School for Feeling. As Sydney Smith wrote, "Where is every feeling more roused in favour of virtue than at a good play? Where is goodness so feelingly, so enthusiastically learnt? What is so solemn as to see the excellent passions of the human heart called forth by a great actor, animated by a great poet?"[33]

Sensibility, the new form of feeling, was the last ingredient in the formula. It was the reagent that would, in the presence of the representation of strong human emotion, make the heart malleable enough to be shaped and changed.

With the advent of sentimental comedy, the theatre changed. It changed in the nature of the subjects it treated, and it changed in the kind and the degree of emotion these subjects were calculated to arouse.

The subjects of this new middle-class genre were middle-class subjects. No longer were they the traditional subjects of tragedy — "sad stories of the death of kings" — or the traditional subjects of comedy — folly, vice, and sin — but incidents from domestic life and the difficulties encountered by the *sensible* human heart. Nor were these subjects intended to arouse feelings of terror and awe, which tragedy traditionally did, or the *saeva indignatio* and the curative laughter, which classical comedy did. They were, instead, intended to arouse blander and shallower emotions: benevolence, which would lead naturally to beneficence, and sympathy, or fellow-feeling, which would lead, through the development of a good heart, to charity.

This was real education, the education of the heart, which should not be denied children. How much more might the heart be educated, if the children not only witnessed but acted in the plays? Could it not be supposed that children who acted "a few domestic scenes, calculated to shew, the happy effects of filial affection, sweetness of temper, and steadiness of mind"[34] might not, in life, become better sons and daughters?

This new "theatre of education" demanded a new kind of play, and the new kind of play demanded a new dramaturgy. Mme de Genlis's questions were raised again. In "plays without intrigue," without strong conflict, and without the depiction of real evil, what would keep an audience in its seats?

In sentimental comedy, as adapted for children, what keeps the audience in its seats is a finely manipulated flush of fellow-feeling that replaces plot suspense as the mainspring of the dramaturgy. In the new genre, the interst lies not in uncertainty but in certainty: in seeing the predictable happen, the scales fall from the imperfect characters' eyes, and the lesson learned. Northrop Frye says that Samuel Richardson in his novels doesn't cast the suspense forward but "keeps the emotion in the continual present."[35] Writers of sentimental comedies for children did the same, rarely providing a climax, much less a catharsis, but keeping the audiences' emotions always gratifyingly warmed, between simmer and low boil.

A strong residuum of sentimental comedy is very much with us today. Even if we no longer recognize the peripheral conventions of the genre in the eighteenth century, we do recognize its center: the kind of subject it treated, the manner in which it treated its subjects, and, perhaps most clearly of all, its subtext: the asumptions about what children are, how they are to be addressed and treated, and what art — particularly theatrical art — can do for them.

Sentimental comedy is with us in even deeper ways. Its subjects, lit by our modern version of Sensibility, have become what we mean by "human interest," which, astonishingly, seems to be found not in the world-shaking headlines but in the Family Section: the lost puppy found or the paralyzed orphan taking her first step.

This displacement of strong, overpowering emotions with smaller, more mangeable ones can, I think, be traced back directly to the Age of Sensibility. The expectation of an uplifting outcome — the puppy is found, the orphan does walk — can be traced directly to the art of that age, particularly the theatre and fiction, which soon became the standard theatre and fiction for children, who took it without irony.

In this instance, at any rate, the child was father to the man. And his patrimony was the benevolent smile, the easy tear, and, perhaps most perniciously, the debasing idea of Cute.

FAIRY TALES AND EASTERN TALES

"I will give my children neither fairy tales nor the Arabian Nights."

Mme de Genlis, 1783, *Adèle et Théodore*[36]

Fairy tales and Eastern (or Arabian) tales have some of their origins in common. They have often been linked and sometimes been confused, for there is indeed considerable overlapping beween them. On the page, and even more on the stage, they share common attributes — magic, improbablity, and otherness. Nevertheless, at their heart, they are entirely different forms.

Fairy tales are, at their essence, a much more austere form than Eastern tales. Eastern tales could be, and often were, used as lightly veiled parables to illuminate the state of England. But fairy tales are much less easily bent to didactic ends. They are powerful mythic stories, refined to their core by years of anonymous telling. Any change in their basic structure weakens their tensile strength. Any moral tacked on to them is bound to seem trivial, as would a moral tagged on to any archetypal story, because no moral is capable of summing up the whole meaning of the original. Fairy tales are, moreover, predicated on pre-Christian, non-Christian magic. Writers as different as Locke and Rousseau disapproved of them. At their best, fairy tales are at once irreducible pagan myth and pure imagination. On both these counts they are deeply suspect.[37]

Historically, fairy tales have been denounced as either dangerous or trivial or sometimes, bizarrely, as both. On stage, they have been crossbred and domesticated, in England most familiarly in Pantomime, which diminishes them by transformations, crosscutting their mysteries with comic English stage business.[38]

But a fairy tale is always diminished when it is staged. Despite the charms of *féerie*, no lighting, no costumes, no sets, no music, no ballet and, particularly, no stage effects can compare in power to the vision of the original imagined in the mind.

Eastern tales on the other hand, were fun, lavish, and exotic. Moreover, when they were done by or for children, they could be quite easily adapted to uplift.

Eastern Tales

The earliest Eastern, or Arabian, tales date from approximately the eighth century. They were, according to Darton, "already present in some sort in Aesop and to a less extent in details of the Romances and the Gesta Romanorum — even in Chaucer's Squire's Tale."[39] They were published in France by Antoine Galland between 1704 and 1717 and in England almost immediately afterward and very quickly became immensely popular in all of Western Europe. The East was the other side of the world, the antipodes to Paris and London. It was a locus in which philosophers could speculate on what was common to human nature. When one of *them* came here, it could be an occasion for self-criticism, seeing ourselves afresh through new eyes. And when one of *us* went there, it could be an occasion for unflattering comparison betwen the customs and character of the visitor and those of the indigenous people.

The East was essentially an imaginary place but, unlike other imaginary places that were the destinations of other imaginary voyages — Swift's Laputa or Cyrano's Land of the Moon — it was already well furnished with manners, customs, decor, and plots. And of course, it was a designer's dream.

Fairy Tales

Madame d'Aulnoy published her *contes des fées* in 1698. They were translated into English the year afterward. Perrault published his *Histoires ou contes du temps passé* in 1696–97, some of which appeared in bilingual editions in England and America almost immediately. A collection of Perrault's stories appeared in England, in English, in 1729. Mlle de la Force, Mme de Murat, and the Chevalier de Mailly also published stories, and in 1768 Newbery reissued Perrault's *Contes.* So, although the Grimm brothers did not publish their *Tales* until 1815, and Hans Christian Andersen did not publish his until 1835, playwrights from the eighteenth century on had a great variety of fairy tales to dramatize.

Mme de Beaumont published a version of *Beauty and the Beast.* But perhaps the greatest writer of fairy tale plays of the period was the Venetian Carlo Gozzi, who, as a challenge to Goldoni, dramatized ten *fiabe da putei* — "tales for little children" — including King Stag and Turandot, and for a time did actually drive Goldoni's realistic comedies off the stage with them.

By the late eighteenth century, fairy tales had become subjects for Christmas pantomimes in England. They were regularly adapted for the stage, often with music and ballet, all through the nineteenth century. In America, as early as 1807, *Cinderella, or the little glass slipper, a Grand Allegorical Spectacle,* was performed in Philadelphia. But the doyenne of the fairy tale on stage was an English woman of the mid-nineteenth century, "the ingenious Mrs. Julia Corner," whose ten fairy tale plays charmed audiences of the time and can still charm them today.

FAMILIAR DIALOGUES

Nothing tends more to make good readers and speakers, than the reading or speaking of familiar Dialogues; for these are generally well understood by the young, and inflections of the voice are more frequently required, and more naturally made, than in other lessons.

William Fowle, *Familiar Dialogues*, [3]–4.

Fowle meant by a "familiar dialogue" a short scene taken from ordinary life, written in colloquial speech, and playable by children. His six collections of dialogues include scenes about home and scenes about school, scenes between parents and children, scenes between teachers and pupils, boys and boys, girls and girls, and a very few scenes between boys and girls. The subjects of these scenes are generally small, domestic, and topical: "familiar" in the etymological sense of having to do with family matters. Fowle collected and wrote his dialogues for his own pupils at the Boys' Monitorial School in Boston, "to supply a great defect in our school books, and to relieve the tediousness of school exhibitions."[40] He hoped that, in time, they would be performed at home as well as in school. They were for him an extension of his schooolmaster's work, a kind of journalism rather than a branch of literature, written on the spot for particular occasions, with the sound of his pupil-actors' voices in his mind's ear. By so doing, he managed to present, unselfconsciously and unintentionally, some of the most vivid vignettes of American children's life in our dramatic literature.

The familiar dialogues are the descendants and the cousins of several forms and trends, theatrical, educational, and social. They are, first, the grandchildren of the purely didactic school dialogue, the prototype of which is the catechism, in which the matter of a lesson is divided for pedagogic reasons between or among different speakers. They are, second, children of the *drame bourgeois*, which took ordinary domestic life seriously enough to put it on stage. They are, third, cousins to home entertainments, which relaxed the formalities of the theatre and which often included children. They were, finally, the godchildren of a new interest in, and a new ear for, actual human speech, including the speech of children. This last connection deserves a separate word.

Sometime in the last quarter of the eighteenth century, writers began to listen to and try to reproduce the way ordinary people spoke. Of course, good writers always had. But in the last quarter of the eighteenth century, writers began to perceive "common" speech not merely as curious, comical, or indicative but as expressive in ways that standard speech was not, and therefore valuable. A similar value was beginning to be found in other non-standard English as well: in Scots and Scottish English, by Sir Walter Scott and Robert Burns, and in Irish English by Tom Moore.

Wordsworth has traditionally been given a lion's share of the credit for the introduction of common speech into literary English. In the celebrated Advertisement to the *Lyrical Ballads* of 1798, he wrote:

The majority of the following poems are to be considered as experiments. They were written chiefly with a view to ascertain how far the language of conversation in the middle and lower classes of society is adapted to the purposes of poetic pleasure. [Some may think] the author has sometimes descended too low, and that many of his expressions are too familiar, and not of sufficient dignity.[41]

In *Lyrical Ballads*, mixed in with the language of adults of the middle and lower classes, is occasionally found the language of a child. The most famous and memorable occurrence is surely the speech of the eight-year-old cottage girl quizzed by the benign blockhead in "We Are Seven." She says:

> "The first that died was sister Jane;
> "In bed she moaning lay,

"Till God released her of her pain;
"And then she went away.

"So in the church-yard she was laid,
"And when the grass was dry,
"Together round her grave we played,
"My brother John and I.

"And when the ground was white with snow,
"And I could run and slide,
"My brother John was forced to go,
"And he lies by her side.

And her inquisitor asks again:

"How many are you then," said I,
"If they two are in heaven?"
The little Maiden did reply
"O Master! we are seven."

"But they are dead; those two are dead!
"Their spirits are in heaven!"
Twas throwing words away; for still
The little Maid would have her will,
And say, "Nay, we are seven!"

Wordsworth thought that some readers might find that
"wishing to avoid the prevalent fault of the day, the author
has sometime descended too low, and that many of his expressions are too familiar." "Low and familiar" this speech may be,
but it is not the speech of a real child. It is *faux-naif* rather
than simple, despite the monosyllables, and its inversions (e.g.,
"moaning lay") are "poetical" in the most old-fashioned
way.[42]
     Wordsworth's stated object was to try to turn common speech
into poetry. But when common speech is fitted into poetic form,
it sometimes ceases to be common speech without managing to
become poetry, which is the case here. The language is not
popular merely because it is fitted into the poetic form
traditionally associated with popular diction, the alternating

three-four ballad stanza, and it is not childlike merely because it is mostly monosyllables.

Admittedly, the problem Wordsworth set himself — to make poetry out of the language of children — was an extremely difficult one, one which no one, except perhaps Blake, successfully solved. But Wordsworth's problem was, I think, compounded by his idealization of Childhood and The Child, which made it difficult for him to draw children as they really were.

Humbler writers came closer to the truth. Charles Stearns's farmhands, William Fowle's schoolboys, and Eliza Follen's brats are all recognizable children, in their speech as well as in their actions. And the child's voice in this anonymous 1841 dialogue, on a subject close to Wordsworth's, rings truer than Wordsworth's.

Charles. Mother, may I play with the baby a little while before I go to school?

Mother. She is asleep now, my son; but you may go softly and look at her.

Charles. She is just going to wake up, mother! She is smiling and moving her little hands.

Mother. No, she is only dreaming; don't hold the curtain back so far, the sun shines on her face.

Charles. I wonder what she is dreaming about; she looks very sober now; what a pity she can't tell us when she wakes! Mother, I shall be glad when Susan grows a little bigger, and can run about, and talk, and play with me; I don't think a little baby is good for much.

Mother. And what if she should never wake up, Charles?[43]

Useful as this division by genres may be for academic purposes, the last thing that must be said on the subject is that none of the genres is sacrosanct. School plays were done at home. Home entertainments were done in schools. Some Eastern tales are also history plays. Some dramatic proverbs are fairy tales. And most of the plays are, in some way or another, whatever else they may be, Moral Tales.

In addition, the canon can never be complete. Many of these plays and entertainments were never written down. Many, perhaps most, of those that were written down were never printed. School plays and home entertainments were most often private and informal events, not entered into any public record any more than large dinner parties or balls were.

It is perhaps because of this fact that the body of plays we have is of such great interest, an interest which often transcends their purely dramatic merit. Archeologists say that it is frequently not the ruins of great public structures that give us the clearest insight into the civilizations they are excavating, but rather the scrap heaps and dumps, where objects and artifacts too common to be noted were discarded. It is from these, they say, that we can often get the clearest picture of what daily life was like for ordinary people.

To a great degree, the same is true of plays for children written in this period. It is particularly true of the familiar dialogues in which playwrights who did not think of themselves as playwrights set down, in haste and with no thought of posterity, images from the daily lives of children. Unlike images in fiction, these images are recorded *without comment*, without the novelist's explanation of a scene or a motivation, and with no more editorializing than is posible in a short stage direction.

All the plays in this collection are, I believe, interesting for their historical importance or for their literary and theatrical merit or for both. But some are doubly interesting because they are additionally the closest thing we have to candid snapshots of the real lives of children from the end of the eighteenth century to the middle of the nineteenth: vivid images that speak eloquently for themselves.

NOTES

1. Quoted in *The Oxford Companion to the Theatre,* ed. Phyllis Hartnoll, 3rd ed. (London: Oxford University Press, 1967).

2. Other systems of education, most notably the Jesuit, made the regular performance of plays by students a central part of their curricula very early. The practice and its rationale are excellently discussed in William McCabe, *An Introduction to Jesuit Theater* (St. Louis: Institute of Jesuit Sources, 1983). For examples of plays presented in Jesuit schools, see *Jesuit Theater Englished: Five Tragedies of Joseph Simons,* ed. Louis J. Oldani, S.J., and Philip C. Fischer, S.J. (St. Louis: Institute of Jesuit Sources, 1989).

3. *The Theatre of Education. A New Translation from the French of Madame la Marquise de Sillery, late Madame la Comtesse de Genlis* (London: J. Walter, 1787), vi.

4. The first *Theatre of Education* in English (London: T. Cadell and P. Elmsley, 1781) combined Mme de Genlis's *Théâtre à l'Usage des Jeunes Personnes,* her *Théâtre de Societé,* and her *Drames Sacrés.*

5. See James Herbert Davis, Jr., *The Happy Island: Images of Childhood in the Eighteenth-Century French Théâtre d'Education* (New York: Peter Lang, 1987), chapter 10, for background. By her own report, Mme de Genlis had had as a girl quite an extensive, if haphazard, theatrical education. She read the plays of Mary Anne Barbier and began to compose comedies at eight, wrote Dialogues of the Dead in imitation of Fontenelle, and acted in a wide variety of plays. Cf. *Memoirs of the Countess de Genlis, illustrative of the History of the Eighteenth and Nineteenth Centuries. Written by Herself,* 8 vols. (London: Henry Colburn, 1825), vol. 1, especially 238 ff.

6. The stricture against raising strong passions in young people, particularly girls, through acting is further articulated by Anna Barbauld. She wrote:

> "To wake the soul by tender strokes of art
> To raise the genius, and to mend the heart" —
> Hold, hold! that's not my cue, we've no intention
> By "tender strokes" to sharpen girls' invention:
> The soul will waken time enough, ne'er fear;
> No lines shall rouse the slumbering passions here.

"Prologue to a Drama," *The Works of Anna Laetitia Barbauld, With a Memoir by Lucy Aikin*. 2 vols. (London: Longman, Hurst, Rees, Orme, Brown, and Green, 1825), vol. 1, 298. Mme de Genlis further limited herself by writing one volume of plays exculsively for the "children of shopkeepers and mechanics; [though] people of even lower rank, may find useful instruction in it." *Theatre of Education, Translated from the French of the Countess de Genlis*, 4 vols. (London: T. Cadell, P. Elmsly and T. Durham, 1781), vol. 4, ii.

7.   "Occasionally I imagine that the theatre will be a place where the most important moral problems will be discussed without interfering with the swift and violent action of the play. How to go about it?" Denis Diderot, quoted in *European Theories of the Drama with a Supplement on the American Drama*, ed. Barrett Clark, revised by Henry Popkin (New York: Crown Publishers, 1965), 241.

8.   *The New-England Primer improved for the more easy attaining of true reading of English. To which is added the Assembly and Mr. Cotton Mather's Catechism* (Boston: Edward Draper, 1777). These sentiments echo those of a sixteenth-century dialogue called *The Interlude of Youth* (1557), which is a kind of *Everyman* for the young.

9.   The Translator ("A Friend to Youth"), *Juvenile Theatre. Containing the Best Dramatic Productions of the Celebrated Madam de Genlis* (New York: Printed for the Translator, by D. and C. Bruce, 1807), Preface, iv.

10.   Frances Ann Kemble, *Records of a Girlhood*, 2 vols. (New York: Henry Holt and Company, 1878), vol. 1, 2–3. For a record of translations and reprintings of de Genlis's works, see Jonathan Levy and Martha Mahard, "Preliminary Checklist of Early Printed Children's Plays in English, 1780–1855," in *Performing Arts Resources*, ed. Barbara Naomi Cohen-Stratyner (New York: Theatre Library Association, 1987), vol. 12, 1–97, 50–56. For a record of reprintings of Berquin's work, ibid., 30–36. Eliza Follen, *Home Dramas for Young People* (Boston and Cambridge: James Monroe and Company, 1859), Preface, p. [iv].

11.   Eliza Follen, *Home Dramas*, Preface, p. [iv].

12.   *Evenings in New England, Intended for Juvenile Amusement and Instruction. By an American Lady* (Boston: Cummings, Hilliard and Co., 1824), iii.

13.   Anna Cora Mowatt, *Autobiography of an Actress: or, Eight Years on the Stage* (Boston: Ticknor, Reed, and Fields, 1854), 21.

14. Arnaud Berquin, *The Children's Friend* (Newburyport, [1794]), iv.

15. Augustus J. C. Hare, ed. *The Life and Letters of Maria Edgeworth* (Boston and New York: Houghton Mifflin Company, n.d.), 159.

16. "[T]hese distinguished amateurs ... affected a species of drama invented for their purposes by Carmontelle, the *proverbe*. Here, under the veil of illustrating some familiar apothegm, such as 'Petit pluie abat grand vent,' a scandal of the day was related in more or less piquant dialogue, and little or nothing beyond clearness of elocution and ease of deportment was needed to carry the players through their ordeal. . . . 'In brief,' says Fleury, 'this passion for private theatricals was a serious misfortune to the Comédie Française. Our boxes were empty; the boxes of the amateur theatres were nightly crowded with the rank and fashion of Paris.'" Frederick Hawkins, *The French Stage in the Eighteenth Century*, 2 vols. (London: Chapman and Hall, 1888), vol. 2, 260.

17. For a fuller discussion, see Clarence Brenner, *L e Développment du Proverbe Dramatique en France et sa Vogue au XVIIIe Siècle avec un Proverbe Inédit de Carmontelle* (Berkeley: University of California Press, 1937) and Davis, *Happy Island Images*, especially pp. [9]–16.

18. "En jouant des proverbes on est occupé de rendre exactement le personnage que l'on doit représenter: quand on a trouvé qu'il ressemblait à quelqu'un de sa connaissance, on l'a observé davantage; cela accoutume à devenire spectateur dans le monde, et de sortir de soi-même." Carmontelle, *Théâtre de campagne, Preface, Lettre à Madame la baronne de Joyenval*, quoted by Davis, *Happy Island Images*, 11.

19. Seneca maintained that it "may be very helpful to the uninitiated and those who are still novices, for individual aphorisms, in a small compass, rounded off in units rather like lines of verse, [to] become fixed more readily in the mind." *Letters from a Stoic, Epistulae Morales ad Lucilium*, selected and translated with an introduction by Robin Campbell (London and New York: Penguin Books, 1969), Letter 33, 80.

20. For further discussion of this question, see Jonathan Levy, *A Theatre of the Imagination* (Rowayton, Conn.: New Plays Incorporated, 1987), 43–55.

21. Quoted in Davis, *Happy Island Images*, 11.

22. Henry Wadsworth Longfellow, *The Letters of Henry Wadsworth Longfellow*, edited by Andrew Hilen, 2 vols. (Cambridge: Harvard University Press, Belknap Press, 1966), vol. 1, 328. I have changed the order of this letter slightly.

23. Quoted by P. H. Newby, *Maria Edgeworth* (London: Arthur Barker, Ltd., 1950), 89–90.

24. *Annual Review* (1805), vol. 4, 639. The anonymous review ends: "But in thus recommending sacred dramas, we do not mean those of Mr. John Collet, unless it be thought advisable to represent them as afterpieces for the sake of sending the audience home sleepy." For a thorough discussion of the topic, see Murray Roston, *Biblical Drama in England from the Middle Ages to the Present Day* (Evanston: Northwestern University Press, 1968).

25. Louis J. Oldani, and Philip C. Fischer, eds. *Jesuit Theater Englished*, quoted on back cover.

26. Quoted by T. H. Vail-Motter, *The School Drama in England* (Port Washington, [N.Y.]: Kennikat Press, [1968]), 298.

27. Barbara Hofland Wreaks Hoole, *Little Dramas for Young People, on subjects taken from English History: intended to promote among the rising generation an early love of virtue and their country* (London: Longman, Hurst, Rees and Orme, 1810), p. [v].

28. R. S. Storrs, *A Dialogue, exhibiting Some of the Principles and Practical Consequences of Modern Infidelity* (Sag Harbor, N.Y.: Alden Spooner, 1806; reprinted Tarrytown, N.Y.: William Abbot, 1932).

29. Northrop Frye, "Towards Defining an Age of Sensibility," in *Eighteenth Century English Literature: Modern Essays in Criticism*, ed. James Clifford (New York: Oxford University Press, 1959), 311.

30. Davis, *Happy Island Images*, 143.

31. See Allardyce Nicoll, *A History of English Drama, 1660–1900*, 6 vols. (Cambridge: Cambridge University Press, 1967), vol. 3, 35 ff.; and, especially, Ernest Bernbaum, *The Drama of Sensibility: A Sketch of the History of English Sentimental Comedy and Domestic Tragedy* (Gloucester, Mass.: Peter Smith, 1958), passim.

32. Davis, *Happy Island Images*, p. [i], in part quoting Robert Pattison.

33. Sydney Smith, *The Works of Sydney Smith*, 3 vols. (Philadelphia: Casey and Holt, 1844), vol. 1, 158–59. Smith particularly recommends the salutory effect of Mrs. Siddons in *The Gamester* and *Jane Shore*.

34. "I. P.," *Dramatic Pieces calculated to exemplify the mode of conduct which render young ladies both amiable and happy, when their school education is completed*, 3 vols. (London: John Marshall, [c. 1786]), vol. 2, v.

35. Frye, *Towards Defining an Age of Sensibility*, 312.

36. Quoted in Meigs, Eaton, Newbitt and Vigeur, eds., *A Critical History of Children's Literature* (New York: Macmillan, 1969), 108.

37. For a thorough discussion of the historical origins of the mistrust of fairy tales, see Samuel F. Pickering, Jr., *John Locke and Children's Books in Eighteenth-Century England* (Knoxville: University of Tennessee Press, 1981), 40–69.

38. "There are pantomimes on Aladdin and other Eastern heroes. . . . The way is being slowly prepared for the Christmas shows of the succeeding century." Nicoll, *History of English Drama*, vol. 3, 210.

39. F. J. Harvey Darton, *Children's Books in England: Five Centuries of Social Life* (Cambridge: Cambridge University Press, 1982), 91.

40. William B. Fowle, *Familiar Dialogues and Popular Discussions, for Exhibition in Schools and Academies of either Sex, and for the Amusement of Social Parties* (Boston: Tappan and Dennet; New York: Mark H. Newman; Philadelphia: Thomas, Copperthwait & Co., 1844), [3]. Fowle did not invent the form, or the name. Collections of Familiar Dialogues had appeared in Boston and in Philadelphia before Fowle's first collection appeared in 1817. But if Fowle did not invent the form, he did develop and embellish it. He is the author of six collections of Familiar Dialogues and other short scenes adapted for the use of young people, many taken from other writers but at least as many, including many of the best, his own.

41. William Wordsworth and Samuel Taylor Coleridge, *Lyrical Ballads* ed. W. J. B. Owen (London: Oxford University Press, 1967), advertisement, pp. [3]–4.

42. W. H. Auden makes a similar point about Wordsworth and adult speech:

> The case of Wordsworth, the greatest of the Romantic poets, is instructive. While stating that he intended to write in the language really used by men, in particular by Westmorland farmers, whenever he tries to do so his work is not completely successful, while in his best work, the Odes and the Preludes, his diction is poetic and far removed from the spoken word.

W. H. Auden, *The Oxford Book of Light Verse* (London: Oxford University Press, 1938), introduction, xiv.

43. "Charles and his Mother," in *Robert Merry's Museum*, ed. S. G. Goodrich (Boston: Bradbury and Soden, 1841), vol. 2, no. 3, 124–26. For a fuller discussion of deathbed scenes in Victorian literature, see Nina Auerbach, *Private Theatricals: The Lives of the Victorians* (Cambridge, Mass. and London: Harvard University Press, 1990), especially 21 ff.

L'AVEUGLE
DE SPA,
COMÉDIE.

Le Conquérant est craint, le Sage est estimé,
Mais le Bienfaisant charme, & lui seul est aimé.
VOLTAIRE.

SCÈNE PREMIÈRE.

Le Théâtre représente une Promenade.

Madame AGLEBERT, JEANNETTE.

Madame AGLEBERT, *tenant un paquet.*

ARRÊTONS-NOUS un moment, il fait si beau !....

JEANNETTE.

Notre maison n'est qu'à deux pas,

THE BLIND WOMAN OF SPA

1781

Stéphanie Félicité Ducrest, Comtesse de Genlis

Mme de Genlis was born at Autun, France, on January 25, 1746. At sixteen, she married Charles Brûlart de Genlis, Colonel of Grenadiers and later Marquis of Silery. The young Countess performed amateur theatricals in the Count's private theatre and, ashamed of her lack of education — except in music, for which she had showed an early talent — proceeded to educate herself. She did this so successfully that in 1770, the Duc de Châtres (whose mistress she was said to be) made her governess to his daughters.

Her educational methods were strongly influenced by Rousseau, but she was an imaginative and innovative teacher in her own right. She taught her pupils history with magic-lantern slides, which offered "instruction to the mind and . . . to the eye . . . figures of a pure style and design."[1] She taught them practical botany, with the help of a gardener; she insisted that they do regular physical exercise; and, most tellingly for our purposes, she made the theatre a central part of their education, taking them regularly to the Comédie Française and writing plays for them to act.[2] The Duc de Châtres was so pleased with her methods that in 1781 he took the unusual step of making her tutor to his sons.

Mme de Genlis's husband, from whom she was by then estranged, was guillotined in 1793 under the Girondin. She was obliged to flee with her pupil, Mlle d'Orléans, first to

Switzerland, then to Berlin, and finally to Hamburg, where she supported herself by writing and painting. Napoleon, who had once said of her that she wrote of virtue as if she had just discovered it, permitted her to return to France in 1799 and gave her an apartment and a pension of 6000 francs, which he later reduced and finally cut off entirely. Maria Edgeworth visited her in 1803 and left this chilling portrait.

She looked like the full-length picture of my great-great-grandmother Edgeworth ... very thin and melancholy ... dark eyes, long sallow cheeks, compressed thin lips, two or three black ringlets on a high forehead, a cap that Mrs. Grier might wear — altogether an appearance of worn-out health, and excessive, but guarded irritabilty.... I went to see her after seeing her *Rosière de Salency* with the most favorable disposition, but I could not like her; there was something of malignity in her countenance and conversation that repelled love, and of hypocrisy which annihilated esteem, and from time to time I saw, or thought I saw through the gloom of her countenance, a gleam of coquetry.[3]

Mme de Genlis died in Paris on December 31, 1838, with her former pupil Louis Phillipe on the throne of France.

THE BLIND WOMAN OF SPA

The first play in the second volume is *The Blind Woman of Spa*. It is a most touching tableau of the simplest and most naive beneficence, which makes us love humanity by presenting in it virtue in opulence and virtue in poverty, both equally noble, equally respectable, the one paying homage to the other through the sentiment with which it accompanies its good works.
Journal Encyclopédie, April, 1780, pp. 103–4

Nothing changes more quickly than the height of fashion, and no fashion changes more quickly than fashion in feelings. Sensibility becomes sentimentality, sentimentality becomes kitsch, and kitsch becomes camp without the substance of the emotion changing greatly. What changes is what we feel about our feelings.

The Blind Woman of Spa may seem, at first glance, naive and bathetic to modern readers. Certainly, many plays of the period do, especially the *comédies larmoyantes*, of which this play is a short example. Diderot's *Le Père de Famille*, so praised in its time, is barely readable today.

The defects of *The Blind Woman of Spa* are not hard to find and are generally the defects of the *comédie larmoyante* in the period: its easy tears, its clumsy humor, its abrupt French scenes, and, to modern eyes, its simplistic and reactionary moral: If the rich are good to the poor, God will be good to the rich.

Yet even if there were no more to the play than this, it would be worth reprinting as an example of the *Théatre d'Education*, which has had such an enormous influence on what theatre for children has been since Mme de Genlis, down to our own day. But the play, I believe, is of considerable interest in its own right.

Dramaturgically, *The Blind Woman of Spa* is a small miracle. According to its author, it is a true story, told without imaginative embellishment. But this is modesty on the author's part. The mere act of turning any story into a play requires both craft and imagination. What is extraordinary about *The Blind Woman of Spa* is that it is not held together by the usual sinews of dramatic construction: complexity of plot, the contrast between good and evil, and, most particularly, conflict. *The Blind Woman of Spa* contains virtually none of these. Yet it plays, and the younger its audience, the better it plays. Why?

It plays partly because of the small touches it contains, like the praise of the English by a Frenchwoman, which gives patriotic pleasure to an English audience and the even more poignant pleasure of self-criticism to a French audience. But it plays chiefly because, to a surprising extent, it does what Mme de Genlis said it would do: It pleases the viewer with the virtually continual exhibition onstage of active goodness.

If it is true that fashions in feeling change but the raw material of feeling does not change and that no human emotion is lost in our evolution; if a newborn baby is in fact equally programmed to cry at *Jane Shore* as at *La Boheme* or *Death of a Salesman*; then it is possible, unfashionable as that possibility may appear, that Mme de Genlis might have been essentially right. She may have been right to believe that good and delicate emotions can be taught and can be taught in a play, both to young performers and to a young audience, which might lead us to imagine that under the right conditions even modern children, given *The Blind Woman of Spa* to act or to see, might be touched and changed by the exhibition of triumphant human goodness in it.

NOTES

1.   Stéphanie de Genlis, *Lessons of a Governess to her pupils: or Journal of the method adapted by Madame de Sillery-Brulart in the education of the children of M. d'Orléans. Translated from the French*, 3 vols. (London: Printed for G. G. J. and J. Robinson, 1792), vol. 3, 211.

2.   "In the winter season I accompanied them every eight or ten days to the Comédie Françoise, taking care to select such pieces as they had never before seen. During the representation, attentive solely to my pupils, I studied their sentiments and feelings, corrected their ideas when they were erroneous, and the next morning I made them dictate an analysis of the performance, which was brought to me and instantly corrected. . . . We also represented plays, confining ourselves to the pieces in my Theatre of Education. At other times we have recited in a dramatic form different passages in the history of voyages, the scene of the exhibition being the garden and every person belonging to the house taking a character in his turn." de Genlis, *Lessons of a Governess*, vol. 3, 222–23, 229.

3.   *Maria Edgeworth: Chosen Letters*, with an introduction by F. V. Barry (Boston and New York: Houghton Mifflin Company, [1931]), 137–39.

THE BLIND WOMAN OF SPA

A COMEDY

Le Conquerant est craint, le Sage est estimé, Mais le Bienfaisant charme, & lui seul est aimé.

Voltaire

Advertisement

The subject of the following little piece is not a work of fancy. The Author saw the worthy Catherine Aglebert at Spa three years ago, and learnt the history from the poor blind woman herself: All the particulars of this Comedy are strictly true; even the name of the woman, the names of her children, and the profession of her husband are preserved. It is likewise true, that an English Lady who was at that time in Spa, behaved very generously to that respectable family.

The Persons

Mrs. AGLEBERT, the wife of a Shoemaker.

JENNET,
MARY,   } Mrs. Aglebert's daughters.
LOUISA,

GOTO, a blind woman.

LADY SEYMOUR, an English lady.

FELICIA, a French Lady.

FATHER ANTHONY, a Capuchin Friar.

The Scene is at the Waters of Spa.

Scene I

The Stage represents a walk.
Mrs. Aglebert, Jennet.

Mrs. Aglebert [holding a bundle]: Let us step a little, the weather is so fine! —

Jennet: We are almost at home mother, and if you will give me leave, I will carry the bundle which encumbers you.

Mrs. Aglebert: No, no, it is too heavy. It is our provision for to-morrow and Sunday.

Jennet: There is nothing but potatoes! —

Mrs. Aglebert: Well, Jennet? —

Jennet: For these eighteen months we have had no other food but potatoes.

Mrs. Aglebert: My child, when people are poor —

Jennet: You was not so eighteen months ago mother? We had such good bread and pies, and cakes. —

Mrs. Aglebert: Ah, if you knew my reasons! — But Jennet, you are too young to comprehend these things.

Jennet: Too young! I am almost fifteen.

Mrs. Aglebert: Your heart is good, and I will tell you all one of these days.

Jennet: Ah mother! tell me now. —

Mrs. Aglebert: Hush, I hear a noise, here are some ladies coming. —

Jennet: Ha, mother!

Mrs. Aglebert: What is the matter? —

Jennet: It is she; it is the lady that gave my sisters and I, our new gowns.

Mrs. Aglebert: Did you not go and thank her this morning?

Jennet: Yes, mother.

Mrs. Aglebert: Now let us begone! and the rather as our poor blind girl Goto has not had a walk today, and I dare say is in expectation of your coming. Come, you shall lead her to the Capuchin garden, where I will join you when my work is done. Come then. —

Jennet: I will follow mother. [Mrs. Aglebert goes before, Jennet slackens her pace. Lady Seymour and Felicia pass by her, without observing her. Jennet looks at Felicia, and says]: She did not see me; I am sorry for it, because I greatly love her. [She runs to overtake her mother.]

Scene II

Lady Seymour, Felicia.

Lady Seymour: There is no moving a step in this place without meeting some unhappy wretches! — It grieves me to the heart. —

Felicia: You have such sensibility! — besides, I think in general the English women are more compassionate than we; they have less whim, less coquetry; and coquetry stifles and destroys every worthy sentiment.

Lady Seymour: What you said just now reminds me of an incident with which I was struck this morning. You know the Viscountess Roselle?

Felicia: A little.

Lady Seymour: I met her about two hours ago in the square; there was a poor old lame beggar asked her for charity, and told her his family were dying for want and hunger. The Viscountess hearkened to him with compassion, and pulling her purse out of her pocket was going to give it to him; when unfortunately a person with caps and feathers to sell, drew near. He opened the band-box, and the Viscountess no longer heard the complaint of the old man, but with coldness and inattention. However, to get rid of him, she threw him a trifle and purchased the whole contents of the band-box.

Felicia: I am sure your Ladyship relieved the old man.

Lady Seymour: Hear me to the end. The poor man picked up the money, exclaiming: "My wife and my children shall not die this day!" These few words kindled some emotions in the heart of the Viscountess which is naturally good and humane; she called back the old man, and after a moment's reflexion, said to the person with whom she had been dealing, you may charge me more for these things I have just now taken, but you must give me credit; the proposal was accepted, and the purse given to the unhappy old man, whose joy and surprise had almost made him expire at the feet of his benefactress. Seated under a tree and concealed by the covered walk, I could easily attend to this interesting scene, which has furnished me with abundant matter for reflexion.

Felicia: You should take a journey to Paris, and since you are fond of making reflexions, we will supply you with many other subjects. You will there see for instance, that we value ourselves on imitating you in every thing, except one, I mean benevolence. We carry all your fashions to the extreme, we take to your customs and manners; but we have not yet adopted that generous custom universally established with you, to raise subscriptions for encouraging merit, or relieving the distressed.

Lady Seymour: So you mimic rather than imitate us, since you make no mention of what renders us truly valuable; and by overdoing our customs and manners, you turn us into ridicule.

Felicia: I hope in time you will communicate some of your virtues to us, as you have already given us your manners. But, my lady, to continue this conversation more at our ease, will you go to the mountain where we shall find shade? —

Lady Seymour: I cannot, for I must wait the coming of a person whom I appointed to meet me here.

Felicia: Will your business delay you long?

Lady Seymour: No, I have but one word to say. Ha, here he comes!

Felicia: So, it is Father Anthony! I can guess the motive for such an appointment. You want to be informed where you can best do a generous action, and for such a purpose the venerable Father Anthony is worthy of your confidence. Farewell my Lady, I shall expect you on the mountain.

Lady Seymour: Where shall I find you?

Felicia: In the little temple.

Lady Seymour: I will be with you in a quarter of an hour.
[Felicia goes out.]

Scene III

Lady Seymour, Father Anthony.

Lady Seymour: Poor Father Anthony, with how much pain he walks; what a pity he is so old, he has an excellent heart! — Good day to you Father Anthony; I have been waiting for you an hour.

Father Anthony [a nosegay in his hand]: I did not care to leave home without a little nosegay for your ladyship, and I had not a rose: but at last one of our brothers gave me a couple. — These carnations however are from my own garden.

Lady Seymour: They are very fine.

Father Anthony: O, as to carnations I fear no body — without boasting I have the finest carnations! but my Lady you have not been to see my Garden since I have had carnations in blow! —

Lady Seymour: I will certainly go. But in your public garden there is always such a number of people, and I am so unsociable. — But Father Anthony let us talk of our affairs. — Have you found out a family for me that are very poor, and very worthy? —

Father Anthony: I have found one — Ah! my lady I have found a treasure: — a woman, her husband, five children, and in such want! —

Lady Seymour: What employment is the husband?

Father Anthony: He is a shoemaker, and his wife makes linen; but she is a woman of such piety and virtue. She is the daughter of a schoolmaster; she reads and writes; she has had an education for her station in life. Then if you knew the charity of which these people are capable, and the good they have done. Ah, my lady they richly deserve your fifty guineas.

Lady Seymour: You give me great pleasure, Father; — well!

Father Anthony: O, it is a long history. In the first place the husband's name is Aglebert. — But will you go to his house — you must witness it to believe all. —

Lady Seymour: Hear me father; come back to this place in two hours, and we will go together to these good people, but in the meantime tell me their history in two words.

Father Anthony: In two words! — It would take me three quarters of an hour for the bare preamble; and what is more, I never could tell any thing in two words.

Lady Seymour: So I find. Well father, farewell till the evening, I hear people coming towards us, and we shall be interrupted.

Father Anthony: And for my part. I have some little business; but I will be here with you by seven.

Lady Seymour: You will find me here. Farewell Father Anthony.

Father Anthony [makes some steps and returns]: My Lady, you will come and see my carnations won't you?

Lady Seymour: Yes, Father Anthony, I promise you, you may depend upon it.

Father Anthony: O they are the worthiest people!

Lady Seymour: Who your carnations.

Father Anthony: No, I was speaking of the worthy Agleberts. It is a family of God. [He moves some steps, turns back, and speaks with an air of confidence.] Then I have one variegated red and white; 'tis a non-such in Spa.

Lady Seymour: I will certainly go and see it to-morrow.

Father Anthony [in going out]: Farewell my Lady; what a worthy action you are going to do this evening! —
[He goes out.]

Lady Seymour: The Agleberts and the carnations make extraordinary confusion in his brain. To relieve the poor, and cultivate his flowers, make the sum of his pleasures and his happiness. The greatest virtues are always accompanied with the most simple desires. But I must go and find Felicia. — Ha, what a sweet pretty girl! —

Scene IV

Lady Seymour, Jennet, Goto, Mary.

> [*Jennet*, leading *Goto* to the bottom of the stage, where she stops and sits down. *Mary* her sister comes forward to look at *Lady Seymour*.]

Mary: No, it is not she.

Lady Seymour [looking at her]: She is charming. — Come hither my little dear; what are you looking for?

Mary [making a courtsey]: It is that — I took you for a very good Lady, and who is likewise very amiable, and I find I am mistaken.

Lady Seymour: But perhaps I am good too, as well as your lady.

Mary [shaking her head]: ***** —

Lady Seymour: *** do not believe it?

Mary: The Lady gave me a gown.

Lady Seymour: O, that is another affair. — Is that it you have now?

Mary: Yes madam, and then I have a fine cap which I shall wear on Sunday. And my sister Jennet, and my sister Louisa have new gowns.

Lady Seymour: And all from the good Lady?

Mary: Yes, indeed.

Lady Seymour: What is her name?

Mary: I never saw her till this morning, and I have forgot her name, but she is a French lady, and lodges at the Prince Eugene.

Lady Seymour: O 'tis Felicia. — And are your sisters as pretty as you?

Mary: There is Jennet below.

Lady Seymour: That young girl who sits knitting?

Mary: Yes, that is she.

Lady Seymour: Who is with her?

Mary: It is Goto, our blind woman.

Lady Seymour: Who is your blind woman?

Mary: Marry our blind woman, as my mother calls her, whom we walk with, and lead about. As to me, I have only led her these three months, because I was too little, and still I am not allowed to lead her in the streets for fear of the crowd. —

Lady Seymour: She is surely one of your relations?

Mary: Yes, a relation very possibly. I don't know, but my mother loves her as much as she loves us; for she sometimes calls her, her sixth child.

Lady Seymour: It is very right to take care of relations, especially when they are infirm. — What is your name?

Mary: Mary, at your service.

Lady Seymour: Well Mary, come and see me to-morrow morning, I live upon the terrace at the large white house, and bring your blind woman with you. I shall be very glad to be acquainted wth her.

Mary: O Goto is a very good girl.

Lady Seymour: Farewell Mary till to-morrow.

[She goes out.]

Scene V

Mary, Jennet, Goto.

Mary: Here is another good Lady. — I'll lay a wager she will have a gown made for Goto; she loves blind people, I see that. — I am very glad of it. I shall keep my pretty apron, but if it had not been for this, I would have given it to Goto. — Ah! there they come. — They want to know what the lady said to me.

Jennet: Mary tell us who that fine lady is, that was talking with you?

Mary: Is she not a pretty lady? She lives upon the terrace; I shall go there to-morrow and lead Goto with me.

Jennet: Not alone, there are too many streets.

Mary: Yes to be sure, and in the streets too. The fine lady said I was tall enough to do that. She knows these things very well, perhaps.

Goto: Mary, you are not strong enough to support me.

Mary: O, to be sure — but it is because you love Jennet better than me — that is not fair.

Goto: Alas! my children, I love you equally; you are all so charitable!

Jennet: Well Mary, I will only lead Goto through the streets without entering the lady's house.

Mary: No, no, you shall come with us: don't be uneasy; but going along the road, Goto shall likewise lean upon me. Let her promise me that, and I shall be satisfied.

Goto: Yes Mary, yes my girl. — Poor dears, God will bless you all.

Mary: By the by, Goto, are you our relation? The lady asked me, and I did not know what answer to make.

Goto: Alas! I am nothing to you, and I owe you every thing — But heaven will reward you.

Mary: What is it then you owe us Goto? — Is it, that it is a trouble to us to take care of you! It is with such good will. O! I wish I was but big enough to dress, serve, and lead you, like my mother and Jennet. —

Jennet [low to Mary]: Hold your tongue, you vex her; I believe she is crying. —

Mary [going to the other side of Goto taking her by the hand]: Goto, my dear Goto, have I said any thing that gives you pain? Are you offended?

Goto: On the contrary my dear children, your good hearts make me forget all my sorrows. —

Mary: O! We are very happy then. — But I hear my mother's voice, it is she and Louisa.

Scene VI

Mary, Jennet, Goto, Mrs. Aglebert, Louisa.

Mrs. Aglebert: There they are. — Jennet, we were looking for you; come, it is time to go home.

Jennet: O mother, allow us to work here half an hour longer.

Mrs. Aglebert: Very well, I have no objection. Mary go and fetch my wheel, and bring some work for yourself at the same time. [Mary goes out.]

Louisa: And for me mother?

Mrs. Aglebert: You shall stay with Goto, in case she wants anything; you shall execute her commissions. You must accustom yourself to be of use as well as your sisters. Come let us sit down. [She draws a form and sits down; She takes Goto by the hand and places her between herself and Jennet.]

Louisa [to Jennet]: Sister give me your place, I must be there to serve Goto.

Mrs. Aglebert: Sit down on the ground by her.

Louisa: With all my heart. [She places herself upon her knees at Goto's feet.]

Jennet: Mother there is your wheel. [Mary gives her mother the wheel, who begins immediately to spin: Jennet knits; Mary sits upon a large stone in the corner near the form, by the side of her mother, and hems a handkerchief; and Louisa takes some violets out of the pocket of her apron to make a nosegay.]

Mrs. Aglebert [after a short silence]: Mary, is your father come home?

Mary: No mother.

Jennet: Is he not gone to the capuchin convent?

Mrs. Aglebert: Yes, to speak with Father Anthony.

Mary: O, Father Anthony has fine carnations!

Louisa [crying]: Ah Goto, you have thrown down all my violets by your turning, on the ground.

Goto: Forgive me my dear child. — I could not see them.

Louisa [still crying]: My God, my violets. —

Mrs. Aglebert: What is the matter little girl?

Louisa: Mary, she has thrown down all my violets. So she may gather them up, and that too. [She throws away the nosegay she had begun, in a passion.]

Jennet: O fy, Louisa.

Mrs. Aglebert: Louisa, come hither. [Louisa rises, and Mrs. Aglebert takes her between her knees.] Louisa are you angry with Goto.

Louisa: Yes, she has thrown down my violets.

Mrs. Aglebert: We shall talk of that by and by, but in the first place, take my wheel and carry it home.

Louisa: With all my heart mother. — O, it is too heavy, I cannot even lift it.

Mrs. Aglebert: Well Louisa, I will no longer love you, since you cannot carry my wheel.

Louisa [crying]: But mother, I have not strength; is it my fault?

Mrs. Aglebert: So you think I am wrong to desire it?

Louisa: Yes mother you are wrong. And then you know very well that I am too little to carry that great ugly wheel.

Mrs. Aglebert: It is very true I know it; but don't you likewise know that Goto is blind? Can she see your flowers, and can she help you to gather them up?

Louisa: Well I was wrong to cry, and to be provoked with her.

Mrs. Aglebert: Is she not sufficiently unhappy, poor girl, not to see; to be blind from her birth?

Goto [taking Mrs. Aglebert by the hand]: Ah! Mrs. Aglebert, I am not unhappy; no, your goodness, your charity. —

Mrs. Aglebert: Don't speak of that, my dear girl. — Hear me Louisa, if you do not look upon Goto as your sister, I will no longer look upon you as my child.

Louisa: I love Goto very well, but however, she is not my sister.

Mrs. Aglebert: It pleased God to make this poor girl fall quite helpless into my hands; was it not to say to me, there is a sixth child which I give you?

Jennet: O yes, just the same thing.

Mary: I likewise can conceive that.

Mrs. Aglebert: And Louisa too will be able to conceive it in time: goodness of heart must come with reason. My dear children there is no such thing as content, without a good heart; I repeat it to you, and desire you will remember it. Your father and I have worked hard, and have had a great deal of trouble, but by always doing our duty, life passes smoothly; and then one good action consoles us for ten years of toil and vexation.

Mary: Mother, I think I hear some ladies coming.

Mrs. Aglebert: Very well, let us be gone.

Jennet: Mother, mother, it is the French Lady.

Mrs. Aglebert: No matter, let us go home. Come, put back the bench.

[They all rise.]

Scene VII

*Mary, Jennet, Goto, Louisa, Mrs. Aglebert,
Lady Seymour, Felicia.*

Lady Seymour: Father Anthony is not yet come. — Ha! there are the young girls, of whom we were just now speaking.

Felicia [to Jennet]: Is that your mother?

Mrs. Aglebert [making a courtesy]: Yes madam — and I proposed to go tomorrow to thank you madam, for your goodness to my children; but I have been so busy yesterday and to-day. —

Felicia: This blind girl is one of your family, no doubt?

Mrs. Aglebert: No madam.

Goto: No, but it is the same thing.

Mrs. Aglebert: Jennet, take my wheel. — Let us go, lest we disturb the ladies. —

Lady Seymour: I beg you will not go away. — I have something to say to you. [low to Felicia]: She seems to dread our questions about the blind woman. It is somewhat singular.

Felicia [low to lady Seymour]: I made the same remark. [aloud to Mrs. Agelbert]: What is your situation in life, your business?

Mrs. Aglebert: I spin and make linen.

Lady Seymour: And is your work sufficient to support your family?

Mrs. Aglebert: Yes madam, we have wherewithal to live.

Felicia: That day however when I met your daughters on Annette and Lubin's hill, I was equally struck with the poverty which was evident from their dress, and with their charming figures. — And you yourself don't seem to be in a more prosperous state.

Mrs. Aglebert: It is true we are not rich, but we are content.

Lady Seymour [to Felicia]: Does not she interest you?

Felicia: Beyond expresison. — [to Mrs. Aglebert]: You have three charming little girls there — [All the three courtesy.] Have you any more children?

Mrs. Aglebert: I have two boys likewise, thank God.

Goto: And I, whom she entirely supports. —

Mrs. Aglebert: Ah Goto! —

Lady Seymour: How? —

Goto: It is to these worthy people I owe every thing. This family of Angels, lodge, feed, clothe and serve me, who am a poor infirm girl, frequently sick, and always useless. I find in them a father, mother, brothers, sisters and servants, for they are all equally disposed to do good offices, all equally good, equally charitable. Ah ladies, they are angels, real angels whom you see before you.

Felicia: What, is it possible! — O Heavens!

Lady Seymour: Surprise and compassion have struck me motionless.

Mrs. Aglebert: My God! what we have done, was so natural! — This good girl had no other resource; we could comfort and help her; could it be possible to abandon her? —

Mary [low to Jennet]: Why are these ladies so very uneasy at this? See, they are in tears.

Jennet: It is because they are surprised at it; but however there is no reason.

Felicia: Be so good as to let us know the particulars of such an affecting story.

Lady Seymour [to Mrs. Aglebert]: How did this poor girl fall into your hands?

Goto: We lodged in the same house, when an old aunt of mine, who took care of me, and upon whose labour I subsisted, happened to die, and with her, I lost every means of support. I fell sick, and this dear good woman came to see me; she began by sitting up with me, paying a doctor for me, making my drinks, in short, serving me as my nurse. When I recovered she took me home to her house, where I have been treated these two years as if I had been the eldest daughter of the family.

Felicia [embracing Mrs. Aglebert]: O incomparable woman, with such a soul, into what a condition has your destiny placed you.

Lady Seymour: Let me too embrace her.

Mrs. Aglebert: Ladies, you make me ashamed —

Lady Seymour [to Mrs. Aglebert]: Tell us your name, that respectable name, which shall never be effaced from our remembrance.

Mrs. Aglebert: My name is Catharine Aglebert.

Lady Seymour: Aglebert! — It is she whom Father Anthony mentioned to me. — Do you know Father Anthony?

Mrs. Aglebert: Yes madam, he came to our house this morning, and this evening has sent for my husband, but I don't know what he wants with him.

Goto: I saw him yesterday at the Capuchin Gardens; he asked me some questions, and I told him my whole story.

Felicia: But how comes it that your story is not known to all the people in Spa? How is it possible that such an instance of virtue and benevolence should remain unknown.

Goto: Because Mr. and Mrs. Aglebert have never mentioned it; besides, I am frequently sick, and of course confined to the house a part of the year, and Jennet, who takes care of me, leads me, by her mother's desire, to the walks which are the least frequented; and when she observes people coming, she leads me a different way. It is only when she is greatly hurried with her work, that I am taken to the garden of the Capuchins, which is near at hand, and that has only happened three or four times.

Lady Seymour [to Felicia]: Here is virtue in all its lustre, and we enjoy the inexpressible happiness of discovering and contemplating it in all its purity. Simple, sublime, natural; without vanity, without ostentation, and finding within itself, both its glory and its reward.

Felicia: Ah! who can see it in this light without paying their adorations? Who can look upon this woman without feeling a delightful emotion of respect and admiration!

Lady Seymour: And that conformity of disposition, that general agreement for the good of the whole family! — And that girl, the affecting and virtuous object of so many kindnesses, how she expresses her gratitude, how she is penetrated with whatever she ought to feel! — No, nothing is wanting to compleat the delightful picture.

Mary: O mother, I think I see Father Anthony. —

Louisa: I am glad of it, for he always gives me a violet.

Lady Seymour: Stay Mrs. Aglebert, and we will go home with you presently.

Mrs. Aglebert: Madam. —

Scene VIII

Mary, Jennet, Goto, Louisa, Mrs. Aglebert,
Lady Seymour, Felicia, Father Anthony.

Lady Seymour: Come, Father Anthony, come, I fancy I have discovered the treasure you spoke of to me. —

Father Anthony: Just so, there they are; it is Mrs. Aglebert. Well then my Lady, you know her history? —

Lady Seymour: I know all.

Father Anthony [to Mrs. Aglebert]: Mrs. Aglebert, learn to know and thank your benefactress. Lady Seymour wanted to give fifty guineas to the most worthy family in Spa, and her choice has fallen upon yours.

Goto [raising her hands to Heaven]: O my God! —

Mrs. Aglebert: Fifty guineas! — No, madam, it is too much; there are a number of worthy people in Spa, still more needy than we. My neighbour Mrs. Savard is a worthy woman, and in such misery! —

Lady Seymour: Very well, I will take care of Mrs. Savard, I promise you. — Father Anthony shall give you fifty guineas this night, and I will add a hundred more, as a portion for Jennet.

Mrs. Aglebert: O my Lady, it is too much — it is too much indeed. —

Goto: O God! is it possible — O where is this good Lady, that I may embrace her knees. — Jennet where is she?

> [Jennet leads her to lady Seymour's feet.]

Felicia: Poor girl, how affecting to see her! — And you my lady, you must be happy! —

Goto [laying hold of Lady Seymour's robe]: Is this she? —

Lady Seymour [reaching her hand to Goto]: Yes my Girl! —

Goto [throwing herself at her feet]: Ah madam, I will pray for you all the days of my life. You have made the fortune of this respectable family, but you have done still more for me. I owe to you their content, and the only happiness poor Goto can find upon earth, which is the knowledge of these worthy people being made as happy as they deserve. I have nothing more to wish, and now I can die satisfied. —

Lady Seymour [raising her up and embracing her]: O, I conceive your happiness, and enjoy it with transport.

Mrs. Aglebert: We shall all join, madam, in our prayers to heaven for you, while we live.

Jennet: O yes indeed.

Mary: And with all our hearts.

Louisa: And I too.

Lady Seymour: Pray then that it may preserve to me a feeling heart; you prove to me that it is the most precious gift heaven can bestow.

Father Anthony: My lady, I just now came past Vauxhall, where they are playing and dancing, but I will wager, the pleasure of the people who are there, are not equal to those you have been just now tasting.

Felicia: How they are to be pitied, if the happiness we have been enjoying is unknown to them! —

Lady Seymour: Come, let us go home with Mrs. Aglebert, I am impatient to see her husband. —

Mrs. Aglebert: Madam, you are very good, but we live so high —

Lady Seymour: Come and conduct us; with what pleasure shall I enter that house, which contains such virtuous inhabitants!

Mrs. Aglebert: My God, Father Anthony, speak for us: I am so surprised, so affected, I do not know how to express himself. —

Father Anthony: Come, come, my Lady's heart can see into yours. — But Mrs. Aglebert, there is one favour you must obtain for me with my Lady; it is to come and see my garden when she leaves you.

The End

J. Porter.   T. Pollock.

TEACHING THE SCRIPTURES.

Engraved expressly for this Work.

MOSES IN THE BULRUSHES

1782

Hannah More

Hannah More was born in Gloucestershire, near Bristol, England, on February 2, 1745, the fourth of the five daughters of Jacob More, a schoolmaster. Hannah was bred to his profession. She was, apparently, a prodigy as a child, teaching herself to read at age four and to write at five. In her teens, she added French, Italian, Spanish, and Latin to English. At twenty-two, she became engaged to a Mr. Turner, who was twenty years her senior. When Turner backed out of the marriage at the last moment, Hannah More resolved never to marry, and she never did.

After her engagement was broken off, More went to London, where, with Garrick's encouragement, she "began to study drama in earnest"[1] and eventually saw four of her plays produced professionally. When Garrick died on January 20, 1789, her strongest tie to the professional stage was broken. At the same time, her religious convictions were growing stronger. She came to believe playgoing sinful and proved the strength of her convictions by refusing to attend Mrs. Siddons's revival of her greatest theatrical success, *Percy*, in 1787.

More devoted the remainder of her long life to teaching and writing. Under the influence of Wilberforce, she wrote powerfully against slavery. She also wrote about the abuses and hypocrisies of the rich, the necessity of serious education for girls, and the need for the reform of religious education. To promote this last end, she and her sisters established a group of Sunday schools in Somerset, where they had a summer cottage. In 1794, they began writing a series of Cheap Repository Tracts for the poor children who were learning to read in these Sunday schools. A hundred and fourteen of these tracts were printed, of which Hannah had written about half. In 1808, she wrote *Coelebs in Search of a Wife*, a social rumination in the form of a novel. It was the most successful thing she ever wrote, running to eleven editions in its first year of publication alone.

She continued to write, chiefly on religious and educational subjects, well into her last years of retirement. She died, the last of her sisters, in 1833 at the age of 88 and left an estate of 30,000 pounds almost entirely to charity.

SACRED DRAMAS

> Mrs. Hannah More is another celebrated poetess, and I believe still living. She has written a great deal which I have never read.
>
> William Hazlitt

If we think of Hannah More at all today it is as "the old bishop in petticoats," "trembling at the idea of being entertained and thinking no Christian safe who was not dull."[2] There is some truth in this portrait, but it is not a portrait of Hannah More the playwright. The plays belong to Hannah More's youth and young womanhood, when she was a very different person indeed.

Hannah More the *wunderkind* wrote, according to family legend, original compositions at four. At sixteen, she wrote her first play, *The Search after Happiness: A Pastoral Drama*, which she wrote to be acted by the girls at her school as "a substitute for the very improper custom of allowing plays, and they not of the purest kind, to be acted by young ladies in boarding schools."[3] The play passed from school to school in manuscript before it was published in 1773. When it went into its ninth edition, in 1787, it had sold over ten thousand copies.[4] Her second play, *The Inflexible Captive*

(1774), was taken from a subject in Metastasio and was produced at Bath and Exeter.

As a young woman in London, Hannah More wrote *vers de societé*, "quipped with Garrick and scribbled with Walpole."[5] She knew everyone, the charming lightweights as well as the moral heavyweights. It was Garrick who encouraged her to continue writing her plays, and he himself wrote a prologue and an epilogue for her third play, *Percy* (1778), which Allardyce Nicoll calls "unquestionably her *chef d'oeuvre*." *Chef d'oeuvre* or not, it was an enormous success. It ran for 21 nights at Covent Garden, sold 4,000 copies in two weeks, and earned her 600 pounds. Her last play to be produced professionally was *A Fatal Falsehood* (1779), which had a prologue by Sheridan.

The *Sacred Dramas*, then, were not the work of a naive or inexperienced playwright. Hannah More wrote the plays as she did consciously and purposefully, not because she lacked the expertise to write them otherwise. The plays' limitations are self-imposed, outgrowths of the occasion they were written for and of the sacred subjects they were taken from. They were an experiment in education, and More's modern biographer believes that they were the boldest experiment Hannah More ever made.

The *Sacred Dramas* grew directly out of More's experience of teaching religion in school. She found the traditional method of learning texts by rote deadening and ineffective. More was apparently a friendly and lively teacher. She told her pupils nursery rhymes and fairy tales to pique their interest in secular subjects; and when she came to teach them religion, she used the same vivid method. She told them stories of the Children of Israel (as one of her puils remembered) "with such eloquence and force that I fancied that she must have lived among them herself."[6] The step from telling Bible stories dramatically to dramatizing them was a natural one for her to take.

But it was a step she took with enormous caution and forethought, both because of her subject and because of her purpose. Her subject was the Word of God. When she dramatized it, she

believed, "the place on which she stood was holy ground."[7]
She was therefore forbidden to take any dramatic liberties,
either with her plot or her characters.

Her purpose was avowedly educational, not literary or
dramatic. Her aim was moral instruction, and her actors and
audience were "young [girls], in whom it will always be time
enough to have the passions awakened."[8] This meant two
things. It meant that she could not represent the strong emotions
that are the customary material of serious drama, and it
meant that all her actors, though not all her characters, would
be girls.

What was left to her was language. But in language she was
always vividly aware of the giant shadow of Milton, who was
for her, "God's poet" and with whom she knew she could not
compete. With the cold eye she always had for her own work,
she recognized the faults of the *Sacred Dramas*, most
accurately and damningly in a work for the stage that "some of
the speeches are so long as to retard the action."[9]

Nonetheless, the *Sacred Dramas* were gladly and, for the
most part, well received. They were acted regularly in schools
for many years and were often reprinted. In 1786, when Mme de
Genlis's *Sacred Dramas* appeared in English in Thomas
Holcroft's translation, an anonymous reviewer wrote:

As we have in our own language, Sacred Dramas, executed with much
judgement and taste, and adorned with all the graces of simple and
elegant verse, there was less necessity for transplanting an exotic of
this kind, especially from a country where, the use of the Bible in the
mother tongue being prohibited, a close adherence to the original
narrative may be easily dispensed with.[10]

Hannah More's *Sacred Dramas* had run to eighteen editions
by 1815.

MOSES IN THE BULRUSHES

Modern readers may find it difficult to understand the
success of More's plays. They may find the plays' faults so

glaring that they may not see any virtues in them. Nonetheless, there are virtues, all present in *Moses in the Bulrushes*: the dramatic tact with which the holiest events are treated, the charm of the hymnlike song and its metrical contrast with the steady, unrhymed pentameter of the dialogue, and the occasional good, ringing Handelian line.

Yet even if there were no special virtues in *Moses in the Bulrushes*, it would be worth including here as an illuminating document in the history of taste and as an essential document in the history of childhood. It is worth reprinting because of the enormous influence it had on the generations of pupils who read and acted in it and the other *Sacred Dramas*, the generations of teachers who taught and directed them, and the generations of playwrights writing for children for whom they were the *locus classicus* of religious drama, either to be imitated or to be revolted against.

The play is, finally, worth reprinting because it did what it was written to do: teach. It taught the story of *Moses in the Bulrushes*, indelibly, to generation after generation of young children. It is a *lehrstück* that worked and was perceived to work with children as far afield as Ceylon. Hannah More meant her *Sacred Dramas* to teach, and teach they did, perhaps more deeply and surely than the more sophisticated didactic plays of today do. Hannah More's work is good, wrote her descendant E. M. Forster, if education is good.[11] If history's judgment on the *Sacred Dramas* is that they are awkward theatre but good education, no one would be more pleased than Hannah More.

NOTES

1. M. G. Jones, *Hannah More* (Cambridge: Cambridge University Press, 1952), 17.

2. It was William Cobbet, according to *The Oxford Companion to Children's Literature*, 361, who called her "the old Bishop," and Sydney Smith, *The Works of Sydney Smith* (Philadelphia: Casey and Holt, 1844), vol. 1, 159, who said the rest.

3.   Jones, *Hannah More*, 15, note 40.
4.   Allardyce Nicoll, *A History of English Drama* (Cambridge: Cambridge University Press, 1967), vol. 3, 213, suggests that the play was first printed privately in 1765.
5.   E. M. Forster, *Abinger Harvest* (New York: Meridian Books, 1955), 230.
6.   Jones, *Hannah More*, 15, note 37.
7.   Hannah More, *The Works of Hannah More*, 2 vols. (New York: Harper and Brothers, 1835), vol. 1, 75.
8.   Ibid.
9.   Ibid. She also observed that her Jewish characters often sounded too Christian. A contemporary reviewer added that sometimes characters speak sentiments that are not appropriate to them. See John Genest, *Some Account of the English Stage, from the Restoration in 1660 to 1830*, 10 vols. (Bath: H. E. Carrington, 1832), vol. 6, 250.
10.   *The Monthly Review, or literary journal*, 81 vols. (London: R. Griffiths, 1786), vol. 75, 397.
11.   Forster, *Abinger Harvest*, 232.

MOSES IN THE BULRUSHES

A SACRED DRAMA

Let me assert eternal Providence,
And justify the ways of God to man.
Paradise Lost

The Persons

HEBREW WOMEN:
JOCHEBED, mother of Moses.
MIRIAM, his sister.

EGYPTIANS
The PRINCESS, king Pharaoh's daughter.
MELITA; and other attendants.

Scene — On the banks of the Nile.

This subject is taken from the second chapter of the book of
Exodus.

Part I

Jochebed, Miriam.

Joch: Why was my pray'r accepted? why did heaven
In anger hear me, when I ask'd a son?
Ye dames of Egypt! ye triumphant mothers!
You no imperial tyrant marks for ruin;
You are not doom'd to see the babes you bore,
The babes you fondly nurture, bleed before you!
You taste the transport of a mother's love,
Without a mother's anguish! wretched Israel!

Can I forbear to mourn the different lot
Of thy sad daughters! — Why did God's own hand
Rescue his chosen race by Joseph's care?
Joseph! th' elected instrument of heaven,
Decreed to save illustrious Abraham's sons,
What time the famine rag'd in Canaan's land.
Israel, who then was spar'd, must perish now!
   Thou great mysterious Pow'r, who has involv'd
Thy wise decrees in darkness, to perplex
The pride of human wisdom, to confound
The daring scrutiny, and prove, the faith
Of thy presuming creatures! hear me now:
O vindicate thy honour, clear this doubt,
Teach me to trace this maze of Providence:
Why save the fathers, if the sons must perish?
   Mir: Ah me, my mother! whence these floods of grief?
   Joch: My son! my son! I cannot speak the rest;
Ye who have sons can only know my fondness!
Ye who have lost them, or who fear to lose,
Can only know my pangs! none else can guess them.
A mother's sorrows cannot be conceiv'd
But by a mother — would I were not one!
   Mir: With earnest pray'rs thou didst request this son,
And heaven has granted him.
   Joch: O sad estate
Of human wretchedness; so weak is man,
So ignorant and blind, that did not God
Sometimes withhold in mercy what we ask,
We should be ruin'd at our own request.
   Too well thou know'st, my child, the stern decree
Of Egypt's cruel king, hard-hearted Pharaoh;
That every male, of Hebrew mother born,
Must die! Oh! do I live to tell it thee!
Must die a bloody death! My child, my son,
My youngest born my darling must be slain!
   Mir: The helpless innocent! and must he die?

Joch: No: if a mother's tears, a mother's prayers,
A mother's fond precautions can prevail,
He shall not die. I have a thought my Miriam,
And sure the God of mercies who inspir'd,
Will bless the secret purpose of my soul,
To save his precious life.
   Mir: Hop'st thou that Pharaoh —
Joch: I have no hope in Pharaoh, much in God;
Much in the Rock of Ages.
   Mir: Think, O think,
What perils thou already hast incurr'd,
And shun the greater which may yet remain,
Three months, three dangerous months thou has preserv'd
Thy infant's life, and in thy house conceal'd him!
Should Pharaoh know!
   Joch: Oh! let the tyrant know,
And feel what he inflicts! Yes, hear me, heaven!
Send thy right aiming thunderbolts — but hush,
My impious murmurs! is it not thy will;
Thou, infinite in mercy? Thou permitt'st
The seeming evil for some latent good.
Yes, I will laud thy grace, and bless thy goodness
For what I have, and not arraign thy wisdom
For what I fear to lose. O, I will bless thee
That Aaron will be spar'd; that my first born
Lives safe and undisturbed! that he was giv'n me
Before this impious persecution rag'd!
   Mir: And yet who knows, but the fell tyrant's rage
May reach *his* precious life.
   Joch: I fear for him.
For thee, for all. A doating parent lives
In many lives; through many a nerve she feels;
From child to child the quick affections spread,
Forever wand'ring, yet forever fix'd.
Nor does division weaken, nor the force
Of constant operation e'er exhaust

Parental love. All other passions change
With changing circumstances; rise or fall,
Dependent on their object; claim returns;
Live on reciprocation, and expire
Unfed by hope. A mother's fondness reigns
Without a rival, and without an end.
    Mir: But say what heav'n inspires to save thy son?
    Joch: Since the dear fatal morn which gave him birth,
I have revolv'd in my distracted mind
Each means to save his life: and many a thought
Which fondness prompted, prudence has oppos'd
As perilous and rash. With these poor hands
I've fram'd a little ark of slender reeds;
With pitch and slime I have secur'd the sides.
In this frail cradle I intend to lay
My little helpless infant, and expose him
Upon the banks of the Nile.
    Mir: 'Tis full of danger.
    Joch: 'Tis danger to expose, and death to keep him.
    Mir: Yet, oh! reflect. Should the fierce crocodile,
The native and the tyrant of the Nile,
Seize the defenceless infant!
    Joch: O forbear!
Spare my fond heart. Yet not the crocodile,
Nor all the deadly monsters of the deep,
To me are half so terrible as Pharaoh,
That heathen king, that royal murderer!
    Mir: Should he escape, which yet I dare not hope,
Each sea-born monster, yet the winds and waves
He cannot 'scape.
    Joch: Know, God is every where;
Not to one narrow, partial spot confin'd:
No, not to chosen Israel: he extends
Through all the vast infinitude of space:
At his command the furious tempests rise —
The blasting of the breath of his displeasure.
He tells the world of waters when to roar;

And, at his bidding, winds and seas are calm:
In him, not in an arm of flesh, I trust;
In him, whose promise never yet has fail'd,
I place my confidence.
   Mir: What must I do?
Command thy daughter; for thy words have wak'd
An holy boldness in my youthful breast.
   Joch: Go then, my Miriam, go, and take the infant.
Buried in harmless slumbers there he lies:
Let me not see him — spare my heart that pang.
Yet sure, one little look may be indulg'd,
And I may feast my fondness with his smiles,
And snatch one last, last kiss. — No more my heart;
That rapture would be fatal — I should keep him.
I could not doom to death the babe I clasp'd
Did ever mother kill her sleeping boy?
I dare not hazard it — The task be thine.
Oh! do not wake my child; remove him softly;
And gently lay him on the river's brink.
   Mir: Did those magicians, whom the sons of Egypt
Consult and think all-potent, join their skill
And was it great as Egypt's sons believe;
Yet all their secret wizard arts combin'd,
To save this little ark of bulrushes,
Thus fearfully expos'd, could not effect it.
Their spells, their incantations, and dire charms
Could not preserve it.
   Joch: Know this ark is charm'd
With incantations Pharaoh ne'er employ'd;
With spells, which impious Egypt never knew:
With invocations to the living God,
I twisted every slender reed together,
And with a pray'r did every ozier weave.
   Mir: I go.
   Joch: Yet e'er thou go'st, observe me well;
When thou hast laid him in his wat'ry bed,
O leave him not: but at a distance wait,

And mark what Heaven's high will determines for him.
Lay him among the flags on yonder beach,
Just where the royal gardens meet the Nile.
I dare not follow him, Suspicion's eye
Would note my wild demeanor! Miriam, yes,
The mother's fondness would betray the child.
Farewell! God of my fathers. Oh, protect him!

Part II

[Enter *Miriam* after having deposited the child.]

Mir: Yes, I have laid him in his wat'ry bed,
His wat'ry grave, I fear! — I tremble still;
It was a cruel task — still I must weep!
But ah, my mother! who shall sooth thy griefs!
The flags and sea-weeds will awhile sustain
Their precious load; but it must sink ere long!
Sweet babe, farewell! Yet think not I will leave thee:
No, I will watch thee till the greedy waves
Devour thy little bark: I'll sit me down,
And sing to thee, sweet babe; thou can'st not hear;
But 'twill amuse me, while I watch thy fate.

>   [She sits down on a bank, and
>   sings.]

SONG
I.

Thou, who canst make the feeble strong,
    O God of Israel, hear my song!
Not mine such notes as Egypt's daughter's arise;
'Tis thee, O God of Hosts, I strive to praise.

II

Ye winds, the servants of the Lord,
Ye waves, obedient to his word,
Oh spare the babe committed to your trust;
And Israel shall confess the Lord is just!

III

Though doom'd to find an early grave,
This infant, Lord, thy power can save,
And he, whose death's decreed by Pharaoh's hand,
May rise a prophet to redeem the land
                    [She rises and looks out.]
What female form bends thitherward her steps?
Of royal port she seems; perhaps some friend,
Rais'd by the guardian care of bounteous Heaven,
To prop the falling house of Levi. — Soft!
I'll hasten unperceiv'd; these trees will hide me.
                    [She stands behind.]

[Enter the *princess* of Egypt, attended by a train of ladies.]

Prin: No farther, virgins, here I mean to rest.
To taste the pleasant coolness of the breeze;
Perhaps to bathe in this translucent stream.
Did not our holy law* enjoin th' ablution
Frequent and regular, it still were needful
To mitigate the fervours of our clime.
Melita, stay — the rest at distance wait.
                    [They all go out, except one.]

---

* The ancient Egyptians used to wash their bodies four times every twenty-four hours.

[The *Princess* looks out.]

Sure, or I much mistake, or I perceive
Upon the sedgy margin of the Nile
A chest; entangled in the reeds it seems:
Discern'st thou aught?
 Mel: Something, but what I know not.
 Prin: Go and examine what this sight may mean.
          [Exit maid.]

[*Miriam* behind.]

O blest, beyond my hopes! he is discover'd;
My brother will be sav'd! — who is the stranger?
Ah! 'tis the princess, cruel Pharaoh's daughter.
If she resemble her inhuman sire,
She must be cruel too; yet fame reports her
Most merciful and mild. — Great Lord of all,
By whose good Spirit bounteous thoughts are given
And deeds of love perform'd — be gracious now,
And touch her soul with mercy!

[Re-enter *Melita*.]

 Prin: Well, Melita!
Hast thou discover'd what the vessel is?
 Mel: Oh, princess, I have seen the strangest sight!
Within the vessel lies a sleeping babe,
A fairer infant have I never seen!
 Prin: Who knows but some unhappy Hebrew woman
Has thus expos'd her infant, to evade
The stern decree of my too cruel sire.
Unhappy mothers! oft my heart has bled
In secret anguish o'er your slaughter'd sons;
Powerless to save, yet hating to destroy.
 Mel: Should this be so, my princess knows the danger.
 Prin: No danger should deter from acts of mercy.

[*Miriam* behind.]

A thousand blessings on her princely head;
Prin: Too much the sons of Jacob have endur'd
From Royal Pharaoh's unrelenting hate;
Too much our house has crush'd their alien race.
Is't not enough that cruel task-masters
Grind them by hard oppression? not enough
That iron bondage bows their spirits down?
Is't not enough my sire his greatness owes,
His palaces, his fanes magnificent,
Those structures which the world with wonder views,
To much insulted Israel's patient race?
To them his growing cities owe their splendour:
Their toils fair Rameses and Pythom built;
And shall we fill the measure of our crimes,
And crown our guilt with murder? and shall I
Sanction the sin I hate? forbid it, Mercy!
   Mel: I know thy royal father fears the strength
Of this still growing race, who flourish more
The more they are oppress'd: he dreads their numbers.
   Prin: Apis forbid! Pharaoh afraid of Israel!
Yet should this outcast race, this hapless people
Ere grow to such a formidable greatness,
(Which all the gods avert whom Egypt worship)
This infant's life can never serve their cause,
Nor can his single death prevent their greatness.
   Mel: Trust not to that vain hope. By weakest means
And most unlikely instrument, full oft
Are great events produc'd. This rescued child
Perhaps may live to serve his upstart race
More than an host.
   Prin: How ill it does beseem
Thy tender years and gentle womanhood,
To steel thy breast to Pity's sacred touch!
So weak, so unprotected is our sex,
So constantly expos'd, so very helpless,

That did not Heaven itself enjoin compassion,
Yet human policy should make us kind,
Lest in the rapid turn of Fortune's wheel,
We live to need the pity we refuse.
Yes, I will save him — Mercy, thou has conquered!
Lead on — and from the rushes we'll remove
The feeble ark which cradles this poor babe.

> [The *Princess* and her maid go
> out.]

[*Miriam* comes forward.]

How poor were words to speak my boundless joy!
The princess will protect him; bless her, Heaven!

> [She looks out after the
> princess, and describes her
> action.]

With what impatient steps she seeks the shore!
Now she approaches where the ark is laid!
With what compassion, with what angel sweetness,
She bends to look upon the infant's face!
She takes his little hand in hers — he wakes —
She smiles upon him — hark, alas! he cries;
Weep on, sweet babe! weep on, till thou has touch'd
Each chord of pity, waken'd every sense
Of melting sympathy, and stolen her soul!
She takes him in her arms — O lovely princess!
How goodness heightens beauty! now she clasps him
With fondness to her heart, she gives him now
With tender caution to her damsel's arms:
She points her to the palace, and again
This way the princess bends her gracious steps;
The virgin train retire and bear the child.

[Re-enter the *Princess*.]

Prin: Did ever innocence and infant beauty
Plead with such dumb but powerful eloquence?
If I, a stranger, feel these soft emotions,

What must the mother who expos'd him feel!
Go, fetch a woman of the Hebrew race,
That she may nurse the babe: and, by her garb,
Lo, such a one is here!
 Mir: Princess, all hail!
Forgive the bold intrusion of thy servant,
Who stands a charm'd spectator of thy goodness.
 Prin: I have redeem'd an infant from the waves,
Whom I intend to nurture as mine own.
 Mir: My transports will betray me! [aside.] Gen'rous Princess!
 Prin: Know'st thou a matron of the Hebrew race
To whom I may confide him?
 Mir: Well I know
A prudent matron of the house of Levi;
Her name Jochebed, is the wife of Amram;
Of gentle manners, fam'd throughout her tribe
For soft humanity; full well I know
That she will rear him with a mother's love.
[Aside.] Oh truly spoke! a mother's love indeed!
To her despairing arms I mean to give
This precious trust: the nurse shall be the mother!
 Prin: With speed conduct this matron to the palace.
Yes, I will raise him up to princely greatness,
And he shall be my son; I'll have him train'd
By choicest sages, in the deepest lore
Of Egypt's sapient son; — his name be *Moses*,
For I have drawn him from the perilous flood.
           [They go out. She kneels.]
 Thou Great unseen! who causest gentle deeds,
And smil'st on what thou causest; thus I bless thee.
That thou did'st deign consult the tender make
Of yielding human hearts, when thou ordain'dst
Humanity a virtue! did'st not make it
A rigorous exercise to counteract
Some strong desire within; to war and fight
Against the power of Nature; but did'st bend
The nat'ral bias of the soul to mercy:

Then mad'st that mercy duty! Gracious Power!
Mad'st the keen rapture exquisite as right;
Beyond the joys of sense; as pleasure sweet,
As reason vigorous, and as instinct strong!

Part III

[Enter *Jochebed*.]

I've almost reach'd the place — with cautious steps
I must approach the spot where he is laid,
Lest from the royal gardens any 'spy me:
— Poor babe! ere this the pressing calls of hunger
Have broke thy short repose; the chilling waves,
Ere this have drench'd thy little shiv'ring limbs.
What must my babe have suffer'd! — No one sees me!
But soft, does no one listen! — Ah! how hard,
How very hard for fondness to be prudent!
Now is the moment to embrace and feed him,
                              [She looks out.]
Where's Miriam? she has left her little charge,
Perhaps through fear; perhaps she was detected.
How wild is thought! how terrible is conjecture!
A mother's fondness frames a thousand fears,
With thrilling nerve feels every real ill,
And shapes imagin'd miseries into being.
                              [She looks towards the river.]
Ah me! where is he? soul-distracting sight
He is not there — he's lost, he's gone, he's drown'd!
Toss'd by each beating surge my infant floats.
Cold, cold, and wat'ry is thy grave, my child!
O no — I see the ark — transporting sight!
                              [She goes towards it.]
I have it here — Alas, the ark is empty!
The casket's left, the precious gem is gone!
You spar'd him, pitying spirits of the deep!

But vain your mercy; some insatiate beast,
Cruel as Pharaoh, took the life you spar'd —
And I shall never, never see my boy!

[Enter *Miriam.*]

Joch: Come and lament with me thy brother's loss!
Mir: Come and adore with me the God of Jacob!
Joch: Miriam — the child is dead!
Mir: He lives! he lives!
Joch: Impossible — Oh, do not mock my grief!
See'st thou that empty vessel?
Mir: From that vessel
Th' Egyptian princess took him.
Joch: Pharaoh's daughter?
Then still he will be slain: a bloodier death
Will terminate his woes.
Mir: His life is safe;
For know, she means to rear him as her own.
Joch [Falls on her knees in rapture.]:
To God, the Lord, the glory be ascrib'd!
O magnify'd forever be thy might
Who mock'st all human forethought! who o'er-rulest
The hearts of all sinners to perform thy work,
Defeating their own purpose! who canst plant
Unlook'd-for mercy in a heathen's heart,
And from the depth of evil bring forth good?
                         [She rises.]
Mir: O blest event, beyond our warmest hopes!
Joch: What! shall my son be nurtur'd in a court,
In princely grandeur bred? taught every art
And ev'ry wond'rous science Egypt knows?
Yet ah! I tremble Miriam; should he learn,
With Egypt's polish'd arts her baneful faith!
O worse exchange for death! yes, should he learn
In yon proud palace to disown *His* hand
Who thus has sav'd him: should he e'er embrace

(As sure he will, if bred in Pharaoh's court)
The gross idolatries which Egypt owns,
Her graven images, her brutish gods,
Then shall I wish he had not been preserv'd
To shame his fathers and deny his faith.
   Mir: Then to dispel thy fears and crown thy joy,
Hear farther wonders — Know, the gen'rous princess
To thine own care thy darling child commits.
   Joch: Speak, while my joy will give me leave to listen!
   Mir: By her commission'd, thou behold'st me here
To seek a matron of the Hebrew race
To nurse him: thou, my mother, art that matron.
I said I knew thee well; that thou would'st rear him,
E'en with a mother's fondness; she who bare him
(I told the princess) would not love him more.
   Joch: Fountain of Mercy! whose pervading eye
Can look within and read what passes there,
Accept my thoughts for thanks! I have no words.
My soul, o'erfraught with gratitude, rejects
The aid of language — Lord! behold my heart.
   Mir: Yes, thou shalt pour into his infant mind
The purest precepts of the purest faith.
   Joch: O! I will fill his tender soul with virtue,
And warm his bosom with devotion's flame!
Aid me celestial Spirit! with thy grace,
And be my labours with thy influence crown'd!
Without it they were vain. Then, then, my Miriam,
When he is furnish'd 'gainst the evil day,
With God's whole armour,* girt with sacred truth,
And as a breastplate wearing righteousness,
Arm'd with the Spirit of God, the shield of faith,
And with the helmet of salvation crown'd,
Inur'd to watching and dispos'd to prayer;
Then may I send him to a dangerous court,

---

*Thess. chap. 5. Ephes. chap. vi.

And safely trust him in a perilous world,
Too full of tempting snares and fond delusions!
   Mir: May bounteous Heav'n thy pious cares reward!
   Joch: O Amram! O my husband! when thou com'st,
Wearied at night, to rest thee from the toils
Impos'd by haughty Pharaoh, what a tale
Have I to tell thee! Yes: thy darling son
Was lost, and is restor'd; was dead, and lives!
   Mir: How joyful shall we spend the live-long night
In praises to Jehovah; who thus mocks
All human foresight, and converts the means
Of seeming ruin into great deliverance!
   Joch: Had not my child been doom'd to such strange perils
As a fonder mother trembles to recal,
He had not been preserv'd.
   Mir: And mark still farther;
Had he been sav'd by any other hand,
He had been still expos'd to equal ruin.
   Joch: Then let us join to bless the hand of Heaven,
That this poor outcast of the house of Israel,
Condemn'd to die by Pharaoh, kept in secret
By my advent'rous fondness; then expos'd
E'en by that very fondness which conceal'd him,
Is now, to fill the wondrous round of mercy,
Preserv'd from perishing by Pharaoh's daughter,
Sav'd by the very hand which sought to crush him.
Wise and unsearchable are all thy ways,
Thou God of Mercies — Lead me to my child.

The End

Ditailly del.   Voisard Sculp.

THE DANCING MASTER'S BALL

1788

Arnaud Berquin

Arnaud Berquin was born in Bordeaux on September 25, 1747.[1] In his short lifetime, he had two essentially separate literary careers. He began as a poet, although his parents believed poetry "would render him incapable of more serious and important studies."[2] His two major poetic works are *Idylles*, published in 1775, which one critic said "served to invest virtue with new charm,"[3] and *Romances*, published in 1776, which made his literary reputation.

In 1782 and 1783, he wrote and published serially twenty-four small volumes of stories, moral tales, dialogues, and plays for children, which he called *L'ami des enfans*. The series won a prize in 1784 for being the most useful literary work published in France that year.

Berquin followed his success with *L'ami des adolescence* in 1784, and, having found his métier, he followed that work with other didactic works for the young. At the outbreak of the Revolution, he was proposed as tutor for Louis XVI's son, but he did not get the post. During the Revolution, he was denounced as a Girondist. He died on December 21, 1791, at the age of forty-four.

Berquin's influence was considerably greater than his talent. His chief gifts were his ability to read his market and his enormous literary energy, which is remarkable even by eighteenth-century standards. He was the first Frenchman to make a living writing for children.[4] His collected works in French run to ten substantial volumes.

Berquin was a prolific translator as well as a writer. His translations introduced the French public to the works of the German writers for children Weisse and Pfeffel, the English writers Thomas Day, Mrs. Trimmer, and Samuel Richardson, in an abridgment of *Le Petit Grandisson* [sic] for children. In turn, his own works were widely translated. *L'ami des enfans* alone was printed in England in two separate translations by 1786, three years after it had first appeared in French, and in America — in Boston, Newburyport, Philadelphia, and New Haven — by 1794. In London, Berquin's plays, along with the plays of Mme de Genlis, when acted by young French immigrants, became "the fashionable frenzy of the day."[5]

THE DANCING MASTER'S BALL

The Dancing Master's Ball is at least as much the work of its translator, the Reverend Mark Anthony Meilan, as of its author, and it is none the worse for that. Meilan was no respecter of the sanctity of the work of others. His work is very free. I print it here because it is lively, playable in English, and full of what Henry James called "felt life," which he asserted was one of the true tests of the value of a work of art. Too often, the English translations of Berquin's plays by his contemporaries are overly respectful of the original and emerge pallid and banal.

The Dancing Master's Ball, short as it is, is an effective and funny piece. It ends with the obligatory moral, but before it does, it is good theatre. Its themes are those of *Les Précieuses Ridicules* and *Le Bourgeois Gentilhomme*, but the easy derision the themes might have produced is softened and humanized here by understanding.

The Dancing Master's Ball is a skillful piece of work by any standards. It opens, effectively, *in medias res*, dispensing with the scene (or scenes) of slow exposition common in the period. It is particularly and specifically imagined, down to the stage directions.

"Oh, yes, indeed she does [says Miss Mushroom]. She has a board that sticks out thus: [*Describing it with her elbows jutting out, and with her forefingers meeting in a point*]. on which she wrote in fine gold letters: YOUNG LADIES GENTEELY EDUCATED."

The play's language, too, is specific. It differentiates its two characters clearly, both in their vocabulary and in the length of their sentences. Speech to speech, even line to line, the dialogue sounds like the talk of real people, up to and including Miss Mushroom's "cork rump." Realism of any kind is very rare in English plays for children of this early period, and realism in dialogue is particularly rare and therefore particularly welcome.

The theme of a pretentious, and consequently ridiculous, middle-class social climber is certainly not new in the eighteenth century. But *The Dancing Master's Ball* is different and more humane than most other plays of the type. Miss Mushroom, describing herself decked out by her mother for the ball, is a pathetic figure as much as she is a figure of fun. What is more, she is willing, even eager, to learn, which is what the young should do and what plays like this are written to help them do. It is the mother who is, in the end, the ridiculous and reprehensible figure. The daughter is merely her creature, or has been up until the end of this dialogue: pensive, uninformed, a little sad, and ultimately admirable. In twenty years, she will not be ridiculous, as her mother is, and she will surely treat her own daughter better than she herself was treated. In short, she will have become educated.

NOTES

1. Darton says he was born in 1749. *Children's Books in England*, 148.

THE DANCING MASTER'S BALL

Miss Lucy Harlow and
Miss Sophronia-Wilhelmina-Josepha Mushroom

Miss Harlow: Yes; so my father told me.
Miss Mushroom: Father, Miss? I thought young ladies said papa.
Miss Harlow: Oh, no.
Miss Mushroom: Ours do, however.
Miss Harlow: Yours! and who are they, Miss Mushroom?
Miss Mushroom: Those I go to school with.
Miss Harlow: Is your school in London?
Miss Mushroom: Yes, in Popping Alley, near Fleet Market, at a chandler's shop.
Miss Harlow: A chandler's shop?
Miss Mushroom: Yes, Miss: I mean the lower part of such a shop. Our school is on the second floor.
Miss Harlow: Tis plain your governess knows nothing of gentility.
Miss Mushroom: Oh, yes, indeed she does. She has a board that sticks out thus: [Describing it with her elbows jutting out, and her forefingers meeting in a point] on which she wrote, in fine gold letters: YOUNG LADIES GENTEELY EDUCATED.
Miss Harlow: Do they call the children ladies, that go to that school?
Miss Mushroom: Yes, every one.
Miss Harlow: And can you tell me of what business, any of the parents, are, that send their children thither?
Miss Mushroom: Yes, at once. First; there is Miss Amelia Medler and her sister: their papa sells greens. Then, Miss Maria Cleaver, at the butcher's shop in Fleet Street; and a dozen others as genteel as they are.
Miss Harlow: Well, believe me, gentlefolk are never called papa, mama, or any thing of that kind by their children, but plain father, mother, and the like; they are as plain in that respect as their clothes.

Miss Mushroom: As in their clothes? and do you think, my dear Miss Harlow, I am plain, as you express it, in my clothes, whenever I go out of a visiting?

Miss Harlow: You should, as you are such a creditable tradesman's daughter. Oil and pickle-men, my father says, are generally very rich; and I should think you the genteelest child of any at your school.

Miss Mushroom: Yes; my mama is often telling me as much: but you are serious, miss, in saying ladies always wear plain clothes? Do you?

Miss Harlow: Yes, Miss.

Miss Mushroom: But what?

Miss Harlow: Why, nothing but a cambric frock and such.

Miss Mushroom: And never have your hair dressed?

Miss Harlow: Never.

Miss Mushroom: And no feathers?

Miss Harlow: Never.

Miss Mushroom: And do no young ladies wear such things?

Miss Harlow: No, if their parents are genteel.

Miss Mushroom: Ah, I am glad you tell me this; for my mama shall henceforth give me nothing but plain clothes: I shall be more at ease, if she will do so.

Miss Harlow: More at your ease! How so?

Miss Mushroom: Why you must know, Miss Harlow, I was this day sennight at our dancing master's ball; and my mama, to make me elegant as all young ladies should be, overloaded me with finery, in such a manner that at night I was rejoiced, when I got home to rest myself.

Miss Harlow: Tell me the whole from first to last: how were you dressed? and what diversion, during the whole night, you met with?

Miss Mushroom: Dressed! and with what diversion! I was never in my life so fine before, or in such pain.

Miss Harlow: Well, tell me regularly; and begin with the story of your dress. What had you on?

Miss Mushroom: Oh, I must give you first of all the history of the day before. Mama began at night to put my hair up into papers. I, for my part, was delighted with the notion of a ball, as I had never been at one before. Alas! I did not know what it would prove! I had been only told about the dancing, and the cakes, and lemonade, and orgeat, and nice things, I should have given me. I desired no better, and with great impatience waited for the happy day, which came at last, and my mama prepared to dress me.

Miss Harlow: Well?

Miss Mushroom: I had a cushion, in the first place, put upon my head.

Miss Harlow: A cushion!

Miss Mushroom: Yes; and it was fastened to my hair beneath it, with large pins, as long as this: [Describing a certain length] and then, upon the cushion, there was placed a plenty of false hair.

Miss Harlow: Why you had surely hair enough!

Miss Mushroom: No matter if I had. Mama said she would positively have me better dressed than any in the ball room, when I once got there. And thus the cushion and false hair, as you may easily imagine, made me up a monstrous head already. But on that, came next a huge-sized hat; and on the last, a deal of gauze and ribbands, and on them, a bunch of flowers; and on the flowers, at least six feathers sticking up, of which the least was two feet long.

Miss Harlow: But how, pray, could you walk about the ball room, under such a burthen?

Miss Mushroom: To say truth, I could not. I was totally incapable of stirring; neither could I move my head. The least position on one side would certainly have made me lose my balance. — Then they finished dressing me: I had a steel-ribbed pair of stays that almost took away my breath. A cork rump was applied behind me; and before, a handkerchief puffed out like a baloon; and over all, a cambric frock, that made me look exactly like a shepherdess, they said. When this was done, our shopman carried me to Kensington, near London, where the ball room was, and said: Take care you do not, when you dance, disturb your hair, or rumple your new frock, and be as merry as you please.

Miss Harlow: And could you dance?

Miss Mushroom: Dance! I could hardly walk: however, *that* you are not come to yet. The dancing master showed me to a seat, where he desired me to sit till some young gentleman should ask me out. I waited long enough. I looked so sorrowful, than no one thought I had the least desire to dance. At last, however, I was taken out; but when we got into the middle of the room, the place was filled already by another couple; so that I returned quite disappointed to my seat.

Miss Harlow: But what meant you, when you said the place was filled already by another couple?

Miss Mushroom: Why I found that those young ladies who ran best, danced most.

Miss Harlow: Such ladies very possibly as go to school in Popping's Alley, may; for had they been genteely educated, as you say is mentioned on your governess's board, they would have know how impolite it was to keep their friends from dancing.

Miss Mushroom: Oh, I found them worse than impolite; for they were cruel, and burst out laughing, when they saw me sitting in such pain.

Miss Harlow: O, fie upon them!

Miss Mushroom: It was certainly ridiculous, but quite uneasy: should they not have pitied me, Miss Harlow?

Miss Harlow: To be sure they should: but tell me, had the rest cork rumps on, and such other fineries as you had?

Miss Mushroom: No.

Miss Harlow: Then let me give you some advice; which I can do, as I remember what my dear mama is often saying to me; that plain clothes are best for children. You will see how I am dressed, while you continue here upon your visit. None but parents that know nothing of the world, says my mama, bedizen out their children like painted dolls in toyshop windows. So that when you go to such a ball again, get your mama to dress you in the plainest way she can.

You will be then not only more at ease, but more respected as a lady.

   Miss Mushroom: Oh, if that be true gentility, I promise I will tell mama: and she will never let me be so ungenteel in future.

The End

THE WOODEN BOY

1798

Charles Stearns

Charles Stearns, the son of Thomas Stearns and Lydia
Mansfield Stearns, was born on July 19, 1753, at Lunenberg,
Massachusetts, and grew up in the nearby town of Leominster.
He graduated from Harvard College in 1773 and spent the next
several years studying theology and teaching school. He
received an M.A. from Harvard in 1776 and was appointed tutor
in the college in 1780. He resigned his tutorship eighteen
months later to become the pastor of Christ Church in Lincoln,
where he remained for forty-five years.

On December 4, 1781, he married Susanna Cowdry of
Reading. They had eleven children, six boys and five girls,
seven of whom lived to their majority.

In 1792, twenty-one prominent citizens of Lincoln organized
themselves as the Associated Proprietors of the Liberal School
in Lincoln, where Stearns taught and of which he became the
first principal. It was for his pupils at the Liberal School that
Stearns, over the next six years, wrote his *Dramatic Dialogues*.

As both minister and teacher, Stearns was the "person —
parson — of the town. . . . Everybody went to him for advice.
He seemed to be invested with a kind of magisterial dignity."[1]
In time, Stearns grew very fat. But despite occasional and
sometimes serious illness, he "retained his bodily and mental
facilities in a remarkable degree" and preached his last sermon
in the same month he died.[2]

In 1809, Stearns was elected a member of the American Academy of Arts and Sciences, and in 1810 he received an honorary doctorate from Harvard. About this time he was apparently approached about accepting the presidency of Harvard, but he declined on the grounds that "he was content with his parish and that he could not maintain his family and meet the increased expenses at Cambridge on the president's salary."[3] He died on July 26, 1826, in his seventy-fourth year. He is buried between his wife, who outlived him by eight years, and his daughter Eliza.

Stearns left four kinds of written works: sermons; *Principles of Religion and Morality*, a religious textbook; *The Ladies' Philosophy of Love*, a long poem in heroic couplets; and his major work, the *Dramatic Dialogues for the Use of Schools*.

The *Dramatic Dialogues* consists of thirty plays, eleven "single pieces" — set pieces for individual speakers — and an introduction. The plays are short. Although they are typically written in five acts, they rarely run to more than ten pages of printed text.

Stearns took his plots where he found them and wrote in conventional genres of his century — Romanoid tragedies, history plays, Eastern tales, comedies of manners, and *comédies larmoyantes*. The best plays are the ones, like *The Wooden Boy*, that he drew from life: scenes of New England town, farm, and school life at the very end of the eighteenth century.

THE WOODEN BOY

> When they [school exhibitions] are properly conducted they enlarge the ideas and polish the manners of students. They show an example of moral precepts as represented in real life.
>
> *Dramatic Dialogues*, Introduction, p. [7]

The Wooden Boy, like all the *Dialogues*, sets out to illustrate a moral precept stated as a subtitle; here, "The Folly of Local Prejudice." The action of the play does this but, it must be said, in a rather perfunctory way. Stearns was a natural and gifted playwright, and his playwright's instincts told him correctly that the dramatic fun of the piece would be in the exhibition of the folly, not the reproof of it. There is some moralizing and editorializing during the play. But the folly is much more strongly reproved by John Hickory's ad hoc wit and indeed by the self-evident, palpable wrongheadedness of the people who believe the foolishness than by the orthodox moral talk.

The characters in the play are (Stearns says) "so exaggerated that young persons, who are always wanting in experience, may better discern the intention of them."[4] The characters in the *The Wooden Boy* are exaggerated, being chiefly, and sometimes only, that quality they were drawn to exemplify. Their names, in the fashion of eighteenth-century comedy, tell the audience what they stand for. Battledore is pugnacious. Plume is a dandy. But, although the characters may have been conceived as embodiments of abstract qualities, they talk like real boys.

Battledore: Think of you — Why as to your own proper self, you look passably well — But then how you dress, all as far from the fashion as from Nova Scotia to Georgia — What do you mean by wearing that old bayonet hat — Your coat is half a yard too short — oh! fun indeed! this is pretty! what a coat! and your hair tied up with a leather — whang — You look like old Jeremy — fact!

II, i.

The girls talk more correctly and genteelly than the boys in this dialogue, and so their talk is less interesting. But in some of the *Dialogues*, particularly in scenes when there are no adults or boys around, the girls let themselves go; although they are never as rough as the boys, they are sometimes as common and frequently as exuberant.

In several of the *Dialogues*, Stearns's own voice is discernible, through a raisonneur. In *The Wooden Boy*, the raisonneur is concerned with the degradation in schools, which may sound something like Harvard College in the 1770s.

Martin: To study one, two, three, or four years, in some seminary of learning — to qualify ourselves, to get drunk as brutally as porters, and grooms — to introduce ourselves to vicious women, who after all prefer the assassin and street robber — and to acquire an aversion to modest ladies, to be embarrassed, and know not how to speak to them. One need not reside in a college to learn these things — They may be learned in taverns, and gaming houses to perfection.

The Wooden Boy is a fair representative of Stearns's *Dramatic Dialogues*. It is one of several *Dialogues* that I believe could be successfully mounted today. Didactic and schematic as the *Dialogues* may be in their plan, they are full of life — the life of late eighteenth-century American children — and are potentially an entree for contemporary American children to that life.

NOTES

The biographical section on Stearns has been edited but is taken virtually verbatim from Jonathan Levy, "The *Dramatic Dialogues* of Charles Stearns" in *Spotlight on the Child: Studies in the History of American Children's Theatre*, ed. Roger L. Bedard and John Tolch (Westport, Conn.: Greenwood Press, 1989), [5]–24.

1.   Charles Stearns, *Proceedings in observance of the one hundred and fiftieth anniversary of the first church in Lincoln, Massachusetts, August 21 and September 4, 1898* (Cambridge: Cambridge University Press, 1899), 71–72.

2   William B. Sprague, ed., *Annals of the American Pulpit* (New York: Robert Carter and Brothers, 1865), 148.

3.   Charles Stearns, *Proceedings*, 73–74.

4.   Charles Stearns, *Dramatic Dialogues for the Use of Schools*, (Leominster, Mass.: John Prentiss and Co., 1798), preface, [29].

THE WOODEN BOY

A DRAMATIC DIALOGUE IN THREE ACTS

The Folly of Local Prejudices

Perhaps there is not a prejudice in human beings more unfriendly to society than that which is properly called *local prejudice*. A remarkable influence of this we have between *cits* and *clowns* — In the exercise of this prejudice it is difficult to say which discovers the most impenetrable stupidity. The cits commonly, however, are most insolent; the clowns have, perhaps, the most settled malice. Differing districts of the same nation often carry it almost to open hostility — How can men so far forget, that they are all of the same species, and have the same feelings?

Persons

Men
Mr. FREEMAN,　　　　 { a polite young gentleman, affecting
or JOHN HICKORY,　　 { to be a rustic.
JAMES HOTSPUR, a young satirist.
JACK BATTLEDOOR, a boxer, affecting to be a high fellow.
HARRY PLUME, a young beau.
TALBOT, a large good natured boy.
MARTIN, a serious sententious lad.
CHRISTOPHER, a waiter in a boarding school.

Women
MYRA, a miss, favorite of Harry Plume.
SISTERS, of Mr. Freeman who appear but do not speak.

Act I

SCENE I

Plume and *Battledoor*

Plume: I wonder what the marvellous cause can be that our young fellows do not study the art of dress!

Bat: I think the art of boxing of much greater consequence.

Plume: Dress recommends us to the ladies, dear creatures; my heart is charmed with them; tho people laugh at me, for taking notice of them because I am so young.

Bat: But you can learn *push, parry, quart* and *tierce,* I mean to learn the art of fencing before I make pretensions to the ladies, and then if a man rivals me, I'll call him out.

Plume: I guess I'm not far from being a man, for when the miss Linnets sung last evening — they are sweet little angels you know — I felt my heart go pit a pat as plain as day light. If I be not pretty near a man, I wonder what in the name of beauty, that could mean.

Bat: I care not, I love to throw every boy in the school of my age; and beat every one of my size in boxing — then, if I like any of the girls, I can defend myself in possession.

Plume: But to make the girls like you, that is a serious matter, to captive their little tender souls, then you may keep them forever.

Bat: I would rather undertake to knock down a boy of twice my size, than to flatter a girl, or even to coax her to walk with me half a mile.

Plume: You and I shall not agree in our notions — But do you know that we are to have a new student, in our school, to day?

Bat: I heard of it — They say his name is John Hickory, and that he comes from the town of Brushwood, a rare wooden fellow — I dare say we shall pick fun out of him.

[Enter *Hotspur*.]

SCENE II

Hotspur, Plume, and *Battledoor.*

Hot: Well boys, they say we shall have a queer fellow come into school to day — We shall have music with him.

Plume: I wonder you should not have the prudence to acquaint yourself with the sweet little angels, and learn genteel manners, as I do.

Bat: If he comes I guess I shall box him, or at least I shall challenge him to wrestle with me at the first dash, that's my way.

Hot: I'll try, and see how he'll bear a joke. They say he dresses very queerly, all out of fashion. We shall joke him all to rags.

Plume: I wonder he should not dress himself when he comes to school, because that's a matter of importance.

Hot: I mean to buy me a jest book, and learn to joke by rule — It will cost only one dollar, and wit, you know, is worth every thing.

Plume: Better lay it out in pomatum to keep your hair slick; and give it an agreeable smell; that will make the young ladies like you.

Hot: When I get all the wit in the world, the ladies will like me for my wit; and then I shall be as smart as any man.

Bat: I am determined to learn boxing and the back sword; for if you and I travel together, as we may; when you affront a man with your wit, then I shall have to fight him.

Plume: Rare work you'll make of it, and I shall have to follow you in order to make peace. So we have business planned out for the rest of our lives.

Bat: We will contrive some way to make fun of neighbor Hickory — I love to take a fellow, who can't say his soul is his own, and give him a hearty sweat.

Plume: Now I had rather please one girl, than plague ten boys, and there is more amusement in it.

[Exit *Plume*.]

SCENE III

Martin, Battledoor and *Hotspur.*

Mar: Nothing gives a greater lustre to learning than prudence and good morals. I cannot join you in afflicting our new companion, it can only render us odious.

Bat: You never had any spirit for fun more than my grandmother — Always preaching your grum morals, what do you say Jack, shall we give up to him?

Hot: Not till he has had a spice of my jokes; I mean to try titles with him for the greatest wit.

Bat: If he can give me a fall, or beat me in boxing, then I'll allow him to be a good fellow.

Mart: I'm ashamed of you both — forever in riots and mischief — a terror to the neighborhood. You'll sooner be in prison than in Congress, at this rate of proceeding.

Hot: What a preacher! Let's collect money to buy him a new black coat — and he shall hold forth to the school.

Mart: You will need no preacher. Soon the consequences of your folly will give you tormenting conviction, *very* soon.

Bat: Think I'll give back for you — I'll only go deeper — I'll get a blanket, and toss Mr. Wooden head in a blanket.

[Exit *Martin*, and after him the rest.]

SCENE IV

Hickory (entering) and *Christopher.*

Hick: Sir can you introduce me into the school?

Chris: No! [in a surly tone.]

Hick: Why not? [complaisantly]

Chris: I have no time to wait on such wooden headed fellows — You came from the town of Brushwood — I must attend to my business.

Hick: Sir it will take you but a moment to introduce me.

Chris: I cannot spend my time to wait on you — You have no more manners than a bear — What sort of people live, where you came from?

Hick: A very rough unsociable people I must say to their dishonor — They will refuse to direct a stranger on his way — ask the town he came from, and tell him he has no more manners than a bear.

Chris: That is pretty much as they do here.

Hick: WIll you please to direct me into the common room?

Chris: You must first cross the yard — then turn over to the left — then you must come to the right again — then you must go back again to the left — then come to the right, and take a winding course up the back stairs into the common room.

Hick: It is impossible to find the way by these directions. Here, I'll give you this if you will show me the way.

Chris: I will wait on you sir. [Looks wishfully at the money.] But I must ask leave of absence of the master of the kitchen.

[Exit *Christopher*.]

Act II

SCENE I

Battledoor [entering] and *Hickory*.

Bat: Well, sir what's your name?

Hick: John Hickory sir.

Bat: What town did you come from?

Hick: Brushwood; a very remote part of the state.

Bat: You are the fellow I have been hearing of a number of days past — they told me there was a strange, woodenheaded fellow coming from Brushwood, a dark obscure hole, and that he had no more manners than a bear.

Hick: Well what do you think of him?

Bat: Think of you — Way as to your own proper self, you look passably well — But then how you dress, all as far from the fashion as from Nova Scotia to Georgia — What do you mean by wearing that old bayonet-hat — Your coat is half a yard too short — oh! fun indeed! this is pretty! what a coat! — and then your hair tied up with a leather—whang — You look like old Jeremy — fact! — Why sir, what sort of people are they at Brushwood?

Hick: They are a very droll people it would make you laugh to see their manners.

Bat: Why, how are they?

Hick: O they are so ridiculous, they say you love fun — it would make you die with laughing.

Bat: I long to hear then — Let us have it.

Hick: The first thing these coarse, rough people do, when they see a stranger — is to ask him what is his name — where he came from — they tell him he is a fellow they have heard of before — that he is a strange woodenheaded fellow, with no more manners than a bear — then they examine his person, and tell him he looks passably, but his dress is out of fashion — his hat is not right, and his coat is half a yard too long or too short — they find fault with the tying of his hair, and ask what sort of people they were in the town from whence he came.

Bat: You lie. Those are not the manners of the people at Brushwood.

Hick: They are sir, and you may enquire of any person you please — They are the manners of all people who have no sense of propriety.

Bat: Very pretty indeed, and so I have no sense of propriety!

Hick: I have never said that sir.

Bat: But you told the manners of the people of Brushwood, to be just like mine.

Hick: If they be alike, you would not have me tell a lie.

Bat: You are a saucy fellow; and I dare you out to box with me.

Hick: There are two things more which the people at Brushwood, are very apt to do — If they do not like what a man says to them, they tell him he lies, and challenge him to box.

Bat: I won't bear this — you mean to impose upon me, I know you do — I'll knock you down.

SCENE II

[Enter *Talbot, Battledoor* & *Hickory*.]

Tal: Stop your fire skull; what are you about to do? Fight a scholar before he enters the school — And for what? Has he ever injured you? It is not possible.

Bat: He has insulted me, and I won't bear it.

Tal: How insulted you?

Bat: He described the manners of the people of Brushwood to be just like mine.

Tal: What then? one unmannerly fellow is just like another.

Hick: O let him alone if he has a mind to fight, let him fight.

Tal: But he shall use fair play.

Hick: Fighting is fighting after all. I am not much concerned about the manner of it.

Bat: Yes I suppose in *your Town* they use the *Indian hug*, and strike a fellow after he is down.

Hick: If the business is to be civil, it is best not to fight at all.

Bat: That is because you are a coward. Yes, because you are a coward, I say, you refuse to fight. [with vehemence]

Hick: No sir, I do not refuse — but as you are the challenger, you must let me have the choice of weapons.

Tal: That's certainly fair — you can have no objection to that.

Hick: Then when I fight, I always fight with a large lemon in my fist — look you here, this is the way I fight, if I fight at all.

Bat: What is that for?

Hick: The business of fighting, you see, is to hurt one another — if you bruise any one, the juice gets into the wound, and the smart is intolerable — and if you strike them in the face, the juice gets into the eyes, and the anguish is inconceivable. Here sir, [offers him a couple of lemons] take a couple and prepare yourself. We must hurt one another very much, before we have done — I mean to fight as long as I can move a finger. I hope if I hurt you ever so much, [civilly] you will not take it ill

Bat: [looking at the lemons] 'Twould be a pity — *really* 'twould be a pity.

Hick: What is a pity?

Bat: To bruise these lemons all up in fighting, it will spoil them entirely.

Hick: Would it not spoil a man's face as much. But that is no matter — it is my way of fighting; and I have a right to chuse.

Bat: I think I don't want to fight much now.

Hick: That's because you are a coward.

Bat: Why I think ——I think, I'm dry, and I want a drink of punch — had we not better make these lemons into punch. I'm very fond of punch.

Hick: With all my heart; I love punch for that matter, as well as I love fighting.

Tal: I like it, so lay the lemons aside for a moment and we will have a drink of punch.

Bat: [clapping Hickory on the shoulder] On my word I ask pardon for being rough with you at first. I begin to think you are a clever fellow. There's Hotspur a coming — don't say a word to him, that we have made all up.

SCENE III

Hotspur, entering — the others as in the last Scene.

Hot: Where's our new genius — Well my friend, did you come here to buy wit?

Hick: I have come, I believe, to a bad market, for I do not find you have any to sell.

Hot: He's sharp, you see, very sharp. He lives upon razors, don't you think he does?

Hick: You had better not meddle with me then, for I have just this moment finished my dinner.

Hot: You came from Brushwood, I think, where foxes are plenty.

Hick: Yes sir, and when I dine on razors, I have foxs brains for sauce — that makes me very keen, you see.

Hot: And so you mean to deal out your fox wit by wholesale among us.

Hick: There is no need of that; a very small portion will serve for you.

Hot: I fancy you have been used to fox hunting; do you mean to pursue it here?

Hick: No, I'm hunting for fools, and have had great luck — the game is plenty.

Hot: You will find one if you look in the glass.

Hick: Then I won't look, for I am satisfied with what I see already.

Hot: How his wit bites; he stings close; he has been a pepper merchant, you may depend on it.

Hick: Yes, and have enough of it yet to season a dozen such fellows as you.

Hot: You are a proper blackguard — I am ashamed to talk with you.

Hick: A *cur* is always ashamed when he is beat.

Hot: I'll be revenged on you for this.

Tal: O shame on you — You began the attack, and are only angry because you are out witted.

Hot: I'll go and call a number of boys, and I'll be revenged on you.

Tal: How common it is for boys who begin with joking, soon to get angry — I think we may fairly draw the consequence from this; that judgment is much better than wit.

[Exeunt omnes.]

Act III

SCENE I

Battledoor and *Myra*

Bat: Ah how do ye do, my pretty Miss.

Myra: You are not to be very conversant with me sir, till you behave yourself better.

Bat: Why, have I done you any harm?

Myra: No, but I am told that you this day contrived to insult a new scholar, just as he was entering the school.

Bat: That does not concern you that I know of.

Myra: It concerns me to keep such rude, unmannerly wretches at a due distance. I hope, you will not have admittance, where we dance this evening.

Bat: You are always very particular about your company.

Myra: I wish every girl were as particular, then we should cure you of your high-goes — that is to say of your low frolics.

Bat: Madam, if you are out of temper, it is not worth my while to stay here?

[Exit *Battle*.]

SCENE II

Plume [entering] and *Myra*.

Plume: Your servant Miss — I am happy in hoping for the pleasure of dancing with you, this evening.

Myra: Sir if it be agreeable to you, and the company choose partners I have no objection.

Plume: For one thing Miss you must suffer me to blame you a little gently — I saw you walking with Jack Battledoor; he has not the best character in the school.

Myra: O never fear my growing fond of his company — he seized my arm, 'tis true, but I obliged him soon to quit it — I do not like him, his manner is quite too rough.

Plume: Shall I conduct you home.

Myra: You may if it be agreeable — tho it is but a little way — it will not be unpleasant to have company — yet now I wish you to stay here and prevent the boys from insulting Mr. Freeman. [*Plume* takes his leave of *Myra* very gentelly — comes to the middle of the stage and sings.]

SCENE III

Plume and *Hotspur*.

Plume sings:

'Tis the loveliest season of life,
When the spirits so merrily flow,
Our heart quickly rises with joy,
And is suddenly melted at woe.

Our minds are as simple as doves,
Our hearts yet not hardened with crimes,
Admit the first dartings of love,
And have their sweet meltings betimes.

Why, Myra came tripping to me,
So livelily over the green,
Thro all our fair village, than I,
Not a happier lad could be seen.

But when I walked o'er the green furrow,
Deeply musing on every charm,
I saw my sweet maiden with sorrow,
With another lad, locked in her arm.

Yet surely I welcome the joy,
Altho it be mixed with much pain.
The sensible heart, touched with love,
Never wished to be senseless again.

Hot: Well, Harry, wont you join us, we mean to have a high go?

Plume: I am always afraid of you, you carry matters to such a violent extreme.

Hot: You are a soft hearted thing, just fit to please the girls; and for nothing else.

Plume: What marvellous plan have you on foot, that you urge me so much, to take a part in it?

Hot: We have a scheme to take John Hickory, and toss him in a blanket.

Plume: Have your rough play to yourself, I will have nothing to do with it.

Hot: Go, then, and tie yourself to the girls apron strings; and let them coax, and wheedle, and befool you forever.

Plume: I have no taste for such rough play — It always ends in something disagreeable. As for my misses, they will soften, and polish my manners; and teach me to be a gentleman.

[Exit *Plume*.]

SCENE IV

Hotspur, Battledoor, [entering here]
with other boys and *Martin*.

Hot: Come lads; see John Hickory cut capers in the air — We mean to toss him in a blanket.

Mar: You are forever inventing mischief. What has John Hickory done to you, that you shall bear malice against him?

Hot: He is a new scholar you see.

Mar: The very reason why he should be treated kindly — if he be not polite at present it is his unhappiness not his fault.

Hot: We *know more* than he does.

Mar: Give credit to your knowledge then, and behave yourselves well.

Hot: Wonderfully wise to be sure.

Mar: Ignorant people have some excuse for bad morals — but to those who profess to be the *knowing ones* — nothing can be more infamous, than to despise the manners of civil life.

Hot: It always is the custom among scholars to play the rogue.

Mar: For that very reason seminaries of learning become odious. If men professing learning behave worse than they, who inhabit the woods — who can wonder that men hate the idea of a scholar — by such methods too, they are bred up to be the pests of human society — and the more learned the more pernicious they are.

Hot: But seminaries of learning are the resorts of politeness — the seats of the muses.

Mar: They ought to be; but such fellows as you give them the character of the seats of illiberality, and vice. If we find in colleges and academies, the rough stoic the contemptuous cynic, the coarsest pedants, and the sons of riot and debauchery, who can wonder if the public conceives an aversion to such societies?

Bat: A fig for your morals — There are your high fellows in all the seminaries of learning.

Mar: Yes, a worthy object to be sure. To study one, two, three, or four years, in some seminary of learning — to qualify ourselves, to get drunk as brutally as porters, and grooms — to introduce ourselves to vicious women, who after all prefer the assassin and street robber — and to acquire an aversion to modest ladies, to be embarrassed, and know not how to speak to them. One need not reside in a college to learn these things — They may be learned in taverns, and gaming houses to perfection.

Bat: Come on, boys — down with this preacher — Does he think we came here to hear sermons of terror? Let us all sail on, have him in the blanket, and give him a shaking.

Mar: Stand off you villains; if you attack me, I shall defend myself.

[*Hickory* enters.]

Hot: Well he is a great heavy lubber, we will let him alone; and take Hicory; he is the very man we want.

Hick: What do you mean, by this rude assault on me?
[*Talbot* enters.]
Tal: Silence ye young villains — Let this young gentleman alone — unhand him. There now, be easy; or I will bring every soul of you before the government.
[They desist. — The rest go out.]

SCENE V

Martin, Hotspur, *and* Battledoor.

Bat: I see we are likely to have no fun to day — I will go and see some of the misses — I do that when I can find nothing better.

Mar: What could you have better, than to recommend yourself to the best part of the human species?

Hot: Why do not our instructors then let the masters and misses perform their excercises together — or why in schools where they study together, do they make them sit in different parts of the house.

Mar: It is to save them the pain of being corrected in the presence of each other — to preserve their delicacy, and increase their mutual respect — There is nothing which makes the intercourse of men and women so happy as preserving mutual respect and esteem.

Bat: On my word, I believe you are right, for I have found when we had been from the misses all day — and had a nice genteel dance after school — it was the finest pleasure, I ever experienced in my life.

Mar: That's always the case — The more decent and proper we are in conversation with women, the more we enjoy their society, which is in fact, and truth, the greatest blessing of human life.

Bat: That's what I have not tho't of so much before — But there seems to be good sense and reason in what you say.

SCENE VI

Talbot, [entering] *Hotspur, Battledoor,* and *Martin.*

Tal: Young men you are very fortuante indeed, that you did not meddle with Hickory, for he is indeed a very genteel young man — He lived in Brushwood but one fortnight — as he knew you to be saucy, he contrived this way to mortify you; so he makes you the fools of the play, his real name is Freeman.

Mar: Yes, boys you will be mortified with a witness — The wooden boy you laughed at is really as genteel a lad as any in the school, and has permission to invite the young gentlemen and ladies to a dance after school.

Bat: O I shall die to appear before him.

Hot: I must excuse myself — How he must despise me — I may as well be annihilated as to appear before him.

Mar: I have often told you, young gentlemen, that you would bring yourselves into disgrace by such proceedings — But see, he is coming with his two sisters — sweet girls as ever lived. He looks like a Wooden Boy to be sure.

SCENE VII

Mr. Freeman entering with his two Sisters,
richly dressed.

Free: Gentlemen, I have the honor to invite you to dance with my sisters, and a number of the other misses after school; at the house of Mrs. Careful, the Governess.

Bat: Mr. Freeman I ask a thousand pardons — if I had but known you I should not —

Free: No matter, it afforded me some amusement — no matter,

Hot: If you will only pardon my jokes. I was wrong, perfectly wrong, I confess.

Free: I think sir, your jokes were quite harmless. Gentlemen I shall wait on you at four.

[Exit *Freeman*.]

Battledoor and *Hotspur* walk across the stage,
with their heads down.

Hot: My jokes quite harmless — That is worse than all the rest — He must think meanly of me, and cannot think otherwise. In fact, I feel very small.

Bat: And I too, as small as a mouse — I wish I had been in France before ever I heard of the Wooden Boy.

Martin Epiloguizes.

We see, in contests of the prize of wit;
The biter oft by his own malice bit.
In circles, boasting of politeness, find
Low manners the disgrace of human kind.
Ignorance in colleges may find a place;
And profligacy in a man of grace.
Cits think that Clowns are brutes, and Clowns again,
Esteem poor Cits the dullest sons of men.
The town Belle sneers at every rural lass —
The lass despising madam, *lets her pass.*
Thus mutual prejudice, and malice reign;
And all the joys of social life profane.
Yet banish prejudice, and love revives,
And social bliss, in fields, or cities, lives.

[*All leave the stage.*]

The End

THE FIB FOUND OUT

1808

William Godwin

William Godwin is remembered today as a social critic and a
novelist and chiefly as a pivotal if secondary member of the
brilliant, doomed circle of Shelley and Byron. Nevertheless,
he was also the author and publisher of a large and varied
body of work, including, surprisingly, given the proprieties of
the times and the impropriety of so much of Godwin's life, a
considerable number of works for children.

Godwin was born on March 3, 1756, in Wisbech, Cambridge-
shire, the seventh of the thirteen children of a dissenting
minister. He was a precocious and literary child, who, as a
small boy, asked, "What shall I do when I have read through
all the books that have been written?" He was educated at
Hoxton College, where his stern, Calvinistic upbringing was
reinforced. He was, at the time, politically a Tory.

In his early twenties he served as minister in several
parishes, but lost his Calvinism through reading Joseph
Priestley. He went to London in 1783 and supported himself by
doing literary hackwork. In 1786 he met and became friends
with Thomas Holcroft, the playwright and the translator of
Mme de Genlis's *Théâtre d'Education*. Partly through his
friendship with Holcroft, Godwin moved from religious
skepticism to atheism. His Toryism was eroded as well, and by
1791 he had become a member of a committee to publish Tom
Paine's *Rights of Man*.

In 1793, he published *An Enquiry Concerning the Principles of Political Justice*, a rebuttal of Burke, which gained him considerable success and made him a little money. In 1796 he began to live with Mary Wollstonecraft, the author of *The Vindication of the Rights of Women*. Although both she and Godwin disapproved of marriage, they married in 1797, before the birth of their daughter, Mary, who was to marry Shelley and write *Frankenstein*. Mary Wollstonecraft died giving birth to this child.

Godwin, a widower with a small child, married Mary Jane Clairmont in 1801. She had children of her own (one of whom later bore Byron's daughter, Allegra), and soon they had another together.

Godwin was, from this period on, always short of money. With Holcroft's help, he tried writing for the theatre, but without much success. In 1804 he went to work for Tabart, a publisher of books for children; and in the following year, with capital supplied by Thomas Wedgewood, he and his wife opened a shop in Soho that they called the Juvenile Library. The Juvenile Library published varied and often distinguished books for children, among them Charles and Mary Lamb's *Tales from Shakespeare* (1807), Godwin's own *Dramas for Children* (1809) — probably written in collaboration with his wife — and the first English translation of J. D. Wyss's *The Swiss Family Robinson* (1814). But the venture was undercapitalized, and in 1822 Godwin declared bankruptcy. His last major work was a *History of the Commonwealth of England*, which appeared between 1824 and 1828. He died on April 7, 1836, and was buried beside Mary Wollstonecraft.

THE FIB FOUND OUT

It is puzzling how so unconventional a man as Godwin could have written so conventional a play as *The Fib Found Out* until we realize that the play was taken, almost unchanged, from a French model, L. F. Jauffret's *La Réparation d'Honneur*.[1] But if

The Fib Found Out is a conventional play, it is at the same time a paradigm of an entire class of moral teaching plays of the period, and it is chiefly as such that I include it.

The play does have several virtues. The talk of baby Edmund rings true, and the life of the Wilmots, which we piece together from small touches like Mr. Wilmot's laboratory, is intriguing. But what is perhaps most interesting about the piece is the striking way it differs from the French original, that is, the way it draws its moral.

In Jauffret's play, the guilty children — for the sister is guilty too, in Jauffret's eyes — are obliged to earn their forgiveness. Flouricour, the children's father, says, "Quand on a calommié qulqu'un, on est obligé de lui faire réparation d'honneur en présence de témoins. . . . Vous allez d'abord remplir ce devoir."[2] And the children do. With their father's insistent coaching, they apologize to their innocent little brother in the most abject terms. They are then put *en pénitence*, forced to remain at home while the rest of the family goes out for the day and made to dine on bread and water.

By comparison, Godwin's children get off very lightly. They confess to their father, are forgiven immediately, and are not punished. Mr. Wilmot, their father, ends the play by saying:

Enough — enough, my children. I have suffered some moments of such grief as only a parent's heart can feel, for the fault you have committed, but I now feel a parent's joy, for that ready and ingenuous avowal, which tells me, that the twelve years devoted to your moral improvement, have not been spent in vain. Come and receive from your mother and myself, a kiss of reconciliation, and our promise to forget this morning's vexations.[3]

The lesson of Jauffret's play is clear. Honor must be satisfied, and satisfied in front of witnesses, and wrong actions must be punished.

But what did Godwin believe the easy forgiveness of the children in their play would teach? What did he think the sight of two guilty children, the loathesome Lionel and his accomplice, the poisonous Dorothy, forced at last by circumstances into confessing their duplicity to their father, would teach an audience of children or the child actors playing those characters about the morality of lying? Most particularly, what lesson would the children draw from their father's immediate forgiveness?

It is, of course, possible that Godwin, always short of money, simply truncated Jauffret's play in order to get it into print more quickly. But there is another possibility worth considering. It is that they believed that, *in a play*, the exhibition of a mistake corrected or a wrong righted is enough to remind us of what we already know to be true and that the details of a protracted correction are unimportant or even counterproductive. That is, a moral play, the *morale mise en action*, is not to be thought of as a proof of a new principle but rather as an *aide-mémoire*, to jog the moral sense into remembering what it already knows. Indeed, protracting and explaining the punishment, as Jauffret does and real parents might do usefully in life, merely dulls and blurs the lesson children learn in a play.

Thus the difference between Jauffret's play and the Godwins' is profound. It illustrates clearly two opposing positions about how, *exactly*, a lesson is learned in the theatre — not *taught* but *learned*. That, of course, is the central question at the heart of didactic drama: what it was, is, or could be.[4]

NOTES

1. *La Réparation d'Honneur* is the second play in the first volume of L. F. Jauffret, *Théâtre de Famille*, 2 vols. (Paris: Impr. de Guilmet, an VIII [1800]), vol. 1, 34–73. Jauffret's Avant-Propos to his collection of plays is a classic justification of children's playwrights of the period and as such is worth quoting in full.

> Je publie séparément le receuil de ces petits drames, en faveur des pères de famille et des instituteurs qui veulent exercer la mémoire de leurs enfans ou de leurs élèves, et former en même temps leur coeur à la vertu et à la sensibilité. Si ces deux

volumes sont goûtés du public, et attaignent le but que je me suis proposé en les mettant au jour, je ne tarderai pas à leur donner une suite; heureux de continuer, par ce moyen, à remplir le doux et honorable emploi auquel je me suis voué, celui d'instruire l'enfance en l'amusant! [1]–2.

There does not seem to have been a sequel, although two years later Jauffret did edit a comrephensive edition of the works of Berquin: *Oeuvres de Berquin, mises en ordre par L. F. Jauffret*, 22 vols. (Paris: Chez Le Clere, An X (1802).

2   *La Réparation*, 67.

3.   William Godwin, *The Fib Found Out*, in *Dramas for Children Imitated from the French of L. F. Jauffret* (London: M. J. Godwin, at the Juvenile Library, 1808), 117–18.

4   Another possible explanation is that Godwin took the children's offense less seriously than Jauffret did. "Fib," after all, is a light word. "Lie" would be the word of corresponding weight to "honneur," even if they determined not to translate the title of the play literally. Or, perhaps, Godwin may have felt that the *admission* of a lie was itself the lesson.

THE FIB FOUND OUT

The Persons

Mr. WILMOT.
Mrs. WILMOT.
LIONEL, their Son.
DOROTHY, their Daughter.
EDMUND, their little Child.
Mrs. ANSON, Mother to Mrs. Wilmot.
THOMAS, a Servant

The Scene is in London, in Mr. Wilmot's House.

Scene, a Parlour.

Lionel [coming out of Mr. Wilmot's Study.]: Oh heavens! What have I done! — What a terrible misfortune — what will become of me. — Papa *must* know it the minute he comes in — The nasty parrot, how I shall hate the sight of him. 'Twas all his fault — Ah, I really think I heard papa's voice — Then there is no hope left. I must run and hide myself.
[He is going.]

Enter *Dorothy*.

Dorothy: How frightened you look Lionel! What is the matter?
Lionel: Is it only you, Dorothy, how glad I am it was not papa!
Dorothy: Why should you be so afraid to see him? — Well, *I love* to see him, dearly, and the moment I hear his voice, I jump all the way to meet him, and then if he does not seem to be *thinking*, I get to kiss the back of his hand, which is sure to make him smile.

Lionel: If you were in my place, you would be afraid too, Dorothy.

Dorothy: What, have you not got your lesson ready? What a shame! It was so short. — We had to day only two pages of geography and one of grammar — I could say mine perfect in a quarter of an hour. — Now I'll just say it over — "The earth is divided into two great continents; called the *old* and the *new* world. The old world consists of three parts, which are named *Europe, Asia,* and *Africa.* The new world consists of only one part, and it is called *America.*"

Lionel: Don't be so provoking, Dorothy. — Don't I tell you I am in a shocking scrape. — I don't know what in the world to do.

Dorothy: Why don't you learn it then, lazy bones? — "*Europe* is the least extensive of the four quarters of the globe; it is bounded on the *north*"—

Lionel: You ill-natured creature, you care for nothing but teasing. — Papa will be so angry for what I have done.

Dorothy: "On the *north*, by the Frozen Sea; on the *south*, by the Mediterranean Sea; on the *west*, by the Ocean."

Lionel: Oh what an accident I have had!

Dorothy: Have you had an accident? I thought it was only that you could not say your lesson.

Lionel: Oh dear, if you did but know what I have done — I am *very very* sorry; but that can do no good.

Dorothy: Good gracious! Yes, I see now how frightened you look — do tell me what it is.

Lionel: But it will be of no use. Papa *must* know it.

Dorothy: I'll help you to hide it if I can.

Lionel: You know the large machine in papa's study —

Dorothy: Which do you mean?

Lionel: That which stands by the window, with which papa makes experiments upon little birds, to take away their breath, and to shrivel the skin of an apple.

Dorothy: I know which you mean — I wrote the name of it in my pocket-book, because I thought I could not remember it. —

Let us see [takes out the pocket-book] — it is — it is a very hard name —

Lionel: I wouldn't give a fig to know the name —

Dorothy: [looking earnestly for the place]: The — The —

Lionel: Pish, that's your way, you never will be satisfied without learning the *exact* name — how tiresome it is.

Dorothy: The *air-pump* —

Lionel: Yes, — how I wish I had never touched such a provoking, ugly, ridiculous thing. — But let me tell you how it all happened. — The other day, you remember papa was making some experiments with this machine. — First: he put an apple under the glass —

Dorothy: Which is called the *receiver*, you know.

Lionel: Just so. Well, then he drew all the air out of the receiver in some way or other, and the apple instantly became shrivelled, so that you could scarcely believe it to be the same.

Dorothy: I remember very well. — Then he filled the glass with air again, and the apple was as fresh as ever.

Lionel: Another day he put a sparrow into the receiver, and as soon as the air was drawn out, the sparrow fell down, in appearance dead.

Dorothy: Yes, I was so sorry for the poor sparrow, till papa brought him to life again by letting in the air.

Lionel: Well, now then listen to what has happened. — To day there was no one in the study, and I thought I would just try to use the air-pump myself —

Dorothy: Oh heavens! how could you think of venturing?

Lionel: I knew I should not be caught; for I could get the air out and in again in ten minutes, and papa never comes in to dress till one o'clock. — When I first went into the study, it was so nice to be there all alone, *like papa* — shouldn't you think so, Dorothy?

Dorothy: Y-e-s — but I should never have ventured — did any one see you?

Lionel: Not a creature. — And if it had not been for the nasty parrot —

Dorothy: Ha, ha, ha, you are afraid that he will tell of you. How silly — he can say nothing but *Jacco, Jacco*, and *what's o'clock*.

Lionel: I am quite enraged with him, and if I had him now —

Dorothy: Why how can you be so angry with Jacco?

Lionel: I wanted to make my experiment upon Jacco; and only meant to do the same to him as papa did to the sparrow, which you know did not hurt him the least, and I should have let in the air in less than half a minute. Well I took him upon my finger, and put him under the receiver, and what do you think, the provoking creature began to be frightened, and beat his wings all round the glass till he broke it all to pieces, and then flew out at the window.

Dorothy: And didn't you catch him?

Lionel: No, he flew to a distance, and I quite lost sight of him before I could recover from my fright.

Dorothy: I am afraid papa will be *very, very* angry. What can you say to him about your being in his study, where he so strictly forbids us to go? It was, too, papa's favourite machine — and Jacco was grandmamma's favorite bird.

Lionel: Won't you help me all you can, dear Dorothy?

Dorothy: Yes, Lionel, I will beg and pray papa and grandmamma to forgive you.

Lionel: Oh that will be no use at all. — If it was but *one* thing, it wouldn't be so bad, but it was papa's favourite machine, and grandmamma's favourite bird — and then I am so unlucky in meeting with accidents you know, Dorothy — but — you never meet with any, so they would not be half so angry with *you*.

Dorothy: Oh heavens! Lionel, you want me then to say I did it —

Lionel: If you would say you did only *one* of the things — I will give you my new globes, and —

Dorothy: No, no, I am sure I never can — I could not go into the room and say it was I that did it for all the world.

Lionel: What shall I do? What shall I do?

Dorothy: I wish we could think of any thing —

Lionel: Suppose I were to say little Edmund did it —

Dorothy: O papa would never believe us.

Lionel: Why not? Doesn't he touch everything he sees? And isn't mama always telling Sally to take care he he does not go into papa's study? Well, might he not have got in while Sally stepped up stairs, and then he would be sure to take papa's cane to play with, and jumping with it about the room, might strike the receiver and break it to pieces. — Then you know, he cannot speak plain enough to contradict us, for he can only say, *papa*, *mamma*, *Jacco*. — So it is quite certain he would not be questioned — What say you, Dorothy? Promise me that you will tell mamma it all happened so —

Dorothy: I don't know what to do, dear Lionel — How can I bear to accuse poor Edmund, who I know is quite innocent.

Lionel: What great harm would it be to Edmund? And it would save me from such a punishment. — Now do, do, Dorothy.

Dorothy: But *Sally* would contradict every word.

Lionel: Oh never mind her, I can get her to say any thing, I am quite sure, for you know it was but yesterday that she went out with Edmund as soon as mamma got into the carriage, so I may tell of that — Hearken — that's papa's voice — dear Dorothy, you will be good-natured, won't you? —

[Enter *Mr. Wilmot*]

Lionel and Dorothy together: Good morning, papa.

Mr. Wilmot: Good morning, my dears! What, both in the parlour — A game of play, no doubt —

Dorothy: Oh but papa, I have not wasted my time — I know my two pages of geography and my one page of grammar quite perfect. — Will you hear me, papa, I shall not miss one word.

Mr. Wilmot: And what say you, Lionel?

Lionel: I should have known my lesson too, papa, if it had not been for a sad accident —

Mr. Wilmot: An accident! Pray what might it be?

Lionel: You will be angry I am afraid, papa —

Mr. Wilmot: Do not keep me in suspense — Pray tell me what it is —

Lionel: I was here in the parlour, getting my lesson by heart, and in comes little Edmund tossing about his marbles; he seemed to want me to play with him, but I was determined to learn at least one of my lessons first, so then the little rogue began to chatter, *aba, abou, nana, nona*, in his way, you know, papa — Well, he put me out so that I was obliged to go and learn my lesson in mamma's room by myself —

Mr. Wilmot: You called Sally first, I hope —

Lionel: No, papa, for I thought she would be sure to fetch him in a minute.

Mr. Wilmot: What then? —

Lionel: Then, just as I got to the division of Europe — I heard the sound of glass broken —

Mr. Wilmot: And it was Edmund breaking the window —

Lionel: Worse than that — I am afraid to tell —

Mr. Wilmot: One of the looking-glasses? —

Lionel: I ran as quickly as I could, and found Edmund in your study.

Mr. Wilmot: I imprudently left it open this morning.

Lionel: I found him with your cane in his hand, and I saw that he had broke the glass of the air-pump.

Mr. Wilmot: This is Sally's fault, and I must instantly —

Lionel: And besides this, papa, he had opened Jacco's door —

Mr. Wilmot: And Jacco bit his fingers?

Lionel: I believe not, papa, but Jacco was flown out at the window.

Dorothy: Grandmamma will be so vexed.

Mr. Wilmot: But where was Sally? I must have her called — I must make her sensible of her neglect.

Lionel: Oh papa, she will deny it all, I dare say — and very likely will try to make you believe that I and Edmund were playing together, and that —

Mr. Wilmot: We shall see; but step directly and fetch her to me. — In the mean time I will look at what the little mischief-maker has done.

[*Mr. Wilmot* goes into his study.]

Lionel: Oh be joyful ! Than Dorothy all is safe! Now I will step to Sally and tell her what she is to say, and then we have nothing more to fear.

Dorothy: Go quickly then, for papa will be with us in two minutes, you may be sure.

[*Lionel* goes.]

[Enter *Mr. Wilmot*]

Mr. Wilmot: Come to me, Dorothy. Now tell me all about this accident. Where were you when it happened?

Dorothy: I was in my own room, papa, studying my lesson.

Mr. Wilmot: How then did you know all the circumstances? Did Lionel call you and tell you what had happened? Or did you come in by accident?

Dorothy: When I came down, Lionel told me, papa.

Mr. Wilmot: And were not Edmund's fingers cut with the glass of the receiver? And was he not frightened?

Dorothy: No, papa; his fingers were not cut, and he was not frightened.

Mr. Wilmot: Pray how long ago did all this happen?

Dorothy: About half an hour, papa.

Mr. Wilmot: Very well. Here comes Lionel. Now leave us, Dorothy. I wish to ask him some questions. [*Dorothy* goes.] — [Aside] I begin to suspect this tale; I must learn the truth.

[Enter *Lionel*.]

Lionel: I have looked every where for Sally, papa, and I cannot find her. I think she must be gone out to walk with Edmund.

Mr. Wilmot: I am extremely sorry, for I intended to reprimand her most severely. An infant not two years old, left to run thus about the house, exposed to a thousand dangers! It is truly shameful.

Lionel: It is very sad indeed, papa.

Mr. Wilmot: While we are waiting for her, let me hear from you, Lionel, all the particulars of the affairs, that I may be the better prepared to reprove her effectually.

Lionel: I thought I had told you all, papa.

Mr. Wilmot: Where was your sister at the time?

Lionel: As she had learned her lesson, she was playing in the garden, and I saw Jacco flying over the roof of the house — I — I — called her — to tell her — a-n-d — I called Sally too —

Mr. Wilmot: And Edmund was still in the study?

Lionel: Yes, papa.

Mr. Wilmot: The falling of the pieces of glass must have frightened him?

Lionel: Yes, papa. He cried so I knew not what to do to quiet him.

Mr. Wilmot [discomposed]: Lionel! — Ungrateful boy — I am no longer deceived. I am convinced that you, Lionel, broke the receiver, and that your little brother is innocent.

Lionel [endeavouring to cry]: Indeed, papa, it was not I who did it — only ask my sister — here she comes.

[Enter *Dorothy*.]

Dorothy: Here is a letter for you, papa, and "with speed" is written on the cover.

Mr. Wilmot: Give it to me — [He reads].

Dorothy [in a whisper to *Lionel*]: Papa looks angry — Do you think he suspects?

Mr. Wilmot: Come to me Lionel. And you, Dorothy. I have a letter, which it is proper you should hear read. It comes from your mamma.

Dorothy: Mamma has been out ever since breakfast. I wonder —

Mr. Wilmot: She went to see your aunt Andrews, where she is detained — But I will read her letter, and see what you will then have to say —

"I cannot resist my sister's kind entreaties, my dear, and therefore you will kindly give us leave to spend the whole day with her; that our pleasure may be complete, she begs that you, and Lionel, and Dorothy will join us. The weather is so tempting that we propose going all together to the park; we shall therefore call for you in my sister's carriage in half an hour. Pray then be so good as to tell Lionel and Dorothy to be dressed in time. They will both I suppose be mightily pleased."

Dorothy: How kind of mamma! — Shall I run and dress directly, papa?

Mr. Wilmot: We must first say a few words more about the accident. — Lionel, you are quite sure, are you, that you saw Edmund in my study, and that he broke the receiver — you are *quite* sure?

Lionel: Oh yes, papa, quite sure.

Mr. Wilmot: Suppose I were to tell you, that Sally and Edmund went out with your mamma, and have not since been within this house.

Dorothy [aside]: Oh heavens! what will poor Lionel do!

Mr. Wilmot: Dorothy, I beg you will read aloud the remaining lines of your mama's letter —

Dorothy: Here — are — the — l-e-t-t-e-r-s, P, and S, in this corner.

Mr. Wilmot: Go on if you please: I will tell you what *P.S.* means another time. Read —

Dorothy: "Do not be uneasy, my dear, about the little one. This once I think I can answer, that he has had nothing improper to eat, for I mentioned his being poorly to my sister. He breakfasted at our table, and Sally has been with him in the nursery and in the garden ever since. Little Emily and he are excellent companions."

Mr. Wilmot [angrily]: Unworthy children! What have you now to say for yourselves?

[Enter *Mrs. Anson*.]

Mrs. Anson: Yes, yes, your serious faces tell me that the news is really true. — Little mischievous boy! — But where were you, Dorothy, you who only yesterday begged mamma to let Edmund be your child — Pretty care you would take of him truly. — Oh my poor Jacco —

Mr. Wilmot: Our serious faces, my dear mother, but too truly indicate, that none of us are happy. — Nor is Jacco the only subject of our uneasiness. Your upright heart I know will partake the anguish of a father, who fondly hoped —

Lionel, Dorothy [speaking eagerly together, and bursting into tears]: Oh dear papa! O spare us, dear papa!

Mrs. Anson: What can this mean? May I inquire —

[Enter *Mrs. Wilmot, Mrs. Andrews, Sally, Edmund,* and *Emily.*]

Mrs. Wilmot: Well my dears, we are not too soon I hope — come, quickly, quickly — But — Lionel — Dorothy — something is the matter —

Dorothy [clinging round *Mrs. Wilmot,* hiding her face, and sobbing]: Oh dearest, best mamma, you will hate your poor children — never — never will you forgive us —

Lionel: No, mamma, it was not Dorothy, I did it all myself, and made her tell the story — I wish [sobs] — I wish I had died sooner —

Mr. Wilmot: Enough — enough, my children. I have suffered some moments of such grief as only a parent's heart can feel, for the fault you have committed, but I now feel a parent's joy, for that ready and ingenuous avowal, which tells me, that the twelve years devoted to your moral improvement, have not been spent in vain. Come and receive from your mother and myself, a kiss of reconciliation, and our promise to forget this morning's vexations.

The End

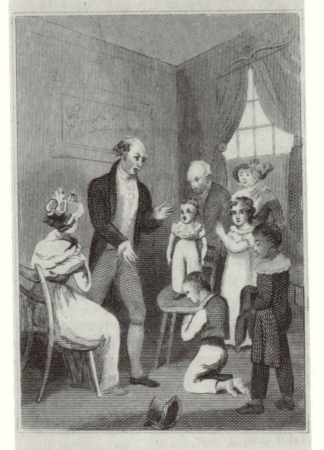

Andy. I do not deserve it. I am not deaf. I am
not dumb. Page 53.

DUMB ANDY

1827

Maria Edgeworth

Maria Edgeworth was born on January 1, 1767, in Oxfordshire, in England, although she lived most of her life in Ireland, which she made the scene of many of her books.

She was the daughter of Richard Lovell Edgeworth, a literary man with a deep interest in education, and Edgeworth's first wife, Anna Maria Elers. Edgeworth encouraged Maria's interest in education and encouraged her to write. (It was at his suggestion she undertook her first literary job, the translation of Mme de Genlis's *Adèle et Théodore*.) After the death of her mother in 1773, Maria was entrusted with the responsibility for the education of her younger brother Henry. When her father was away, as he was periodically, she was responsible for the care of all the younger children. Her first book, *Letters to Literary Ladies*, a defense of the education of girls, appeared in 1775.

From then on, she wrote prolifically, both for adults and for children. Perhaps her best-known works for adults are her Irish novels, *Castle Rackrent* (1800) and *Belinda* (1801), but she also wrote a volume of plays, *Comic Dramas* (1817), and finished her father's memoirs after his death in 1817. For children, she wrote a series of charming books, beginning with *Early Lessons* in 1801, and for their parents several enormously sensible and useful books, including *The Parents' Assistant* (1796–1801) and *Practical Education* (1798), which she wrote with her father.[1]

Through her writing Maria came to know many of the literary lights of her day, including Sydney Smith, Sir Walter Scott, and Jane Austen. Yet, despite her continued literary production and her increasing celebrity in the world, the last third of her life was largely devoted to the business of managing the estate on which her family lived. She proved extremely good at business and took a great interest in improving the condition of the poor on the estate, where she died at eighty-two, on May 22, 1849.

LITTLE PLAYS

> My father has taken me into a new partnership — we are writing
> a comedy; will you come and see it acted? He is making a
> charming theatre in the room over his study; it will be twice as
> large as Old Poz' little theatre in the dining room.
>
> Maria Edgeworth to Sophy Ruxton,
> November 19, 1798

Family theatricals were an important part of life in the Edgeworth household and were performed on birthdays and holidays. The whole family took part, most conspicuously Richard Edgeworth, who loved to act, although parts were provided for everyone old enough to remember his lines. Maria was recognized as the family's most accomplished writer, and the task of writing the plays fell mostly to her.[2]

Maria Edgeworth had little confidence in herself as a playwright, although Sheridan himself urged her to write for the stage. Her doubts were reinforced by her father, who thought the *Little Plays* "inferior performances" and felt that "so many parents would have objections to their children acting plays" that she should "give up the scheme of publishing them."[3] As a result, the *Little Plays* were not published until many years after they had been written and acted.

Maria's method of writing was both practical and imaginative, as she was in everything. Her intention was to amuse her family, particularly the youngest of her father's

eighteen children. She would, typically, begin by writing her
shorter pieces on a slate and copying over in ink the pieces that
pleased the children most. When she had developed an idea,
she would tell it to her father in outline and then revise it after
hearing his criticism.

> Whenever I thought of writing anything I always told him my first
> rough plans and always with the instinct of a good critic, he used to fix
> immediately upon that which would best answer the purpose. . . .
> Sometimes when I was too fond of a particular part, I would dilate on it
> in the sketch; but to this he always objected — "I don't want any of
> your painting — none of your drapery! — I can imagine all that! — Let
> me see the bare skeleton."[4]

Maria took her subjects from life. Very little in them,
according to her biographer, is pure invention.[5] But what she
wrote is art, not reportage, for it is colored and transformed by
her great humor and humanity and by her astonishing ear for
dialogue.

> I could never use notes in writing Dialogues; it would have been as
> impossible to me to get in the prepared good things at the right
> moment in the warmth of writing conversation, as it would be to lug
> them in in real conversation perhaps more so — for I could not write
> dialogues at all without being at the time fully impressed with the
> characters, imagining myself each speaker, and that too fully
> engrosses the imagination to leave time for consulting note-books.[6]

Despite Maria's doubts about her skill as a playwright, the
Little Plays are exemplary. They are funny. They are recog-
nizably human. They are shapely, which is not always the
case with occasional plays, and they are charming. They are, I
believe, worthy to stand with Maria Edgeworth's best work
(which is saying a great deal) and worthy of performance
today.

DUMB ANDY

Winnie: But why must he be dumb? — sure, if he was to speak for himself, I think he'd touch a heart of stone.

Watty: Aye, but not the heart of the rich, that's harder than stone — some, I wouldn't say all. — But, any way, there's so many orphan boys about now, the quality's tired of them, and we must always be having something and out o' the way to draw the tear from the eyes, and the money from the pocket.

Dumb Andy, I, ii

Maria Edgeworth knew and admired *The Beggar's Opera*, and her second Little Play resembles John Gay's ballad opera superficially in many ways. Both plays are about the lot of the poor — in *Dumb Andy* the poorest of the poor, the Irish poor at a time in history between Swift's *Modest Proposal* (1728) and the potato famine of 1848. Both plays are about beggars who feign injury and mutilation to reach the hard hearts of the rich and about the ingenuity and exuberance with which they do so. And both plays are full of music, new words set to old ballad tunes.

But *Dumb Andy* is, at its heart, nothing like *The Beggar's Opera*, because Maria Edgeworth brings a sensibility, sense of humor, and humanity entirely different from Gay's to the subject; because the occasion she wrote her play for was private, not public; and because her moral purpose, which was at least as deep as Gay's, was to teach and cure, not to castigate entertainingly.

Dumb Andy is remarkable in many ways, not least in its skillful construction.[7] It is perhaps most remarkable for its vivid depiction of real people, especially real children, and for the complexity of the moral dilemma at its center.

Each of the three Bridgeman children rings true, and each is drawn different from the others, in character, temperament, and diction. Of course, the actors Maria was writing for were her brothers and sisters, and she could tailor their roles to them. But the fact of the matter is that Maria Edgeworth knew and understood children, and her ability to write believable, *particular* children was extraordinary.[8] Both in her plays and her tales, she wrote, according to one critic, "the first living and breathing children in English literature since Shakespeare."[9]

Maria seems to have begun writing her works for children with a moral, even before she had characters or a plot. She was much better at concealing her hand than most of her contemporaries, but the moral, even the overt moralizing, in *Dumb Andy* is apparent. Although Andy's soliloquies are well written, their substance is conventional. But Andy's moral dilemma, and the dilemma at the heart of the play, is a real and a deep one. It is not like the usual dilemmas in moral works for children of the period, to which there is a clear right answer. It is, somewhat altered, Corneille's classic dilemma of the pull between love and duty or Auden's modern dilemma, so brilliantly exemplified in the work of John Le Carré, between betraying one's country and betraying one's friend. Andy's dilemma — whether to betray his benefactors or his conscience — is a real one, without an easy answer, and it is one of the chief reasons for the play's strength.

But even deeper and closer to the heart of the play is a more profound division: the poignant, unreconcilable difference betwen the views of the world of youth and age, of innocence and experience.

[Enter *Joscelin* running]

Joscelin: Mamma I led the dumb boy all the way myself carefully by the hand.

Mrs. Bridgeman: Was he blind as well as dumb, my dear?

Joscelin: No, mamma, but he could not ask the way, so I showed it to him — and, mamma, I met Kitty, and I asked her to be so good as to give him something to eat, and a great deal too, for his poor jaws look very thin, mamma, as thin as this. — [Drawing in his cheeks.] But mamma, Kitty said that she must know first whether you liked it — for she says she cannot give to all the beggars that want, and that you and papa can tell best who want most. So, mamma, will you come and see this poor, poor thin dumb boy. I am sure you will think he wants, as much as any body can, something to eat. Mamma! — oh! do come, mamma!

> [While *Joscelin* has been speaking, *Mr. Bridgeman* comes down from the gallery, and takes the little boy in his arms, kisses him, and sets him down. Then takes *Bess* and *Caesar* by the hand, and says: —]

Mr. Bridgeman: My dear children, I am glad to see that you are so good natured, but —

That "but" is the point. Explicated, it would fill volumes. As it stands, it has very nearly the same force as Prospero's response to his daughter Miranda's vision of a brave new world. "It is," he tells her, "new to thee."

Andy is given to Margery and Robin Woods for a month in which to see whether anything can be made of him. The Bridgeman children are certain that something can. We, with the elder Bridgemans, *hope* something can, but no adult can be sure any longer that the world is quite as brave as it once seemed.

NOTES

1. For an excellent bibliography of Maria Edgeworth's works, see Bertha Coolidege Slade, *Maria Edgeworth, 1767–1849: A Bibliographical Tribute* (London: Constable Publishers, [1937]).

2 The plays she wrote were *The Grinding Organ*, performed in 1809; *Dumb Andy*, performed in 1814; and *The Dame School Holiday*, whose date of performance is not known. The three plays were published together as *Little Plays* in volume 7 of *The Parents' Assistant* in 1827. Here is Maria's description of a performance of *The Grinding Organ*:

The Grinding Organ went off on Friday night better than I could have expected, and seemed to please the spectators. Mrs. Pakenham brought four children, and Mr. and Mrs. Thompson two sons, Mr. and Mrs. Keating two daughters, which with the Beauforts, Molly, George and the rest of the servants, formed the whole audience. I am sure you would have enjoyed the pleasure the Bristows showed on seeing and hearing Mary Bristow perform her part, which she did with perfect propriety. Sophy and Fanny excellent, but as they were doomed to be the *good* children, they had not ample room and verge enough to display powers equal to the little termagant heroine of the night. William in his Old Man (to use the news-paper-style) correct and natural. Mr. Edgeworth as the English Farmer, evinced much knowledge of English character and humour. Miss Edgeworth, as the Widow Ross, "a cursed scold," was quite at home.

Maria Edgeworth: Chosen Letters, with and introduction by F. V. Barry (Boston and New York: Houghton Mifflin Company, 1931), 159–60.

3. Grace A. Oliver, *A Study of Maria Edgeworth, with Notices of her Father and Friends* (Boston: A Williams and Company, 1882), 311.

4. P. H. Newby, *Maria Edgeworth* (London: Arthur Barker, Ltd., 1950), 51.

5. Marilyn Butler, *Maria Edgeworth: A Literary Biography* (Oxford: Clarendon Press, 1972), 239.

6. Maria Edgeworth, *Maria Edgeworth: Chosen Letters*, 244.

7. Maria Edgeworth took a professional's interest in the craft of playwriting. She criticized the plays of Molière for using the serving men and women only to provide exposition for, and further the plot along for, their masters. She did, of course, fall into the same trap herself. All of Robin and Margery's malapropisms do not disguise the fact that they are being used for exposition. But, to Maria Edgeworth's credit, she does make them an integral part of her plot, giving them charge of Andy for a month in the last scene, to test whether these two good people could make anything of him.

8. Newby, *Maria Edgeworth*, 36.

9. Ibid., 24.

DUMB ANDY

IN TWO ACTS

Dramatis Personae

MRS. BRIDGMAN.
BESS, Mr. & Ms. Bridgman's daughter.
MARGERY WOODS, Wife of Robin Woods.
WINNY BRANNIGAN, Wife of Watty Brannigan — a beggar.
MR. BRIDGMAN.
CÆSAR,
JOSCELIN,   } Sons of Mr. & Mrs. Bridgman.
ROBIN WOODS, Mr. Bridgman's gate keeper.
WATTY BRANNIGAN, a beggar.
ANDY, a beggar boy.
GEORGE, a footman of Mr. Bridgman's.

Act I

SCENE 1

[A porter's lodge belonging to Bridgman Castle. *Margery Woods* and old *Robin* her husband at supper — a stool between them, on which is a large bowl of potatoes and some milk.]

Mar: Robin, dear, the handle's tow'rd ye, take the cup. The milk is fresh from the cow, and I milked her myself.
Rob: Then it's as good as cream to my liking Margery, love.
Mar: That's well — I'm thinking, Robin, how it's forty good year, come Holantide next, we've been this ways, we two, taking our bit and sup together, and not a cross word or look ever come betwix' us.
Rob: Not one, no, nor the shadow of the like; thanks to you Margery and myself too, that had the luck to get such a wife.

Praise be to God for it!

Mar: Why then Robin, I wonder now is there many score of the great folks, in the county, let alone the kingdom, who could say as much.

Rob: Any way there's our own master and mistress, above at the castle, might say as much for themselves, was they as good an age as we two Margery. I don't doubt but they're as happy in the castle as we in the cabin, but it's not always so.

Mar: Well they desarve to be happy, for it's they are good to the poor, and kind to all, to my knowledge; and I never go to sleep without remembering them, next to yourself, Robin, in my prayers, and the house-keeper, she shall have my good word in heaven, was it only for the cure for the asthma she give you, Robin, though it did you no good, my poor man.

Rob: But that was no fault of hers, sure it was the same bottle she took herself, God bless her — and the children, too, well are not they fine childer.

Mar: No better ever lighted the mother's eyes. The mother might well be proud of 'em — even the little cratur itself, Master Jos. See yonder, in the corner, all the chips he gathered for me, to make us a bright blaze at night, Robin, — and Miss Bess, too, who had the thought to pull all them rushes, for the candles, for us; and Master Cæsar! aye, that's the clever little fellow, that will be the very *moral* of his father, Lord love him! see here how he mended my bellows for me, and was kneeling and hammering at 'em, till myself was ashamed.

Rob: To my thinking them bellows are better than new again, it was a pleasure to him, I'll engage, for he has a kind heart, and a good big one too, of his own, in that little body of his, [A bell Rings.] Hark, there's the gate bell.

Mar: Sit you still, Robin, its I will answer the gate.

[Exit *Margery*.]

Rob: Why she's as young and supple on her foot as when first I danced with her, for the cake at the pattern — aye, it's good will that keeps the feet supple and the heart strong. [He sings to the air of Langolee.]

Oh! the quick thought of woman, to help us in all things,
Not a turn of life's troubles, but what she can ease,
Still the worst she can lighten, and laugh at the small things,
And still what she does, it is done all to please,
Dear joy of my old days! warm pulse of my heart's life!
The blessing you've been and the blessing you'll ever-be,
None knows, oh! ma Vourneen! oh! Madgy my-own-wife,
None knows all you've done, all you're doing for me.

All the times that I've felt you my fond heart relieving,
There's none knows but me darling, none knows but me
And the soft word for anger, the hope-look 'gainst grieving.
No, there's none knows but me, dear, that knows them from
thee,
But now thinking it over, the heart-swell I'm taking
'Till my tongue it can't tell it — the faint voice is lost —
And then sooner than speak it my heart would be breaking,
Oh! 'tis he can worst tell it, that feels it the most.

[*Robin* to *Margery* as she returns.] Well Madgy dear, what was
it? who was in it?

Mar: 'Twas only a parcel of beggars that wanted to know,
could they get through the gate, up to the castle, and I *tould*
them no beggars was allowed inside the gate any ways, but if
they had a paper I'd send it up for them to Mistress Lovemore,
the housekeeper, for the charitable ladies. — But they had no
paper, or petition, or certificate, at all, tho' the woman said
she had been burnt out — now if she was burnt out, why had not
she a paper to show, with names as usual.

Rob: Troth that did not look honest.

Mar: And then, too, besides, another thing, the ould man,
tho' he was by way of being blind, *axed* me, was that white
house, on the hill, the parson's or the priest's.

Rob: Then that was a slip of the tongue, but the woman
might have *insensed* him it was a white house.

Mar: No Robin; dear, you're always too good — the woman
was with her back to it, and had never noticed it, she turned
her round that minute to look for it thro' the trees, and by the

same token, she hit me a great thump on the head, with one of her childer's heads, that was on her back, and Lord forgive me for the thought, if I'm wrong — but I could not help thinking to myself, when I heard the child did not cry, and felt the sort of a thump its head give me, that child's no more a child nor I am, nor flesh and blood at all, at all, but wood or stone or the like, dressed up to cheat Christians charitably inclined — which is a shame you know, Robin dear — Lord forgive me if I'm wrong.

Rob: Amen. — Then that would be a shame and a sin — but I cant think they would venture to be so wicked in the country. — The Dublin beggars, they say, have a many tricks with them — but not in the country sure.

Mar: Well I can't take upon me to say — I ax their pardon if I wronged them, any way — but they have taken themselves off, and I'm not sorry for it, for I did not like the looks of them much — any of the *kit* — barring a boy they had with them that did not say a word, good or bad, but looked very pitiful, and my heart warmed to him, and I had a mind to bring him in, to give him a hot potatoe, and a draught of the buttermilk.

Rob: Oh, then, that was like you, and why would not ye.

Mar: Why, Robin, because I was not you — nor ever was half so good! — and sure enough, the thump on my head made me crosser than I ought to be in *rason* — But it's past now, and no more about it — I must be going to look after the white cock, that has taken an ugly fancy to roost down in the tattered barn at Killogenosauce.

[*Margery* puts on her cloak.]

Rob: Then I wonder he would, when he has every convenience here at home that a cock could want — well, I'll be weeding a bit before the door while you're away Margery — its so lonesome to be idle — where's my weeding knife?

Mar: Here, and your straw mat to kneel upon, Robin, I won't have you forget *that*, or the knee will get the rheumatis again — God help it and you till I come back.

[Exeunt.]

SCENE 2

[An old barn — Beggars, viz. *Watty Brannigan,* seemingly an old man with a long beard, *Winny Brannigan* with a large bundle on her back, the heads of two infants peeping out at the top — she carries a kettle in her hand. — *Andy Dolan* follows her — he is a boy about ten years old.]

Win: Bad luck to the ould woman then at the gate that would not let us in to the castle.

Wat: Tut, what matter — sure wel'll find a gap in the hedge, I warrant, and we'll get over the ditch, or the wall, *asy* — there never was a ditch or wall yet I wouldn't get over with pleasure; rather, too, than be beholden to a gate, or gate-keeper that's always saucy and purse-proud more or less.

Win: Andy dear, help me with these childer off my back. That was an unlucky thump the child's head gave that awkward old woman. — I was afraid of my life, she'd have suspected something, so I pinched Sukey to make her cry — come then darling till I give you something to eat — Andy throw the wooden child from ye, Sukey's jealous of her, and won't eat till the other's out o'the way.

Wat: Andy — Get you to the door now, and mount you guard for us — mind and give us notice the minute you'll see any one coming.

> [While *Winny Brannigan* is feeding her child, *Watty Brannigan* is taking off his beard.]

We may rest us here a while and better do so, to give time for them to think us gone. Well, it's a mighty tiresome thing, being an auld man, though you think little of it, Winny Brannigan, and being to be blind into the bargain.

Win: And a very bad blind man you are, Watty Brannigan, as ever begged the road; what made you let on that you saw the white house on the hill.

Wat: What matter! sure I heard of it! and if you go to crossness, Winny Brannigan, I'll tell you a piece of my mind, that you'll be the ruin of us all, one of these days, with those two twins, that you will have, right or wrong.

Win: I must have twins, and I will, Watty Brannigan. There's nothing at all moves the quality so much as a poor *cratur* with twins.

Wat: Aye, if she's a widow and they be orphans.

Win: Well, and I've no objections to being a widow, Watty Brannigan.

Wat: All in good time Winny — but in the mean while, where's my wooden leg? Give it me till I fasten it on smart.

Win: I have not it at all Watty. I had no say to it. [her child cries.] Hush, hush, honey. Then troth here it is, in the bottom of the bundle, and what are you going to be now pray, Watty.

Wat: What should I be, but a disabled soldier, sure didn't we hear at the public house that *abow'*, that the quality at the castle are related or connected, or mighty cronies of the duchess of Wellington, and the Duke's all the go now, and sure they cannot but give half a crown, after the battle of Waterloo, to a disabled soldier — like me.

Win: Waterloo is too *racent* — you'd better have been at the battle of Vemeira.

Wat: Or at the burning of Moscow. But the Duke was not there, was he? Burn me if I know, was he or no?

Win: Sorrow a know know I, so you'd better not be meddling with Moscow at all, Watty Brannigan; come from Spain or Portugal, that's *asy*. And what will you say for yourself now? Have your story pat out of the face, and not bungle it, as you did when you *tould* the gentleman you *sarved* under Admiral Hood, in Gibralter; hush, hush, child.

Wat: I grant ye that was a little mistake to a gentleman — but if it had been a lady, she would never have noticed, and it was all along of my having been a sailor in the morning, which confused my head with the grog I took. But as to getting a story by heart, to tell out o'the face, I lave that to you, Winny Brannigan, its what I could never compass, and scorn to do any way — for my *gen'us* always supplies me with memory enough on the spot.

Win: Oh, you're a great *gen'us*, Watty Brannigan; but they say liars had need of long memories.

Wat: Put on your black bonnet then, will you, Winny, take your red cloak about you, and be *dacent*, for now you're to be a poor soldier's wife, you know. Now mind and don't call yourself a follower of the camp, as you did at Carrick.

Win: Oh, never fear. — Give me the childer on my back.

Wat: Now, Winny Brannigan, I won't stir a step *wid* you, if you have twins — for that cursed wooden child of yours will bring us to the house of industry yet, if you don't wean yourself from it. — Take our own live child in your arms, and a lovely one it is, and be content.

Win: Why, then, it is a lovely child, Watty.

Wat: And, Winny, am not I a good soldier now with my wooden leg, and my cut in my forehead, and my eye that I lost at the trenches at Vimiera?

Win: Trenches — was there trenches in it?

Wat: There was — I'll take my oath.

Win: Whether or no, let me settle the bandage over your eye.

Wat: And now for a glass to good luck, my dear — and we'll be off.

> [Takes out a bottle of whiskey,
> *Watty* and *Winny Brannigan*
> drink by turns.]

Wat: But where's Andy, the boy? — Here, Andy — here's liquor that will make a cat speak, and a man dance.

Andy: I'll take none, I thank you, I have an oath again' it.

Wat: As you *plase* — mores the fool you. — But what shall he be to day? — [turning to *Winny B.*] Shall he be a ballad-singer or Dumb Andy?

Win: Try the ballad-singer — sing a bit, Andy, till we see what's in you.

[*Andy* sings mournfully.]

"My father he lived in the bog of Allen,
And he had neither a house nor place to dwell in,

By the laws, he had neither land nor living,
But what the neighbours chose to give him."

Wat: By the laws! that will never do, that's too dismal a
ditty by half, Andy; try the "Sprig of Shillalah" man alive.

[*Andy* attempts to sing.]

"Who has e'er had the luck to see Donnybrook fair.
An Irishman all in his glory is there,
   With his spring of shillela and shamrock so green."

[His voice fails.]

Win: O, that will never do, Andy.
Wat: Blood! man, can't you put a little life in it, as I do?

[*Watty Brannigan* sings.]

"Och love is the soul of a neat Irishman,
He loves all that's lovely, he loves all he can,
   With his sprig of shillalah and shamrock so green,
His heart is right honest, he's open and sound,
No malice nor envy is there to be found,
He courts and he marries, he drinks and he fights,
He loves, och he loves, for in that he delights,
   With his sprig of shillalah and shamrock so green.
Who has e'er had the luck to see Donnybrook fair,
An Irishman all in his glory is there,
   With his sprig of shillalah and shamrock so green.
His clothes spick and span new, without e'er a speck,
A nice Barcelona tied round his neat neck,
He goes to a tent and he spends half a crown,
Comes out, meets his friend, and for love knocks him down,
   With his sprig of shillalah and shamrock so green."

Wat: Try it now, Andy, can't you sing it as I do, in the true
spirit?

Andy: No, I can't sing since I lost my mother.

Win: Oh! the *cratur*, we wont *ax* him to sing.

Wat: No, I'd bawl my lungs out for him myself sooner — or be a soldier — or a sailor — or a blind man — or any thing at all.

Win: And I the same, Andy.

Wat: No, we'll not be so cruel to ax you to sing against the grain, Andy — nor to do any thing at all but what you like, long as ever we can do for ye.

Andy: Thank yees, I'm ready to do any thing at all I can, and if its *plasing* to you, I'd rather work than no, I would.

Wat: Work! — Troth we'll not set you to work, any how, that would be too bad. — But what will you be the day, Andy?

Andy: Oh! what can I be the day, but what I am every day, a poor orphan boy.

Wat: Then be dumb, Andy, still.

Win: But why must he be dumb? — sure, if he was to speak for himself, I think he'd touch a heart of stone.

Wat: Aye, but not the heart of the rich, that's harder than the stone — some, I would'nt say all. — But, any way, there's so many orphan boys about now, the quality's tired of them, and we must always be having something new and out o'the way to draw the tear from the eyes, or the money from the pocket.

Win: Pocket! sorrow pocket have they now to carry the charity in that they might have, had they the pocket — and what would ladies do with the tear without the white *handkercher*. Oh! its I that knows every turn of them. — But, hush till I hear — what noise is *that* I hear, Andy?

Andy: 'Tis only the pig grunting, Ma'am.

Win: 'Twas not that I *h'ard*. I'd know a pig when I'd hear him, sure. It was more like a cock crow.

Wat: May be then it was the geese you *h'ard*, if there's geese in it. No, faith, I have it now — It was this white cock crowing. Murder! here's a woman coming up the hill. By the laws! it's our old one of the gate — out of that wid yees, — Over the gripe smart, Winny Brannigan. Come along after, Andy, smart.

[Exeunt *Watty* and *Winny*.]

[*Andy*, aside, as he goes off.]

Oh! if it was pleasing to heaven, and it could be without offence to these that has been father and mother to me when mine was took from me, I'd like better to follow some honest industry sooner nor this cheating life of a dumb beggar. But what help. Could I turn traitor, or informer, or runaway? [pausing.] No, I can be nothing else — I must be Dumb Andy.

[Exit *Andy*.]

SCENE 3

[A lawn before the steps of a castle, *Cæsar, Bess*, and *Joscelin*. *Cæsar* has a paper kite in his hand; *Bess* is stretching out the tail of the kite. Little *Joscelin* is looking on, admiring.]

Jos: What a beautiful kite, and what a fine long tail!

C: Bess, what are you about?

Bess: My dear, I am fastening some bobs to the tail, several are wanting.

C [Holding the kite up and looking at it]: Well, my dear kite, you certainly are a beauty! And my father was very good to give me a breast-bone for you, and to help me to make you, as he did with his own hands, and with his own head too, and you know, Bess, he says, and I think it is very true, that *head* is a great deal better than hands — without papa's head you would have been a very different kite from what you are.

Jos: Without papa's *head*; what do you mean, Cæsar?

C: My dear little boy, I mean the inside of papa's head — but you cannot understand, you are not old enough yet to understand about the insides of heads.

[*Cæsar* hums a tune.]

Jos: Stoop down to me, Cæsar — I want to whisper, [whispers,] it is a secret that Bess must not hear. Does Bess know about the song that you are making?

Bess: I hear you.

C [stopping his mouth]: Can you never hold your tongue, Joscelin?

Bess: My dear Cæsar, I knew it long before Joscelin told me.

C: How, pray? — who could tell you? nobody knew it but myself.

Bess: Well, you told me.

C: I!

Bess: Yes, you; you were roaring it out last night after you were in bed — I must have been deaf if I had not heard you.

C: What, through the wall?

Bess: Through twenty walls I could have heard you.

C: And how did you like it?

Bess: If you'll sing it again, now, I shall be able to judge, but I was so sleepy last night.

Jos: Do sing it Cæsar — sing it for me.

C: Well, so I will, while Bess is finishing those bobs for the tail, which will never be finished, I think.

Bess: My dear, it will be finished in five minutes, — if you will sing to Joscelin, and not stand with your eyes fixed upon me, for that makes all the things slip out of my fingers.

C: Now that is the most ridiculous feeling! I never feel that! when I am doing any thing I don't care how many people stand with their eyes fixed upon me.

Bess: Very likely, because you are a man, — but I am a woman.

C: And must not a woman be looked at? I'll be bound she'd soon be sorry for that. What do you curl your hair for?

Bess: Sing your noble kite song for Joscelin, Cæsar.

C [clears his throat]: Now Bess, do you remember what my father told you about Pindar?

Bess: Yes, yes.

C: Then please to remember my kite song is an irregular ode — you comprehend. So, Bess, you are never to mind the length or the shortness of the lines, or the number of the feet; no counting upon your fingers.

Bess: No no, my fingers are too busy; sing, only sing.
Jos: Pray sing.

[*Cæsar* sings.]

My pretty kite fly,
High! high! my kite, high —

C: Now the measure changes.
Bess: Well, we shall find that out — only sing, don't say.

Transparent gauze paper,
As light as thin vapor,
Speeds your elegant form
To contend with the storm.
    My pretty kite fly,
    High! high! my kite, high.

C: These two last lines are the chorus, Joscelin.
Jos: Chorus! — very well, sing on Cæsar — pray sing.

[*Cæsar*, pointing to the kite as he sings.]

Proud arches your outline,
Nice tackle your fine twine,
Full four yards and a nail,
Your magnificent tail.
    Oh my pretty kite fly,
    High! high! my kite, high.

C: Now you are to imagine the kite going up into the air.
Bess: Well, well, we will imagine whatever you please, if
you will only go on.

Yes, yes, Fancy sees thee,
Hard striving to please me,
Now rising, now falling,
Perplexed by my bawling,

It flutters, it flickers,
It rallies, it bickers,
Ah, poor thing! see it dies,
No, it mounts to the skies.
  My pretty kite fly,
  High! high! my kite, high.

Loose the string,
Give it wing —
Have your will,
Take your fill —
Breast the air,
Have a care —
Clear the trees,
Catch the breeze.
  Fly, fly, my kite fly,
  High! high! my kite, high.

Oh the joy of all hearts,
Look, look, how it darts —
See the tail how it streams,
See the light how it gleams.
  Fly, fly, my kite fly,
  High! high! my kite, high.

It holds its course fair,
A white bird in the air,
Mark the bird as it flies!
Now a speck in the skies!
A bright spot in the gleam!
A black mote in the beam.
  Fly, fly, my kite fly,
  High! high! my kite, high.

Jose: Oh! Bess! Bess! — Cæsar! — look — look at these odd people coming — what are they?
  Bess: Beggars, I believe — a soldier! — a poor soldier with a wooden leg!
  C: With a wooden leg? — poor man! — let me speak to him.

[Enter *Watty* and *Winny Brannigan* and *Andy*.]

Wat [in the character of a soldier]: Oh, long life to you,
pretty Masters and Miss, and may you never know sorrow as we
do.

Bess: Poor man! what sorrow have you known?

Wat: Sure, I've six little childer that has not a bit to ate,
and I a cripple that has lost my limb.

Win: Oh, Miss, if you had seen him in the hospital lying as I
did, when his leg was cut off.

Jos: Leg cut off?

Wat: Aye was it, master! [sighing deeply.]

Jos: Did not it hurt you very much?

Wat: It did, master, terribly, [turning to *Cæsar*] but I lost it in
the service of my country, and I stood my ground in the day of
battle.

C: I like him, Bess, he's a brave fellow.

Wat: But now I'm no more good in the army, on account of my
wooden leg, and of this wound in my head; and if it had not
been for my good wife here, Miss, I should have been lost
entirely, for there I was left, on the field of battle, under heaps
of the bleeding.

Jos [shrinking]: The bleeding, oh!

Wat: The bleeding, and the groaning, and the dying, and
myself; I must have died or been buried alive, but for her that
came to *sarch* for me, and found me, and saved me.

Bess: Oh, what an excellent woman!

C: Come with me, brave man, and I will show you the way to
the servants' hall, and then I will go and ask papa to give you
something.

Win [to the three children]: Health, wealth, and prosperity
to yees.

Wat: The Lord presarve yees, a long-life to you master, and
may you live till the world's tired of you, and a happy death
to yees.

Jos: What is the matter with this poor boy, he looks very
melancholy.

Wat: Because he's a great infliction, he's deaf and dumb from his birth, master.

C: Deaf and dumb!

[*Andy* makes signs that he cannot speak or hear.]

Jos: Cannot he speak? poor, poor, poor boy! [takes him by the hand to lead him.] I will lead, you, dumb boy, but you cannot hear me.

C: And what battles were you in, soldier? I like to hear of battles.

Wat: Then it's I can tell you enough about them, master, and too much. I sarved under the great general Wellington.

C: Oh! did you? then come to papa and tell him all about it — oh! take care! take care! man, you've put your wooden leg through my kite, and the tail — boy you are all entangled in it. — Oh my kite! my kite is spoiled.

[*Jos* and *Cæsar* try to disentangle the man and boy, but they cannot, *Cæsar*, after giving one stamp of anger recollects himself, and says calmly,]

I won't be angry — I'm sure you did not do it on purpose. [He cuts the tail of the kite.] There, now — it is all over — come with me, and I will ask papa to give you something, and I can give the boy a coat of my own, only it will be rather too short, I am afraid — but I can give him a hat and a pair of shoes, for his poor bare feet.

[Exit *Cæsar* and *Bess*.]

Andy [aside]: What a kind hearted little fellow! now it's a sin to go to impose upon him.   [Exit *Andy*.]

Wat: It's likely we shall make something of our visit to this castle. It's not every castle we find the likes of these.

[Exit *Watty* and *Winny*.]

SCENE 4

A Hall in Bridgman Castle, a gallery at one end of the hall and a stair-case leading to it. *Mr. & Mrs. Bridgman* and *Bess. Mrs. Bridgman* watering some geraniums. *Mr. Bridgman* walking down and up in the gallery.

[Enter *Bess* out of breath, yet eagerly speaking, and looking at her father and mother by turns.]

Bess: Oh papa! oh mamma! she's the most excellent woman, she dragged her husband off the field of battle, with her own hands — papa, she's a most excellent woman, and her nose is very like mamma's, I assure you, and his leg, he has a wooden leg, Sir; and do you know, mamma, he can tell you all about the duchess of Wellington, I am sure, for he is perfectly well acquainted with the duke of Wellington — yes, perfectly, Ma'am, I assure you — he served under him — he said so; and then another misfortune — they have a dumb boy, Sir.

Mrs. B: A dumb boy, have they? I am sure I have not a dumb girl?

> [*Mr. Bridgman* leaning over the rails of the gallery.]

Mrs.B: I dont understand one word of your whole story, Bess — you have so mixed a leg, and a nose, and the duke of Wellington, and a dumb boy, together — suppose you were to take breath and time to separate these things.

> [Enter *Cæser* running, out of breath.]

Bess: Here comes Cæsar, Sir! and he can tell it you a great deal better than I can.

C: [Holding his sides] Oh! oh! oh! if I had not run so very fast!

Mr. B: Why all this desperate hurry, good folk? — Is your man with a wooden leg running away?

C: Running away? — He, Sir! running away? No, papa, I assure you he is not a man to run away. — He is too brave to run away! Oh! Sir, I wish you had but heard all the things he has been telling me about himself and the duke of Wellington. He has been in I cannot tell you how many battles — and he has a great cut, this long, across his forehead — and he speaks of it just as I would of a cut in my finger — and he lost his right eye in one battle, and his leg was shot off at last — and he says, papa, that he lost all in doing his duty, and therefore, as he says that a soldier can do no more than his duty, he is content — and if he could he would march again to-morrow and fight in the defence of his king and his country — he must be a brave man, must not he? Oh, papa, do come down stairs and see him — I think such a man as he is does deserve to be rewarded; and I am sure you will give him something, wont you, papa?

Mr. B: Certainly, if he *is* such a man as you have described him to be.

Bess and C: [clap their hands] I thought so! — I thought so! — I was sure papa would!

Bess: And mamma, you will give something to the woman, the exellent wife — wont you, mamma? — Do Cæsar tell her about his wife's dragging him and saving him from being buried alive — you can tell it much better than I can.

[Enter *Joscelin* running.]

Jos: Mamma I led the dumb boy all the way myself carefully by the hand.

Mrs. B: Was he blind as well as dumb, my dear?

Jos: No, mamma, but he could not ask the way, so I showed it to him — and, mamma, I met Kitty, and I asked her to be so good as to give him something to eat, and a great deal too, for his poor jaws look very thin, mamma, as thin as this: — [Drawing in his cheeks.] But, mamma, Kitty said that she must know first whether you liked it — for she says she cannot give to all the beggars that want, and that you and papa can tell best who wants most. So, mamma, will you come and see this poor, poor thin dumb boy. I am sure you will think he wants, as much as any body can, something to eat. Mamma! — oh! do come, mamma!

[While *Joscelin* has been
speaking, *Mr. Bridgman* comes
down from the gallery, and
takes the little boy in his arms,
kisses him, and sets him down.
Then takes *Bess and Cæsar* by
the hand, and says: —]

Mr. B: My dear children I am glad to see that you are so good
natured, but —

Bess: [interrupting] Yes, papa, if you had seen how Cæsar
bore his kite's being all torn by this soldier's wooden leg, and
the tail all entangled by the dumb boy, you would have been
pleased with his good nature indeed!

Mr. B: And I am pleased with yours, my dear little girl —
but, as I was saying, or going to say, how can you be sure, my
dear little children, that all that these beggars have told you
is truth?

Bess: Cheat! — Why, Robin, who cheats us?

Marg: Ah! Miss, I am afraid your nice woman, as you call
her, is no better than a cheat, for I looked at her below as I come
in, and though she has new dressed her, to my opinion she is one
and the same woman that came to the gate wanting to come in
this day as we were sitting, Robin and I, after dinner, just as
might be —

C: Oh! nver mind how you were sitting, go on and tell us
about the woman.

Bess: And the doll.

Marg: The doll — the woman — where was I? Oh, why then
I would not let her through the gate, because my master ordered
no beggars to be let up.

C: Yes, we know that, we know all that.

Mrs. B: Gently, gently, Cæsar, if you are so impatient you
will not hear the story one bit the faster, you will put poor
Margery quite out.

C: I beg your pardon, Margery, will you sit down?

Marg: Oh! thank you kindly, no master, it's not for me to be
sitting. So I was keeping, keeping the gate as it might be this

ways, and she turns smart, and her child's head hit me a thump like a post, and my mind misgive me, as I told Robin, it was not flesh and blood even.

Bes: Yes, but this was not that child that I kissed.

Marg: No, Miss, true, but see she had two childer on her back that time.

Bess: Oh, it cannot be the same woman.

C: How do you know it was the same woman, Margery? And how do you know this is the same child, or doll child, that she had on her back?

[*Margery* looks at *Robin*.]

Robin: Why master — Margery wont say she is sure, quite, sure to swear to its being the same child, because she is very careful not to wrong any one, beggar or other; but in my opinion she has good *rason* to think it. Now tell on, Margery, and dont be afeard; you know you dont mean to wrong no one, but only to hinder the master and mistress, and all these young ones, that is so good, from being cheated out of their charity, that should be kept for them that *desarves* it.

Marg: That's true; so I'll tell all; I went up to the ould barn at Killogenosauce, thinking to find my white cock that strayed, and thinking of nothing e'se in the wide world, when what should I find but this doll in the corner, and ever so many scraps of rags about, and this beard of an old man, that I minded was the beard of the old blind beggar man that was with the woman at the gate.

Bess: Then that cannot be our man, because he is not blind, or old, nor has he a beard.

Marg: He took off the beard, may be, Miss, for here it is in my hand.

C: But our man has wooden a leg, Margery.

Marg: May be he put on the leg, Sir.

C: How could he put on the leg, Margery?

Robin: Oh, they have some of them beggars, wicked ways and means of taking off beards and putting on legs, I'm tould, in great great towns, but I did not think till now so much wickedness could get to the country.

C: Wickedness! bit it's impossible! what did he do with his real leg; you don't think he would cut it off?

Robin: No master, but I think he might double it up, as they say them rogues have a knack of doing. Margery, show master, dear.

> [*Margery* tries to bend back
> *Robin's* leg.]

Marg: Oh, it's too stiff, my poor Robin, and your legs are too honest legs for it.

C: [tries] And mine too; and my soldier's too, I hope —

Marg: Well I hope so; I hope it will turn out so; it's good to hope for the best. But I found a shoe too, and a stocking, pulled off; and I looked out and I saw the three beggars making away, and watched till I seen them get over the ditch, and the wall at the end of the lawn, and so up to where you was all playing before the door. [The children look at one another, and are quite silent for a minute and each sighs.] But there's one thing in justice I ought to say Robin — the boy — that is with them, we hear nothing against him, Sir — he seems a poor innocent *cratur*, and he has an honest look, and may be it's his misfortune, not his choice, to be with the likes of them. And they say he's an orphan boy, and God forbid I should wrong the orphan, and the deaf and dumb orphan that cant hear whats brought again him, nor plead for himself.

Bess, Cæsar and *Jos.* [exclaim] Good Margery.

Mr. B: You say he is a dumb boy.

Marg: I think so, Sir, to the best of my opinion; they call him Dumby.

Children: Oh, yes, he is dumb, papa — we all told you so, you know.

Mr. B: True, my dear — but I am not certain of it, nevertheless. — The boy may pretend to be deaf and dumb as easily as the man pretended to be blind and lame.

Bess: Oh, father, do you think that this boy could be so deceitful.

Jos: Oh no — he looks good.

Mr. B: I wish I could be sure that he is good — I should then be as ready to do something for the boy as any of you could wish. — But first I must make myself sure of the truth; Cæsar, Bess, and you, my little Joselin, think, if you can, of some way of finding out whether this boy is really deaf and dumb, or whether he is only pretending to be so — Your mother and I are going to walk; we shall return in half an hour, and if you think of any good way of determining this, you shall try it, or I will have it tried for you.

C: I'll go by myself to think.

> [Exit *Cæsar*.]

Bess: So will I.

> [Exit *Bess*.]

Jos: And so must I.

> [Exit *Joscelin*.]

Robin: God bless them good children — they *are* sure enough.

Mrs. B: Margery — have you said any thing to the woman about the doll?

Marg: Not a word, not a word.

Mrs. B: Do not say any thing of it to anybody, and leave the doll and the beard here with me.

Mrs. B: Go into the housekeeper's room, Robin and Margery, the housekeeper is at tea, and will be glad to see you.

Mr. B: And wait there till we come back, if you please.

> [Exuent *Mr.* and *Mrs.*
> *Bridgman*.]

Marg: [to *Robin*] Then I hope he is deaf and dumb, Robin.

> [Exuent.]

End of the First Act

Act II

SCENE 1

The Hall in Bridgman Castle.
Mrs. Bridgman — Cæsar — Bess, and *Joscelin*.

Bess: Mamma, did papa tell you?

Mrs. B: Tell me what, my dear?

C: Then he has not told her. Now, Bess, let me tell the three ways that we have invented for trying whether deaf and dumb Andy is really deaf and dumb or not.

Jos: Mamma, I have invented a way.

Mrs. B: You — you little creature! you talk of inventing?

C: Well, mamma, and it is a very good invention for him. Mamma, he is to go very softly behind him.

Mrs. B: Who is to go behind who?

C: O, Ma'am! Joscelin is to go very softly behind the deaf and dumb boy, and to tickle him.

Jos: And you'll see how softly and well I'll do it; and if he is not really dumb I am sure he'll cry — *"pray don't."*

C: Mamma, now listen to my way. I have thought, mamma, of a very easy common way, by which I can make a charming horrible noise.

Mrs. B: That I do not in the least doubt, my dear.

C: A noise, mamma, that would startle any stranger who did not know what it is, and might make him think that the whole house was coming down, or somebody tumbling from the top to the bottom of the stairs.

[*Cæsar* runs up the staircase
and calls]

C: George! George! come out and bring the basket full of turf from papa's bed-chamber!

[*George* appears in the gallery,
carrying a large basket full of
turf.]

C: Now, mamma, look how I balance it here, so that the least touch will empty it; and the turf will make such a tremendous noise, thundering down into that empty wooden sarcoph, or whatever you call it, which is just underneath. Shall I let it fall for you, mamma?

Mrs. B: No, thank you, my dear. The hearing it once will be quite sufficient for me.

C: Oh! then you intend to be present at our trials, as well as papa! I'm glad of it! — but I am not quite sure whether overturning this turf, or sounding the bugle horn in his ear, will be the best.

Mrs. B: Worst, you mean. How this poor Andy is to be tormented.

Bess: Now, mamma, for my trial. You know Pretty Poll, Kitty's green parrot — well, she will lend it to me, it is used to me, and I can do what I please with it; so I shall bring it in, without the boy's seeing what I'm about, and when it is close to him, I will stroke his head — Pretty Poll's head, I mean; and that instant it will scream out, for I've taught it long ago, "*Ah! you rogue!*" and if Andy is a rogue, he will start, or —

Cæsar: There now, you've said enough, Bess, let mamma listen to me. Mamma, do you know my father says, if he is convinced that the boy is not a — what was it, Bess, that means a cheat?

Bess: An impostor.

Cæsar: Impostor — if papa is convinced Andy is not an impostor, he will do something good for him — he did not tell us what, mamma; and now we are all ready, and I will run and call papa.

[Exit *Cæsar*.]

Bess: I will run down to Kitty for Pretty Poll.

Mrs. B: Take care Pretty Poll does not bite you.

Bess: It will not bite me, mamma; but perhaps it will bite Andy.

[Exeunt.]

SCENE 2

A Servant's Hall.

Watty Brannigan, Winny and *Andy.*

Win: Watty — Andy — put your heads close to me, till I tell you what I overheard when I was pretending to be asleep, and snoring.

Wat: What is it?

Win: Take care there wouldn't be any one overhearing me there in the kitchen.

Wat: Never fear, they're all of 'em too busy about, the Lord knows what, that they always have to do in these big houses. What did ye year?

Win: I heard one of them little childer, that is cuter than we thought 'em, telling the housekeeper that the father suspects us all to be vagabones and imposters.

Wat: That is very ungenerous of the gentleman, then.

Win: True for ye. But its you, Andy, they most suspect of not being dumb, and they are to make a trial of you, mind, someway with a parrot, and a turf stack, and tickling, and I don't know what, but whatsomdever it bees, Andy, stand to it, and don't be betraying yourself nor us.

Wat: Oh! I hope you would'n't Andy.

Andy: No! not betray you — never! — when you've been so good to me — rather be flogged, I would. But I wish I might confess the truth about myself — might I?

Wat: Oh murder! the truth! never!

Win: Why then he might say it was all a mistake — his being dumb; and that it was only a tooth-ache he took hindered him to *spake*. Could'n't he tell the truth about the rest?

Andy: Aye, let me tell of how good you was to me when my mother died of the *faver*, and you took me, an orphant, and kep' me from starving. Oh! let me tell the truth about that!

Win: Aye, sure, the truth would do no harm there.

Wat: Oh! I'll not have it! — I'll have nothing to do with the truth — for that wont hang together with the rest of the story, that we haven't a bit to put in our own mouths — then how could we help him, the quality would ax. Oh! its what it must be — all truth, or none. The truth will only do for them that sticks to it close, and from the first. Its too late in life, now, Winny Brannigan, for you and me to be taking to it.

Andy: But not for me: its early with me. I wish I'd stuck to the truth, then, from the first. Oh! let me tell the truth now!

Wat: Will you betray *us*, then?

Andy: Never! Oh! I don't know what I'll do!

Win: Be *Dumb Andy*, that's all you can be.

Andy: I'll die before I'll betray yees; but I'm sorry —

Wat: Hush! here's one coming! be dumb!

[Enter *George*.]

George: Whichsomever of you three be deaf and dumb you will be pleased to follow me.

Wat: That's he, poor dumby! — Dumb Andy, Sir — and he's deaf too, from the hour he was born.

Win: I'll speak to him on my fingers, such as they are, and make him sinsible he's to go up and in wid you, Sir.

> [*Winny* speaks on her fingers.
> *Andy* nods, and goes with the footman.]

> [Exeunt *George* and *Andy*.]

Wat: Oh! do ye think Andy will be true to us?

Win: He will — I'll engage.

Wat: Come to the fut of the stairs, where we might hear a bit how he stands the trial. Come off, for this bees no convenient place for listening.

> [Exeunt *Winny* and *Watty*.]

SCENE 3

Hall — *Mr.* and *Mrs. Bridgman* in the gallery,

Cæsar, Bess, and *Joscelin.*

C: Papa, I hope you are near enough to the turf basket to make it empty itself the very minute I put on my hat? — and not till then, remember, of you please —

Bess: And mamma, were you so very good as to desire to have the supper ready for the poor boy, if we find that he really is not a cheat?

Mrs. B: Yes — Whenever I ring the bell supper will come — if —

Bess: Oh, mamma, dont say if — I think I hope.

C: So do I hope.

Jos: So do I, with all my heart — and hope he may have some supper too.

C: Hush, Josecelin, here he is.

[Enter George and Andy.]

George: The deaf and dumb boy, Sir — as you desired.

C: [speaking very loud] Come this way, if you please, my good boy, come to this side of the room.

[Andy stands perfectly still.]

Bess: [repeats it louder still] My brother begs you will go to that side of the room where he is standing — Oh! my dear, he is perfectly deaf you see —

C: Hush, my dear, you know if he is *pretending* he hears every word you say as well as I do.

Bess: Now, Cæsar, can you imagine that he hears you — only look in his face — does he look as if he heard?

C: Indeed I dont think it possible he could look so innocent and honest if he was cheating.

Bess: [low to *Cæsar*.] My dear Cæsar — did you see how he blushed — as red as scarlet when you said honest?

C: [aside to *Bess*.] Now I'll speak to him on my fingers, and ask him if he was born dumb.

[Cæsar speaks on his fingers.
Andy attempts to answer. Bess

> and *Cæsar* repeat the letters as
> he makes the signs.]

I C-A-N-T cant T-E-L-L tell.

C: Cant tell.

Bess: No, how could he — when he was an infant, how could he know? — Did you see how his fingers trembled?

Jos: Hush! hush! now for my trial.

> [*Joscelin* creeps behind him and
> tickles him — *Andy* writhes to
> this side and to that, but makes
> no exclamation.]

Jos: Oh, he is certainly dumb, for any body who was not dumb would have called out, *"Oh, pray! pray dont tickle me"* long before this time.

C: [aside to *Bess*.] Now, if he stands my trial.

> [*Cæsar* puts on his hat, and
> instantly his father empties
> the turf-basket from the gal-
> lery. — The turf falls into a
> turf-box below with a thund-
> erous noise. — *Andy* stands
> with his back to the gallery
> and appears not to hear in the
> least.]

Bess: Now for my trial! and if he stands that — now for it — Poll, Poll, not a word till I bid you. [Bess takes the parrot out of his cage and strokes his head. The parrot screams loudly] "Oh, you rogue, Oh you rogue." —

> [*Andy* stands as still as before,
> and shows no sign of hearing.]

Bess: [Joyfully] Oh, he's deaf, he's deaf indeed — Nobody can doubt it now.

C: [takes down from the wall a speaking trumpet, and roars through it] He is honest, he is honest — Hear ye all men and all women — are you convinced now?

Jos: Mamma, mamma, ring the bell for supper.

> [*Mrs. Bridgman* rings the bell,
> and *Mr.* and *Mrs. Bridgman*,

come down from the gallery,
the children all run to them,
saying]
I hope you are convinced now, papa.
I hope you are convinced now, mamma.
Mrs. B: I am convinced that he is quite deaf — for he was tried when he was entirely off his guard.
Mr. B: I believe you are right my dear children and I am heartily glad of it — I do not want to make you suspicious — you that are young. I hope that, though I am old, I am not very suspicious myself.
C: No, indeed, papa is not suspicious. Now I will go and get the hat and the trowsers that you said I might give him.
[Exit *Cæsar* running.]
Jos: Oh! take me with you, Cæsar!
[Exit *Joscelin*.]

[Enter *George* with supper.]

[*Bess* sets a little table and a chair, and makes signs to the dumb boy to eat. He obeys the signs *Mrs. Birdgman* makes. *Mr. Bridgman* all the time watches him attentively.]
Bess: He does not eat as eagerly as I expected he would, mamma.
[Re-enter *Cæsar* and *Joscelin*, loaded with old clothes of different sorts.]
C: Mamma, may I give him this old, very old, great coat of mine, to keep him warm in the winter?
Mrs. B: Yes, my dear, but I am afraid it will hardly keep him warm.
C: Will this flannel waistcoat, mamma? and these trowsers, papa?
Mr. B: He will never get them on, my dear.

C: Oh yes, papa! you will see they will go on very easily; and this shirt, mamma, Kitty said I might bring to ask you; and these shoes she gives him herself; and this hat of mine, mamma, if you please. Here, poor deaf and dumb boy, here they are all for you.

> [Makes signs to *Andy*, that
> they are all for him. *Joseclin*
> jumps upon the chair behind
> him, and puts the hat on
> *Andy*'s head, *Cæsar* holds the
> great coat for him to put on.]

Bess: Mamma, do you see the tears in his eyes? — how grateful he looks.

> [*Andy* suddenly pushes the coat
> from him, throws the hat from
> his head, falls down on his
> knees, bursts into tears, and
> exclaims]

Andy: I do not deserve it. I am not deaf, I am not dumb; I am a cheat, but, oh, I don't know whether I am doing wrong or right now this minute. [looking up to Heaven] Oh if I knew which was right to do! — But I have no mother, no father, *none* to teach me. Oh, if I'm wrong now, I can't help it; I could not stand your goodness and pity for me, [sobbing] I could not; I could not. That's the trial I could not stand; any thing but that and I would never have spoken. They might have flogged me as long as they could stand over me; oh, I promised I would not tell. [starting up and changing his look and tone] I promised, and I've broke my word, and this is worse; oh worse than all I done.

Bess: What does he mean by that, mamma.

C: I do believe, papa, that he was forced to pretend to be dumb, and forced to be a cheat, by that vile man and woman.

Mr. B: [in a loud voice] Ring the bell — send that man and woman up here.

> [*Andy* throws himself on his
> knees before *Mr. Bridgman*.]

Andy: Send me to jail Sir, do what you will with me, I desarve it all, and am here ready to submit to all. But, oh, spare them, Sir, them that was good to me, an orphan boy, when I'd none other to help me; oh hear me Sir. — They took me, and nursed me, and reared me from the day my mother died of the fever. Whatever else they done bad, they were good and tender to me, and now I am a traitor to them and an informer, and [calmly, and in a tone of despair] twere better for me I was dead — or had never been born; for I dont know, if I was to be killed this minute, what's right and what's wrong, no more nor —

Bess: [Puts her arm within her mother's.] Poor orphan.

Jos: Poor boy — I think he wishes to be good. Oh if he had had such a father and mother as I have.

C: My dear father speak to him; O, tell him he is right *now*.

[*Mr. Bridgman*, while his children speak, appears agitated.]

Bess: Oh, mamma, if he had had such a father and mother as good Robin Woods and Margery.

Mr. B: Send in Robin Woods and his wife — with that man and woman.

[*Andy* clasps his hands in a supplicating attitude.]

Mrs. B: Fear nothing; be assured, poor boy, that I will not make you repent of having told the truth, when you were treated so kindly.

Andy: [aside] Oh if any body, if any human creature, had ever once only spoke to me so before in my whole life!

[He sobs and hides his face.]

Mr. B: [aside to *Mrs. B*.] Poor, ill taught, unfortunate creature, he has quite touched me; but compassion should be of some use — we must have him better taught, we must take him out of the hands of these people.

[Enter *Robin* and *Margery*.]

Robin: Oh! Sir, the birds are flown; they are far away by this time.

Marg: Yes, Ma'am, they left the servant's hall and kept in the passage a while; my mind misgives me that they were near the door here, and heard something that made them take themsleves off in a hurry; and there I see them running across the field, and the man has got both his legs, sure enough. But myself is glad they are gone.

Children: So are we all.

Mr. B: On account of their humanity to this poor boy, I will let them off, otherwise I would have had them pursued and punished. Now we can do something for him — If, as I believe, he really wishes to be good, he shall have an opportunity of being so — I now put him under the care of the most perfectly honest people I know. [turning to *Robin* and *Margery*] This excellent couple, whom I have known now this thirty years, and whom all that time never told a lie, never said or did any thing that could injure man, woman, or child, and who have made themselves respected and loved by all who know them.

> [*Robin* and *Margery* curtsey and
> bow, and say]

Thanks to your honour.

Mr. B: Will you, then, my good Robin, and my good Margery, try for one month, whether this boy can be made good for something.

Robin: Troth we will, with all our hearts.

Margery: And we will never be remembering or throwing the past up again him, so its what he may do well and be happy yet.

Andy: Oh! blessings on yees, will I?

C [to *Andy*.] So, Andy, you find it was best for you to tell the truth.

Andy: Troth it was — no harm, but great good, come of my telling the truth. Then if ever I'm in a condition, I'll show my gratitude, I will, to them that buried my mother, and I'd be bad if I was not good to them that was good to me, wouldn't I? Mane time I'm thankful I'm not forced to play the rogue any more for them, I'm no more Dumb Andy.

> [Exeunt.]

The End

MUCH COIN, MUCH CARE

1829

Anna Jameson

Anna Brownell Murphy was born in Dublin on May 17, 1794, the eldest of the five daughters of Dennis Brownell, a miniaturist. In 1798, the family moved to England and settled in Hanwell. Anna was a precocious student with a particularly good ear for languages. At sixteen, she became governess to the children of the Marquis of Winchester. For the following fifteen years, until she married, she continued to work as a governess, next with the Rowles family of Kent, with whom she toured the Continent, and finally with the Littleton children of Staffordshire. It was for the Littleton children she wrote *Much Coin, Much Care*.

Anna Murphy met Robert Jameson, a lawyer, in about 1821. They married in 1825. The marriage proved tempestuous, perhaps because (as one commentator wrote) "the wife was rudely neglected and the authoress urged to make capital out of her talents."[1] When in 1829 Jameson moved to become a judge in Domenica, his wife did not follow him. Jameson went to Canada in 1833, first as Attorney General of Upper Canada and later as Canada's first Speaker of the Legislature. At his urging, Anna joined him in 1836, but she returned alone to England two years later. Jameson died in Canada in 1854. He made no provision for Anna in his will.

Anna made close friendships while she was in the New World, particularly in New England. It was probably through the Unitarian minister William Ellery Channing that she met Theodore Follen and his wife, Eliza, who admired her and would later anthologize her play.

On her return to England, Anna wrote prodigiously. She wrote books on travel, on the lives of celebrated women, on sculpture and painting, and, near the end of her life, on religion. She died at Ealing, in Middlesex, on March 17, 1860. At the time of her death she was working on *A History of Our Lord.*[2]

MUCH COIN, MUCH CARE

> Mrs. Jameson paid me a long visit; she threatens to write a play; perhaps she might; she is very clever, has a vast fund of information, a good deal of experience, and knowledge and observation of the world and of society.
>
> Fanny Kemble[3]

In fact, in 1831 when Fanny Kemble wrote this, Anna Jameson had written a play. It was *Much Coin, Much Care: A Dramatic Proverb Written for Hyacinth, Emily, Caroline, and Edward,* who were the four Littleton children whose governess she was between 1822 and 1825. Although she was deeply interested in the stage "stagestruck," in fact — she never wrote another play.[4]

Mrs. Jameson's modern biographer, Clara Thomas, dismisses *Much Coin, Much Care* as "a moral little drama . . . undistinguished in invention and technique." I disagree. I think Ms. Thomas underestimates the particular virtues of the play because she takes it at its face value.

A dramatic proverb is as tight a form as a limerick or a sonnet. It requires a moral or ethical dilemma for its plot and a conclusion or solution to that moral dilemma for its title, which is recapitulated in the play's last line. That is the definition of the genre, and *Much Coin, Much Care* fulfills it. Beyond that, the play has no more moral weight than a charade. It is a *jeu d'esprit*, a lark for the actors, that uses the form of the dramatic proverb as its point of departure and its armature.

Anna Jameson was exposed to high moral seriousness in the form of Hannah More's moral tracts, and she loathed and mistrusted it all her life.

It is most certain that more moral mischief was done to me by some of those [tracts] than by all Shakespeare's plays together. These so-called pious tracts first introduced me to the knowledge of the vices of vulgar life, and the excitement of vulgar religion, — the fear of being hanged and the fear of jail became coexistent in my mind; and the teaching resolved itself into this, — that it was not by being naughty, but by being found out, that I was to incur the risk of both.[5]

Much Coin, Much Care is an antidote to Hannah More's humorless moralizing. From its deadpan title on, it is an excuse, not for high seriousness but for high spirits. It gives the children who act it a chance to show off what they can do. It gives them a chance to talk French, both proper (for praise) and fractured (for fun). It gives well brought-up children a chance to talk common, act rowdy, and mock affectations they would themselves be too polite to mock. It gives children who can sing a chance to sing. The fact that it "was written for her young charges to perform"[6] is the reason it is so good. It was precisely and specifically imagined for the occasion on which and the space in which it was going to be performed. And it was tailor-made for its young actors.

Yet it is not perishable, as are many occasional pieces, because it is unbreakably bound to the occasion for which it was conceived. Not despite but because it was conceived so specifically a hundred and seventy years ago, it, like the best drama written for a particular moment, is still so playable today.

NOTES

1. *The Edinburgh Review*, vol. 149, quoted in the *Dictionary of National Biography* (London: Oxford University Press, 1901), 668.

2. Thomas includes a complete bibliography of works by and about Anna Jameson in Clara Thomas, *Love and Work Enough: The*

Life of Anna Jameson (Toronto: University of Toronto Press, 1966), [223]–235.

3. Fanny Kemble, "Records of a Girlhood," in Thomas, *Love and Work Enough,* 394. Anna Jameson says in an endnote to the 1859 edition of her play that *Much Coin, Much Care* was adapted from one of the proverbes dramatique of Leclercq.

4. Anna Jameson did translate the dramas of Princess Amelia of Saxony, under the title of *Social Life in Germany* (1840). The *Cambridge Bibliography of English Literature* lists as Anna Jameson's first work *Cadijah, or the Black Prince: A Tragedy in Five Acts,* 1825. Clara Thomas consulted the general editor of the Cambridge Bibliography, who believes the entry is an error. See Thomas, *Love and Work Enough,* note 5, chapter 5, 237.

5. Anna Jameson, *A Commonplace Book of Thoughts, Memories, and Fancies* (New York: D. Appleton and Company, 1855), quoted by Thomas in *Love and Work Enough,* 6.

6. Thomas, *Love and Work Enough,* 88.

MUCH COIN, MUCH CARE

A DRAMATIC PROVERB

written for

Hyacinth, Emily, Caroline, and Edward

Dramatis Persons

DICK, the Cobbler, a very honest man, and very merry withal, much given to singing.

MARGERY, his wife, simple and affectionate, and one of the best women in the world.

LADY AMARANTHE, a fine lady, full of airs and affectation, but not without good feeling.

MADEMOISELLE JUSTINE, her French maid, very like other French maids.

The SCENE lies partly in the Garret of the Cobbler, and partly in *Lady Amaranthe's* Drawing-room.

SCENE I

A Garret meanly furnished; several pairs of old shoes, a coat, hat, bonnet, and shawl hanging against the wall. *Dick* is seated on a low stool in front. He works, and sings.

And she lay on that day
In the Bay of Biscay O!

Now, that's what *I* call a good song; but my wife, she can't abear them blusteration songs, she says; she likes something tender and genteel, full of fine words. [Sings in a mincing voice.]

Vake, dearest, vake, and again united
Vee'l wander by the sea-he-he-e.

Hang me, if I can understand a word of it! but when my wife
sings it out with her pretty little mouth, it does one's heart
good to hear her; and I could listen to her forever. But, for my
own part, what like is a song that comes thundering out with a
meaning in it! [Sings, and flourishes his hammer with
enthusiasm, beating time upon the shoe.]

March! march! Eskadale and Tiviotdale
All the blue bonnets are over the border!

Marg: [from within]. Dick! Dick! what a noise you do keep!
Dick: A noise, eh? Why, Meg, you didn't use to think it a
noise; you used to like to hear me sing!
Marg: [entering]. And so I did, and so I do. I loves music with
all my heart; but the whole parish will hear you if you go for
to bawl out so monstrous loud.
Dick: And let them! Who cares?
[He sings, she laughs.]
Marg: Nay, sing away if you like it!
Dick: [stopping suddenly]. I won't sing another bit if you
don't like it, Meg.
Marg: Oh, I do like! Lord bless us! not like it! it sounds so
merry! Why, Dick, love, everybody said yesterday that you
sung as well as Mr. Thingumee at Sadler's Wells, and says
they, "Who is that young man as sings like any nightingale?"
and I says [drawing herself up], "That's my husband!"
Dick: Ay! flummery! But, Meg, I say, how did you like the
wedding yesterday?
Marg: Oh, hugeously! such heaps of smart people, as fine as
fivepence, I warrant; and such gay gowns and caps! and plenty
to eat and drink! But what I liked best was the walking in the
gardens at Bagnigge Wells, and the tea, and the crumpets!
Dick: And the punch!

Marg: Yes — ha! ha! I could see you thought *that* good! and then the dancing!

Dick: Ay, ay; and there wasn't one amongst them that footed it away like my Margery. And folks say to me, "Pray, who is that pretty modest young woman as hops over the ground as light as a feather?" says they; and says I, "Why, that there pretty young woman is my wife, to be sure!"

Marg: Ah, you're at your jokes, Dick!

Dick: I'll be hanged then!

Marg: [leaning on his shoulder] Well to be sure, we were happy yesterday. It's good to make holiday just now and then, but some how I was very glad to come home to our own little room again. O Dick! did you mind that Mrs. Pinchtoe, that gave herself such grand airs! She in the fine lavender silk gown, that turned up her nose at me so, and all because she's a master-shoemaker's wife! and you are only — only — a cobbler! [Sighs]. I wish *you* were a master-shoemaker, Dick.

Dick: That you might be a master-shoemaker's wife, hay! and turn up your nose like Mrs. Pinchtoe?

Marg: [laughing]. No, no; I have more manners.

Dick: Would you love me better, Meg, if I were a master-shoemaker?

Marg: No, I couldn't love you better if you were a king; and that you know, Dick; and, after all, we're happy now, and who knows what might be if we were to change?

Dick: Ay, indeed! who knows? You might grow into a fine lady like she over the way, who comes home o'nights just as we're getting up in the morning, with the flams flaring, and blazing like anything; and that puts me in mind —

Marg: Of what, Dick? Tell me!

Dick: Why, cousin Tim's wedding put it all out of my head last night; but yesterday there comes over to me one of those fine bedizened fellows we see lounging about the door there, with a cocked hat, and things like stay-laces dangling at his shoulder.

Marg: What could he want, I wonder!

Dick: O! he comes over to me as I was just standing at the door below, a thinking of nothing at all, and singing Paddy O'Rafferty to myself, and says he to me, "You cobbler fellor," says he, "don't you go for to keep such a bawling every morning, awakening people out of their first sleep," says he, "for if you do, my lord will have you put into the stocks," says he.

Marg: The stocks! O goodness gracious me! and what for, pray?

Dick: [with a grin]. Why, for singing, honey! So says I, "Hark'ee, Mr. Scrape-trencher, there go words to that bargain. What right have you to go for to speak in that there way to me?" says I; and says he, "We'll have you 'dited for a nuisance, fellor," says he.

Marg: [clasping her hands]. A nuisance! my Dick a nuisance! O Lord a' mercy!

Dick: Never fear, girl; I'm a free-born Englishman, and I knows the laws well enough; and says I, "No more a fellor than yourself; I'm an honest man, following an honest calling, and I don't care *that* for you nor your lord neither; and I'll sing *when* I please, and I'll sing *what* I please, and I'll sing as loud as I please; I will, by jingo!" and so he lifts me up his cane, and I says quite cool, "This house is my castle; and if you don't take yourself out of that in a jiffey, why, I'll give your laced jacket such a dusting as it never had before in its life — I will."

Marg: O, Dick! you've a spirit of your own, I warrant. Well, and then?

Dick: Oh, I promise you he was off in the twinkling of a bed-post, and I've heard no more of him; but I was determined to wake you this morning with a thundering song; just to show 'em I didn't care for 'em — ha! ha! ha!

Marg: Oh, ho! that was the reason, then, that you bawled so in my ear, and frightened me out of my sleep, was it? Oh, well, I forgive you; but bless me! I stand chattering here, and it's twelve o'clock, as I live! I must go to market [putting on her shawl and bonnet]. What would you like to have for dinner, Dick, love? A nice rasher of bacon, by way of a relish?

Dick: [smacking his lips]. Just the very thing, honey.

Marg: Well, give me the shilling, then.

Dick: [scratching his head]. What shilling?

Marg: Why, the shilling you had yesterday.

Dick: [feeling in his pockets]. A shilling!

Marg: Yes, a shilling. [Gaily.] To have meat, one must have money; and folks must eat as well as sing, Dick, love. Come, out with it!

Dick: But suppose I haven't got it?

Marg: How! what! You don't mean for to say that the last shilling that you put in your pocket, just to make a show, is gone?

Dick: [with a sigh]. But I do, though; it's gone.

Marg: What shall we do?

Dick: I don't know. [A pause; they look at each other.] Stay, that's lucky. Here's a pair of dancing pumps as belongs to old Mrs. Crusty, the baker's wife at the corner —

Marg: [gaily]. We can't eat *them* for dinner, I guess.

Dick: No, no; but I'm just at the last stitch.

Marg: Yes —

Dick: [speaking and working in a hurry]. And so you'll take them home —

Marg: Yes —

Dick: And tell her I must have seven-pence halfpenny for them. [Gives them.]

Marg: [examining the shoes]. But, Dick, isn't that some 'at extortionate, as a body may say? Seven-pence halfpenny!

Dick: Why, here's heel-pieces, and a patch upon each toe; one must live, Meg!

Marg: Yes, Dick, love; but so must other folks. Now I think seven-pence would be enough in all conscience. What do you say?

Dick: Well, settle it as you like; only get a bit of dinner for us, for I'm as hungry as a hunter, I know.

Marg: I'm going. Good-bye, Dick!

Dick: Take care of theeself, and don't spend the change in caps and ribbons, Meg!

Marg: Caps and ribbons out of seven-pence! Lord help the man! Ha, ha, ha! [She goes out.]

Dick: [calling after her]. And come back, soon, d'ye hear? There she goes — hop, hop, and hop down the stairs. Somehow, I can't abear to have her out of my sight a minute. Well, if ever there was a man could say he had a good wife, why that's me myself — tho'f I say it — the cheerfullest, sweetest temperedst, cleanliest, lovingest woman in the whole parish that never gives one an ill word from year's end to year's end, and deserves at least that a man should work hard for her; it's all I can do, and we must think for to-morrow as well as to-day. [He works with great energy, and sings at the same time with equal enthusiasm.]

> Cannot ye do as I do?
> Cannot ye do as I do?
> Spend your money, and work for more;
> *That's* the way that I do!
> > Tol de rol lol.

Re-enter *Margery* in haste.

Marg: [out of breath]. O, Dick, husband! Dick, I say!

Dick: Hay! what's the matter now?

Marg: Here be one of those fine powdered laced fellows from over the way comed after you again.

Dick: [rising]. An impudent jackanapes! I'll give him as good as he brings.

Marg: Oh, no, no! he's monstrous civil now; for he chucked me under the chin, and says he, "My pretty girl!"

Dick: Ho! monstrous civil, indeed, with a vengeance!

Marg: And says he, "Do you belong to this here house?" "Yes, sir," says I, making a curtsy, for I could do no less when he spoke so civil; and says he, "Is there an honest cobbler as lives here?" "Yes, sir," says I, "my husband that is." "Then, my dear," says he, "just tell him to step over the way, for my Lady Amaranthe wishes to speak to him immediately."

Dick: A lady? O Lord!

Marg: Yes, so you must go directly. Here, take off your apron, and let me comb your hair a bit.

Dick: What the mischief can a lady want with me? I've nothing to do with ladies, as I knows of.

Marg: Why, she won't eat you up, I reckon.

Dick: And yet I — I — I be afeard, Meg!

Marg: Afeard of a lady! that's a good one!

Dick: Ay, just — if it were a man, I shouldn't care a fig.

Marg: But we've never done no harm to nobody in our whole lives, so what is there to be afraid of?

Dick: Nay, that's true.

Marg: Now let me help you on with your best coat. Pooh! What is the man about? Why, you're putting the back to the front, and the front to the back, like Paddy from Cork, with his coat buttoned behind!

Dick: My head do turn around, just for all the world like a peg-top. A lady! What *can* a lady have to say to me, I wonder?

Marg: May be, she's a customer.

Dick: No, no great gentlefolks like she never wears patched toes nor heel-pieces, I reckon.

Marg: Here's your hat. Now let me see how you can make a bow. [He bows awkwardly.] Hold up your head — turn out your toes. That will do capital! [She walks round him with admiration.] How nice you look! There's ne'er a gentleman of them all can come up to my Dick.

Dick: [hesitating]. But — a — a — Meg, you'll come with me, won't you, and just see me safe in the door, eh?

Marg: Yes, to be sure; walk on before, and let me look at you. Hold up your head — there, that's it!

Dick: [marching]. Come along. Hang it, who's afraid?

[They go out.]

SCENE II

A Drawing-room in the House of *Lady Amaranthe*.

[Enter *Lady Amaranthe*, leaning upon her maid,
Mademoiselle Justine.]

Lady Amar: Avancez un fauteuil, ma chère! arrangez les
coussins. [*Justine* settles the chair and places a footstool. *Lady
Amaranthe*, sinking into the arm-chair with a languid air.]
Justine, I shall die, I shall certainly die! I never can survive
this!

Just: Mon Dieu! Madame, ne parlez pas comme çà! c'est
m'enfoncer un poignard dans le coeur !

Lady Amar: [despairingly]. No rest, no possibility of
sleeping —

Just: Et le medecin de Madame, qui a ordonné la plus grande
tranquillité — qui a même voulu que je me taisais — moi, par
exemple!

Lady Amar: After fatiguing myself to death with playing
the agreeable to disagreeable people, and talking commonplace
to commonplace acquaintance, I return home, to lay my aching
head upon my pillow, and just as my eyes are closing, I start, I
wake — a voice that would rouse the dead out of their graves
echoes in my ears! In vain I bury my head in the pillow, in vain
draw the curtains close, multiply defences against my window,
change from room to room — it haunts me! Ah! I think I hear it
still [covering her ears]! It will certainly drive me distracted!

[During this speech *Justine* has
made sundry exclamations and
gestures expressive of horror,
sympathy and commiseration.]

Just: Vraiment, c'est affreux.

Lady Amar: In any more civlized country it never could have
been endured. I should have had him removed at once. But here
the vulgar people talk of laws!

Just: Ah, oui, Madame, mais il faut avouer que c'est ici un
pays bien barbare, ou tout le monde parle loi et metaphysique,

et ou l'on ne fait point de différence entre les riches et les pauvres.

Lady Amar: But what provokes me more than all the rest is this unheard-of insolence! [Rises and walks about the room.] A cobbler, too, a cobbler who presumes to sing, and to sing when all the rest of the world is asleep! This is the march of intellect with a vengeance!

Just: C'est vrai, il ne chante que des marches et de gros chansons à boire — s'il chantait bien doucement quelque joli roman par exemple — [she sings] — *dormez, dormez, mez chers amours* !

Lady Amar: Justine, did you send the butler over to request civilly that he would not disturb me in the morning?

Just: Oui, miladi, dat is, I have sent John; de Butler he was went out.

Lady Amar: And his answer was, that he would sing in spite of me, and louder than ever?

Just: Oui, miladi, le monstre! il dit comme çà, dat he will sing more louder den ever.

Lady Amar: [sinking again into her chair]. Ah! the horrid man!

Just: Ah! dere is no politesse, no more den dere is police in dis country.

Lady Amar: If Lord Amaranthe were not two hundred miles off — but, as it is, I must find some remedy; let me think — bribery, I suppose. Have they sent for him? I dread to see the wretch. What noise is that? allez voir, ma chère!

Just: [goes and returns]. Madame, c'est justement notre homme, voulez vous qu'il entre?

Lady Amar: Oui, faites entrer.

[She leans back in her chair.]

Just: [at the door]. Entrez, entrez toujours, dat is, come in, good mister.

[Enter *Dick*. He bows; and, squeezing his hat in his hands, looks round him with considerable embarrassment.]

Just: [to *Lady Amaranthe*]. Bah! comme il sent le cuir, n'est-ce pas, Madame?

Lady Amar: Faugh! mes sels — ma vinaigrette, Justine — non, l'eau de Cologne, qui est là sur la table. [*Justine* brings her some eau de Cologne; she pours some upon her handkerchief, and applies it to her temples and to her nose, as if overcome; then, raising her eye-glass, she examines *Dick* from head to foot.] Good man — a — pray, what is your name?

Dick: [with a profound bow]. Dick, please your ladyship.

Lady Amar: Hum — a — a — pray, Mr. Dick —

Dick: Folks just call me plain Dick, my lady. I'm a poor honest Cobbler, and no mister.

Lady Amar:]pettishly]. Well, sir, it is of no consequence. You live in the small house over the way, I think?

Dick: Yes, ma'am, my lady, I does; I rents the attics.

Lady Amar: You appear a good civil sort of man enough. [He bows.] I sent my servant over to request that you would not disturb me in the night, or the morning, as you call it. I have very weak health — am quite an invalid — your loud singing in the morning just opposite to my windows —

Dick: [eagerly]. Ma'am, I — I'm very sorry; I ax your ladyship's pardon; I'll never sing no more above my breath, if you please.

Just: Comment! c'est honnête, par exemple.

Lady Amar: [surprised]. Then you did not tell my servant that you would sing louder than ever, in spite of me?

Dick: Me, my lady? I never said no such thing.

Lady Amar: This is strange; or is there some mistake? Perhaps you are not the same Mr. Dick?

Dick: Why, yes, my lady, for that matter, I be the same Dick. [Approaching a few steps, and speaking confidentially.] I'll just tell your ladyship the whole truth, and not a bit of a lie. There comes an impudent fellow to me, and he tells me, just out of his own head, I'll be bound, that if I sung o' mornings, he would have me put in the stocks.

Lady Amar: Good heavens!

Just: [in the same tone]. Grands dieux!

Dick: [with a grin]. Now the stocks is for a rogue, as the saying is. As for my singing, that's neither here nor there; but no jackanapes shall threaten *me*. I *will* sing if I please [sturdily], and I won't sing if I don't please; and [lowering his tone], I don't please, if it disturbs your ladyship. [Retreating] I wish your ladyship a good day, and better health.

Lady Amar: Stay; you are not then the rude uncivil person I was told of?

Dick: I hopes I knows better than to do an uncivil thing by a lady.

[Bows and retreats towards the door.]

Lady Amar: Stay, sir — a — a — one word.

Dick: Oh, as many as you please, ma'am; I'm in no hurry.

Lady Amar: [graciously]. Are you married?

Dick: [rubbing his hands with glee]. Yes, ma'am, I be; and to as tight a bit of a wife as any in the parish.

Just: Ah! il parait que ce Monsieur Dick aime sa femme! Est-il amusant!

Lady Amar: You love her, then?

Dick: Oh, then I do! I love her with all my heart! Who could help it?

Lady Amar: Indeed! And how do you live?

Dick: Why, bless you, ma'am, sometimes well, sometimes ill, according as I have luck and work. When we can get a bit of dinner, we eat it; and when we can't, why, we go without; or, may be, a kind neighbor helps us.

Lady Amar: Poor creatures!

Dick: Oh, not so poor, neither, my lady; many folks is worser off. I'm always merry, night and day; and my Meg is the good temperedst, best wife in the world. We've never had nothing from the parish and never will, please God, while I have health and hand.

Lady Amar: And you are happy?

Dick: As happy as the day is long.

Lady Amar: [aside]. This is a lesson to me. Eh bien, Justine! voilà donc notre sauvage!

Just: Il est gentil ce Monsieur Dick, et à present que je le regarde — vraiment il a une assez jolie tournure.

Lady Amar: [with increasing interest]. Have you any children?

Dick: [with a sigh]. No, ma'am; and that's the only thing as frets us.

Lady Amar: Good heavens! You do not mean to say you wish for them, and have scarce enough for yourselves? How would you feed them?

Dick: Oh, I should leave Meg to feed them; I should have nothing to do but to work for them. Providence would take care of us while they were little, and when they were big they would help us.

Lady Amar: [aside]. I could not have conceived this. [She whispers *Justine*, who goes out.] [To *Dick*]. Can I do anything to serve you?

Dick: Only, if your ladyship could recommend me any customer. I mend shoes as cheap as e'er a cobbler in London, though I say it.

Lady Amar: I shall certainly desire that all my people employ you whenever there is occasion.

[Re-enter *Justine*, holding a purse in her hand.]

Dick: [owing]. Much obliged, my lady; I hopes to give satisfaction, but [looking with admiration at *Lady Amaranthe's* foot as it rests on the footstool] such a pretty, little, delicate, beautiful foot as you, I never fitted in all my born days. It can't cost your ladyship much in shoe leather, I guess?

Lady Amar: [smiling complacently]. Rather more than you would imagine, I fancy, my good friend.

Just: Comment donc — ce Monsieur Dick, fait aussi des compliments à Madame? Il ne manque pas de goût, — [aside] — et il sait ce qu'il fait, apparemment.

Lady Amar: [glancing at her foot]. C'est à dire — il a du bon sens, et ne parle pas mal. [She takes the purse.] As you so civilly obliged me, you must allow me to make you some return.

Dick: [putting his hand behind him]. Me, ma'am! I'm sure I don't want to be paid for being civil.

Lady Amar: But as I have deprived you of a pleasure, my good friend, some amends surely —

Dick: Oh, ma'am, pray don't mention it; my wife's a little tired and sleepy sometimes of a morning, and if I didn't sing her out of bed, I do think she would, by chance, snooze away till six o'clock, like any duchess; but a pinch or a shake or a kiss will do as well, may be; and [earnestly] she's, for all that, the best woman in the world.

Lady Amar: [smiling]. I can believe it, though she *does* sleep till six o'clock like a duchess. Well, my good friend, there are five guineas in this purse; the purse is my own work; and I request you will present it to your wife from me, with many thanks for your civility.

Dick: [confused]. Much obliged, much obliged, but I can't, I can't indeed, my lady. Five guineas! O Lord! I should never know what to do with such a power of money.

Lady Amar: Your wife will not say the same, depend upon it; she will find some use for it.

Dick: My Meg, poor woman! she never had so much money in all her life.

Lady Amar: I must insist upon it; you will offend me.

Just: [taking the purse out of her ladyship's hand, and forcing it upon *Dick*]. Dieux! est-il bête! you no understand? It is de gold and de silver money [laughing]. Comme il a l'air ébahi!

Dick: [putting up the money]. Many thanks, and I pray God bless your ladyship!

Lady Amar: [gaily]. Good morning, Mr. Dick. Remember me to your wife.

Dick: I will, my lady. I wish your ladyship, and you, miss, a good morning. [To himself.] Five guineas! What will Meg say? Now I'll be a master-shoemaker. [Going out in an ecstasy, he knocks his head against the wall.]

Lady Amar: Take care, friend. Montrez-lui la porte, Justine!

Just: Mais venez donc, Monsieur Dick — par ici — et n'allez pas donner le nez contre la porte!

[*Dick* follows *Justine* out of the door, after making several bows.]

Just: Voici Madame Mincetaille, qui vient pour essayer la robe-de-bal de madame.
Lady Amar: Ah! allons donc.
[They go out.]

SCENE III

The Cobbler's Garret

[Enter *Margery*, in haste; a basket in her hand.
She looks about her.]

Marg: Not come back yet! What can keep him, I wonder! [Takes off her bonnet and shawl.] Well, I must get the dinner ready. [Pauses, and looks anxious.] But, somehow, I feel not easy in my mind. What could they want with him? Hard! [Goes to the door.] No — what a time he is! But suppose they should 'dite him for a nuisance — O me! or send him to the watchhouse — O my poor dear Dick! I must go and see after him! I must go this very instant moment! [Snatches up her bonnet.] Oh, I hear him now; but how slowly he comes up!
[Runs to the door and leads him in.]

[Enter *Dick*.]

Marg: Oh, my dear, dear Dick, I am so glad you are come at last! But how pale you look! all I-don't-know-how! What's the matter? Why don't you speak to me, Dick, love?
Dick: [fanning himself with his hat]. Let me breathe, wife.

Marg: But what's the matter? Where have you been? Who did you see? What did they say to you? Come, tell me quick.

Dick: Why, Meg, how your tongue does gallop! as if a man could answer twenty questions in a breath.

Marg: Did you see the lady herself? Tell me that.

Dick: [looking round the room suspiciously]. Shut the door first.

Marg: There.

[Shuts it.]

Dick: Shut the other.

Marg: The other? There.

[Shuts it.]

Dick: Lock it fast, I say.

Marg: There's no lock; and that you know.

Dick: [frightened]. No lock; then we shall all be robbed!

Marg: Robbed of what? Sure, there's nothing here for any one to rob! You never took such a thing into your head before.

[*Dick* goes to the door, and tries to fasten it.]

Marg: [aside]. For sartin, he's bewitched; or have they given him something to drink? Or, perhaps, he's ill. [Very affectionately, and laying her hand on his shoulder.] Are you not well, Dick, love? Will you go to bed, sweetheart?

Dick: [gruffly]. No. Go to bed in the broad day! The woman 's cracked.

Marg: [whimpering]. Oh, Dick, what in the world has come to you?

Dick: Nothing; nothing but good, you fool. There, there, don't cry, I tell you.

Marg: [wiping her eyes]. And did you see the lady?

Dick: Ay, I seed her, and a most beautiful lady she is, and she sends her sarvice to you?

Marg: Indeed! lauk-a daisy! I'm sure I'm much obliged; but what did she say to you?

Dick: Oh, she said, this, and that, and t'other — a great deal.

Marg: But what, Dick?

Dick: Why, she said — she said as how I sung so fine, she couldn't sleep o' mornings.

Marg: Sleep o' mornings! that's a good joke! Let people sleep o' nights, I say.

Dick: [solemnly]. But she can't, poor soul, she's very ill; she has pains here, and pains there, and everywhere.

Marg: Indeed! poor lady! then you mustn't disturb her no more, Dick, that's a sure thing.

Dick: Ay, so I said; and so she gave me this.

> [Takes out the purse, and holds it up.]

Marg: [clapping her hands]. O goodness, what fine purse! Is there anything in it?

Dick: [chinks the money]. Do you hear that? Guess now.

Marg: [timidly]. Five shillings, perhaps, eh!

Dick: Five shillings! five guineas, girl.

Marg: [with a scream]. Five guineas! five guineas! [skips about] tal, lal, la! five guineas! [Runs, and embraces her husband.] Oh, Dick! we'll be so rich and so happy. I want a power of things. I'll have a new gown; lavender, shall it be? Yes, it shall be lavender; and a dimity petticoat; and a lace cap, like Mrs. Pinchtoe's, with pink ribbons — how she'll stare! and I'll have two silver spoons, and a nutmeg-grater, and —

Dick: Ho, ho, ho! what a jabber! din, din, din! You'll have this, and you'll have that! First, I'll have a good stock of neat's leather.

Marg: Well, well, give me the purse; I'll take care of it.

> [Snatches at it.]

Dick: No, thankee, I'll take care of it.

Marg: [coaxing]. You know I always keep the money, Dick!

Dick: Ay, Meg, but I'll keep this, do ye mind?

Marg: What! keep it all to yourself? No, you won't. An't I your wife, and haven't I a right? I ax you that.

Dick: Pooh! don't be bothering me.

Marg: Come, give it me at once, there's a dear Dick!

Dick: What, to waste it all in woman's nonsense and frippery? Don't be a fool! We're rich, and we'll keep it safe.

Marg: Why, where's the use of money but to spend? Come, come, I *will* have it.

Dick: Hey-day! you will? You shan't; who's the master here, I say?

Marg: [passionately]. Why, if you come to that, who's the mistress here, I say?

Dick: Now, Meg, don't you go for to provoke me.

Marg: Pooh! I defy you.

Dick: [doubling his fist]. Don't you put me in a passion, Meg!

Marg: Get along; I don't care that for you. [snaps her fingers.] You used to be my own dear Dick, and now you're a cross, miserly curmudgeon.

Dick: [quite furious]. You will have it then! Why, then, take it, with a mischief; take that, and that, and that!

[He beats her; she screams.]

Marg: Oh! oh! oh! pray don't — pray — [Breaks from him, and throws herself into a chair.] O Dick! to go for to strike me! O that I should ever see the day! you cruel, unkind — Oh! oh!

[Covers her face with her apron, sobs, and cries; and he stands looking at her sheepishly. A long lapse.]

Dick: [in great agitation]. Eh, why! women be made of eggshells, I do think. Why, Meg, I didn't hurt you, did I? Why don't you speak? Now, don't you be sulky, come; it was't much. A man is but flesh and blood, after all; come, I say — I'll never get into a passion with you again to my dying day — I won't — come, don't cry [tries to remove the apron;] come kiss, and be friends. Wont't you forgive your own dear Dick, won't you? [ready to cry.] She won't! Here, here's the money, and the purse and all; take it, do what you like with it. [She shakes her head.] What, you won't then? Why, then, there — [throws it on the ground.] Deuce fetch me if ever I touch it again! and I wish my fingers had been burnt before ever I took it, so I do! [with feeling.] We were so happy this morning, when we hadn't a penny to bless ourselves with, nor even a bit to eat; and now, since all this money has come to us of a suddent, why, it's all as one as if old Nick himself were in the purse. I'll tell you what, Meg, eh! shall I? Shall I take it back to the lady, and give our duty to her, and tell her we don't want her guineas, shall I, Meg? Shall I, dear heart?

> [During the last few words *Margery* lets the apron fall from her face, looks up at him, and smiles.]

Dick: Oh, that's right, and we'll be happy again, and never quarrel more.

Marg: No, never! [They embrace.] Take it away, for I can't bear the sight of it.

Dick: Take it *you* then, for you know, Meg, I said I would never touch it again; and what I says, I says; and what I says, I sticks to.

> [Pushes it towards her with his foot.]

Marg: And so do I; and I vowed to myself that I wouldn't touch it, and I won't.

> [Kicks it back to him.]

Dick: How shall we manage then? Oh, I have it. Fetch me the tongs here. [Takes up the purse in the tongs, and holds it at arm's length.] Now I'm going. So, Meg, if you repent, now's the time. Speak, or for ever hold your tongue.

Marg: Me repent? No, my dear Dick! I feel, somehow, quite light, as if a great lump were gone away from here. [Laying her hands on her bosom.]

Dick: And so do I; so come along. We never should have believed this, if we hadn't tried; but it's just what my old mother used to say — *Much coin, much care.*

The End

QUARTER DAY

1841

William Fowle

William Bentley Fowle was born in Boston on October 12, 1795. His father, a man of considerable literary ability, was a pump-and-block maker by trade. His mother was a sister of William Bentley, a clergyman and diarist, and "a woman of rare intellect."[1]

Fowle entered school at three and proved to be an able and successful student. At ten, he won a medal for excellence in grammar but, when he entered Boston Latin at thirteen, he discovered that he so little understood the rules he had been forced to memorize that he could not conjugate the verb "to love." "It is not to be wondered at therefore," he wrote in later life, "that I hated grammar and had no faith in the utility of teaching it as it was then taught, and determined to reform the method if I ever had a good opportunity."[2]

He was prepared to enter college at fifteen but, because of his father's financial reverses, was apprenticed instead to Caleb Bingham, a bookseller and author of school textbooks, whose shop was frequented by teachers.[3] Bingham died in 1819. Fowle carried on in the business for two years, when he was asked to organize and teach in a school for children "too old for the primary and too ignorant for the grammar schools." In this school for boys and in the school for girls he opened two years later, he instituted many of the educational reforms he was by now convinced were necessary. In both schools he employed the monitorial system, in which the more avanced pupils helped teach the less advanced. He introduced blackboards, map drawing, calesthenics, needlework, and music into the classrooms. Probably for the first time in America, he had scientific apparatus built to illustrate the scientific principles being taught. Perhaps most radical of all, he abolished corporal punishment. During his teaching career he also found time to write or edit more than fifty textbooks on subjects as diverse as grammar and drawing.

In 1842, Fowle became publisher of the *Common School Journal*, which Horace Mann had founded four years earlier. When Mann retired as the *Journal's* editor in 1848, Fowle replaced him and remained its editor until it ceased publication in 1852. In 1843, Fowle was elected to the Massachusetts State Legislature on an antislavery ticket. His last public activity was to open a monitorial school on Washington Street in Boston, which he ran until 1860. He died at his home in Medfield, Massachusetts, on February 6, 1865. At the time of his death, he was working on a book of dialogues to be used in schools.

Fowle wrote his dialogues out of necessity, because of the "scarcity of scenes, suitable for School Dialogues, in our standard and Dramatic writers, and the almost entire neglect of this department by literary men."[4] His books of dialogues ran to many editions. Because of their success, he decided in 1857 to compile a book of Parlour Dramas: "a few pieces of greater length, to be used at family parties or at exhibitions in our higher seminaries."[5]

Fowle's rationale for the usefulness of dialogues in school is practical, sensible, and fairly conventional.

Nothing tends to make good readers and speakers than the reading and speaking of familiar Dialogues; for these are generally well understood by the young, and the inflections of the voice are more frequently required, and more easily and naturally made, than in other lessons.[6]

But the content of the dialogues is not conventional at all, particularly those which deal with the abuses of school: abuses by unenlightened administrators of teachers, by martinet teachers of pupils, by badly behaved pupils of teachers, and by ignorant and pretentious parents of everyone.

QUARTER DAY

A quarter day is, traditionally, one of the four days of the year on which rents and fees, including school fees, are paid. In the United States, the days fall on January 1, April 1, July 1, and October 1.

Although Fowle's play is essentially good-humored, it is clearly written from bitter experience. No one is more powerless than a teacher obliged to solicit paying students. Fowle makes his teacher, Miss Carlton, even more powerless (thereby raising the dramatic stakes) by making her a spinster and the sole support of her orphaned sisters. Miss Carlton is therefore forced to suffer politely the parade of foolish women and their awful daughters who come to interview her. When the parade is done, we fear Miss Carlton will have to starve for her principles, and starve her sisters with her. So we are delighted by the final rush of sensible women eager to enroll their arithmetically progressive daughters in Miss Carlton's school. The conclusion is, admittedly, improbable. But, as with the last minute arrival of the cavalry or of Victoria's messenger, it is deeply satisfying because what should happen does happen, and justice is done.

Fowle did not think of himself as a playwright and often belittles his dramatic abilities. But in *Quarter Day*, as in many of his other dialogues and playlets, he shows himself to be a sound dramatist, perfectly attuned to his occasion and his actors.

He has a wonderful ear for many kinds of real speech. He writes a wide variety of characters and writes them broadly, which makes them fun to play and more plausible when played by inexperienced young actresses. He writes roles that his pupils must have delighted in playing: foolish and pretentious mothers and their wild and disobedient children. (Half-grown children, he knew, love to play little children.) Even his nonspeaking roles are fat. Lucy, Mrs. Frivolous's daughter, does not have a line, but her mother's asides to her — "Lucy, my dear, turn out your toes." "Lucy, dear, take your fingers out your mouth." "Lucy, dear, don't stoop so." — give any spirited young actress an excuse to steal that scene. And awful little Maria, a few minutes later, gets to sass her mother and break a window.

The play's structural weakness is that it is schematic. Each successive mother represents a Wrong Position, which Miss Carlton gently and reasonably disproves but which is even more forcefully disproved by the women and children who embody it. But the play's predictably symmetrical manner is more than offset by its matter which is vivid, particular, and idiosyncratic. Indeed, Fowle's candid snapshot of education, warts and all, in mid-nineteenth-century America is a great deal more telling, memorable and, I suspect, true to life than a great many better-known and more formal portraits.

NOTES

1. *Dictionary of American Biography*, 2d ed. (New York: Charles Scribner's Sons, 1928), 561. All quotations used in this section are from the *Dictionary of American Biography* unless otherwise specified.

2. Fowle was as good as his word. Here is the beginning of a dialogue he wrote to teach the meaning of a verb. It is called "Monsieur and his English master."

Frenchman: No sair, I nevair shall, can, will learn your vile language. De verbs alone might, should, could, would put me to death.

Master: You must be patient, Our verb is very simple compared with yours.

Frenchman: Simple! vat you call simple? When I say que je fusse, you say dat I might-could-could-have been. Ma foi, ver simple dat! Now, sair, tell to me, if you please, what you call one verb?

Master: A verb is a word that signifies to be, to do, to suffer. . . .

The Common School Journal (Boston: Fitz, Hobbs and Co., 1850), vol. 7, 213–31.

3. Caleb Bingham (1757–1817) was a bookseller, an educational reformer, and the author of the second English grammar published in America, as well as many other textbooks.

4. W. B. Fowle, *The Hundred Dialogues* (Boston: Morris Cotton, 1856), [iii]. Fowle wrote or edited six large collections of dialogues and short plays. See Levy and Mahard *Preliminary Checklist of Early Printed Children's Plays in English: 1780–1855*, 49–50. In *Performing Arts Resources*, ed. Barbara Naomi Cohen-Stratyner, vol. 12 [New York: Theatre Library Association, 1987], 1–97), *Quarter Day* is tentatively and wrongly attributed to Elizabeth Sandham. There are many other dialogues, many of them by Fowle, printed in *The Common School Journal* and not reprinted in any of the collections. I strongly suspect many more were not printed at all.

5. W. B. Fowle, *Parlour Dramas, or Dramatic Scenes for Home Amusement* (Boston: Morris Cotton; New York: J. M. Fairchild, 1857), iii.

6. Fowle, *Familiar Dialogues and Popular Discussions for Exhibition in Schools and Academies* (Boston: Tappan and Dennet; New York: Mark H. Newman; Philadelphia: Thomas Copperthwait & Co., 1844), 3–4.

QUARTER DAY

Characters

MISS CARLTON
MRS. WONDROUS and Child.
MRS. SAVEALL and two Children.
MRS. OLDSCHOOL and Child.
MRS. FRIVOLOUS and Child.
MRS. COVENANT and Child.
MRS. LOVEGOOD and Child.
MRS. PLAINSAY and Child.
MRS. DOUBLEREFINED and Child.
MRS. LOFTY and Child.
MRS. GRUMPY and Child.
MRS. WILDER and two Children.
MRS. KINDLY and two Children.
MRS. FAIRPLAY and three Children.
MRS. GOODHEART and four Children.
MRS. WELCOME and five Children.
MRS. LOVELY and six Children.
MRS. BOUNTIFUL and seven Children.

[If the school be large enough, it is desirable to have as many children as are mentioned above. But, without difficulty, seven children, of different sizes, would be sufficient for all the parts. If there are not advanced pupils enough for all the *lady* parts, with a slight change of dress and an exchange of bonnets, a few young ladies may personate all the characters; or some of them may be omitted.]

Miss Carlton: Well, this is my new quarter-day, and on to-day depends the question whether my little school is to be abandoned for want of patronage, and my orphan sisters deprived of this only hope of support, or whether my sincere endeavors are to be rewarded. I have advertised for applications to be made this morning, and never did I feel more anxious to have a morning over. Hark! there is the door-bell.

[Enter *Mrs. Wondrous*, leading in a very small child.]

Mrs. Wondrous: Do I address Miss Carlton?
Miss Carlton. That is my name, madam.
Mrs. Wondrous: Your school has been highly recommended to me by some of my friends, and I have concluded to place my daughter under your care, if we can agree upon the subject of her studies. Pray, what do you teach, Miss Carlton?
Miss Carlton: What is usually taught in genteel schools, madam. How old is your little girl?
Mrs. Wondrous: She is only five; but then she is a child of remarkable capacity.
Miss Carlton: I should not think she studied many branches at present, whatever she may do hereafter.
Mrs. Wondrous: Indeed she is not so backward as you suppose. She has studied botany, geometry, and astronomy; and her teacher was preparing to put her into algebra, when ill health obliged her to give up her school.
Miss Carlton: Have you ever examined her in these branches, madam?
Mrs. Wondrous: O, yes! Fraxinella, my dear, tell the lady something of geometry and astronomy. What is astronomy, my dear? Ask her a question, Miss Carlton — any question you please.
Miss Carlton: What planet do we inhabit, my dear?
Fraxinella: Hey?
Miss Carleton: What do you live on, my dear?
Fraxinella: On meat, ma'am. I didn't know that was what you meant.
Mrs. Wondrous: No, my dear; the lady means, What do you stand on now, my dear? On what do you stand?
Fraxinella: I was standing on one foot then, mother.
Mrs. Wondrous: Fraxinella, dear, you have forgotten your astronomy, the three days you have staid at home. But do now

say a line or two of your last lesson to the lady — now do, dear — that's an angel!

Fraxinella: "The equinoctial line is the plane of the equator extended indefinitely, until it approximates to the calyx or flower-cup supports the corolla for the two sides of a right-angled triangle are equal to the hippopotamus!"

Mrs. Wondrous: There, Miss Carlton! I told you she had it *in* her, only you did not understand the best method of drawing it out. I knew she would astonish you.

Miss Carlton: She does, indeed, madam. You speak of the plane of the equator, my dear. May I ask what is the meaning of the word *plane*?

Fraxinella: *Ugly*, ma'am. I should think every body knew that!

Miss Carlton: How many are three times three, my dear?

Fraxinella: Three times three?

Miss Carlton: Yes, how many are they?

Fraxinella: I don't know. Mrs. Flare never taught me that. She says every body knows how to count.

Miss Carlton: She taught you to read and spell, I suppose.

Mrs. Wondrous: No, I forbade that. I wished to have the mind developed at once, without having the intellect frittered away in attention to such unimportant elements. Mrs. Flare was a nonesuch — a real seek-no-farther. I am afraid her loss will never be made up to poor Fraxinella.

Miss Carlton: I can not agree to receive your daughter, madam, if I am to pursue the course you seem to approve. Until the mind is able to comprehend, I think the child should be employed upon such things as require little or no intellectual effort.

Mrs. Wondrous: I see your school will not do for me. I was *afraid* that you only taught the lower branches. Come, Fraxy, dear, let us go. Good morning, Miss Carlton.

Miss Carlton: Good morning, madam. [The lady goes out.] O dear! I suppose I am a fool, not to help the good lady cheat herself, and ruin her child; but I can not forfeit all my self-respect without a struggle.

[Enter *Mrs. Saveall* and two daughters.]

Mrs. Saveall: Good morning. Miss Carlton, I suppose.
Miss Carlton: Good morning, madam.
Mrs. Saveall: I have heard a good account of your school, Miss Carlton; and, if we can agree upon the terms, I may send you my two girls. Pray, what *are* your terms?
Miss Carlton: How old are your daughters, madam?
Mrs. Saveall: Sarah, dear, how old are you?
Sarah: Nine, mother.
Mrs. Saveall: And you, Jane?
Jane: Seven, mother.
Miss Carlton: The price will be eight and ten dollars a quarter.
Mrs. Saveall: Is that your lowest price?
Miss Carlton: I have but one price, madam.
Mrs. Saveall: What! do you make no allowance for my sending *two*?
Miss Carlton: No, madam, I have never made any.
Mrs. Saveall: That will never answer. My husband, Mr. Saveall, told me you ought to make a discount of twenty per cent.
Miss Carlton: It is as hard to teach two sisters as two strangers, madam.
Mrs. Saveall: Yes, but you have but *one* bill to collect, and a parent who sends two pupils patronizes your school more than she who only sends one.
Miss Carlton: I hope to be faithful to *every* pupil, madam; and sometimes I think the obligation is not *all* on the part of the teacher.
Mrs. Saveall: This never will do, miss. Unless you conduct your school on more liberal principles, you will never get any scholars. I can get my children taught for much less than you ask. Mrs. Slighter, their late teacher, only charged them six dollars each.
Miss Carlton: Why did you not keep your children at her school?

Mrs. Saveall: Why, Miss Slighter is a very good sort of woman, but Mr. Saveall thought the children did not learn any thing under her care, and we thought we would try a change. But your terms are altogether too extravagant; I must find a cheaper school.

Miss Carlton: If I were not interested, I might remark that the cheapest articles are not apt to be the best, madam; but I can not reconcile it to my sense of right to have two prices for the same thing.

Mrs. Saveall: Very well, miss. I shall, no doubt, find some person less scrupulous, and I bid you a good morning. Come, girls, this school will never do for you. Every thing is too narrow and contracted to suit your father's liberal views.

[She goes out.]

Miss Carlton: O dear! Another loss, and two at once! Well, I am almost discouraged. But here comes another patron.

[Enter *Mrs. Oldschool* and daughter.]

Mrs. Oldschool: Have I the pleasure to address Miss Carlton?

Miss Carlton: My name is Carlton, madam. Will you take a seat?

Mrs. Oldschool: No, no, I thank you. I wish to get a school for my only daughter, and I have heard yours highly recommended. But they tell me that, though your pupils are well instructed, you employ some pupils to teach others. Is it so?

Miss Carlton: It is, madam. I think every child should be able to communicate to others what she learns herself.

Mrs. Oldschool: Yes, but I do not wish to pay a teacher for teaching my children, and have them taught by other children.

Miss Carlton: It would be unfair to expect you to do so, madam. But you err in supposing that I perform any the less labor because I employ my pupils as assistants. My whole time is devoted to my pupils; and, as much of the instruction can be given by well-informed pupils under my direction, I can give my personal attention where it is most needed.

Mrs. Oldschool: This all sounds very well; but, after all, children can not teach children any thing.

Miss Carlton: Do you mean, madam, that one child can not teach another that two and two make four — that *t-r-u-t-h* spells *truth* — that Boston is joined to Roxbury — or that the name of a thing is a noun?

Mrs. Oldschool: Perhaps it can; but, then, children have no judgment, and can not *govern* children. I have seen enough of bad discipline; my children have been nearly ruined by shifting schools.

Miss Carlton: Have they ever been taught by monitors?

Mrs. Oldschool: No, never.

Miss Carlton: Surely, you do not bring this as an objection against monitorial schools!

Mrs. Oldschool: Why —— no —— but then, in the nature of things, one child can not be fit to teach another; and if you do not give up this notion, I must put my child elsewhere.

Miss Carlton: I can not give it up until convinced that it is erroneous; nor could you wish me to do so, I think.

Mrs. Oldschool: Well, you may do as you please, but I am too old-fashioned to adopt any such newfangled notions. So, good morning. Come, Sophia, dear, bid the lady good morning.

Miss Carlton: Good morning, miss.

[They go out.]

[Enter *Mrs. Frivolous* and daughters.]

Mrs. Frivolous: Good morning. Miss Carlton, I suppose. I have a little daughter that I wish to place in your school. I understand you teach all the light accomplishments. Who is your teacher of dancing? I have sent my daughter to every teacher that has opened a school in Boston; for I think that, if music and dancing are attended to every thing else follows. *Lucy, my dear, turn out your toes.* As I was saying, we give a ball once or twice every winter, and Mr. Frivolous carries the children to every concert and ball that is respectable.

Miss Carlton: Does not this interrupt their other studies?

Mrs. Frivolous: O, yes; but then ease and grace must be acquired in youth, or never. *Lucy, dear, take your fingers out of your mouth!* As I was saying —— What *was* I saying? What *was I saying?* Strange that I should be so forgetful! But not longer ago than yesterday, I was telling Mr. Frivolous about something, and right in the midst of my story, I forgot what I was going to say; and do what I could, I had to give it up. *Lucy, my dear, you forget to turn out your toes.*

Miss Carlton: May I ask, madam, if your child has never studied any thing but music and dancing?

Mrs. Frivolous: O, yes; she has studied every thing. But then the poor girl sits up so late every night, she can not go to school till it is nearly over; and she practises so much, that she has nearly ruined her health, and has no time to get her lessons. *Lucy, dear, don't stoop so.* She has an ugly stoop in the shoulders; but Doctor Smooth says she will outgrow it one of these days. Now, Lucy, my darling, can't you just dance that horn pipe you learned last?

Lucy: Mother, I don't know how. I have forgotten the steps.

Mrs. Frivolous: My dear, you can't have forgotten them so soon, after spending two quarters in learning nothing else.

Miss Carlton: Don't urge the young lady. I shall be happy, madam, to receive your daughter, if you think fit to place her under my care; but I can only promise her as much instruction in music and dancing as can be given without interruption to her more important studies.

Mrs. Frivolous: No — she must study after she has finished her education. We have but one daughter, and we mean to spare no expense in her education. You are too old-fashioned — excuse me — much too old-fashioned, for my notion; and Lucy, dear, make one of your best courtesies to the lady. [The child does so.] Good morning, miss.

Miss Carlton: Well, what *can* come next? I hardly know

whether to laugh or cry at the ill success of my attempt to enlarge my school. But here is another applicant.

[Enter *Mrs. Covenant* and daughter.]

Mrs. Covenant: Miss Carlton, I presume.

[*Miss Carlton* courtesies.]

I am anxious to give my daughter a religious education, and hearing your school well recommended for every thing else, I am induced to ask what religious instruction is given in your school. Do you teach your pupils how to pray?

Miss Carlton: No, madam. I leave them to follow the teaching of Jesus. He, you know, has told us how we ought to pray.

Mrs. Covenant: But don't you have public prayers in the school?

Miss Carlton: No, madam. I advise the children to pray in secret; for I think few other prayers are sincere and from the heart.

Mrs. Covenant: Do you give no Bible lessons?

Miss Carlton: We read the Scriptures, madam.

Mrs. Covenant: Yes, but do they commit verses to memory, so that they can quote Scripture readily?

Miss Carlton: No, madam. Those who have the most Scripture in their mouths, do not necessarily have the most piety in their hearts. I explain to them the leading principles of our religion upon all proper occasions, and I am careful to set them a good example.

Mrs. Covenant: Then you have no set religious exercises? Your pupils must be little better than heathen.

Miss Carlton: Most of them go to Sunday schools, madam; all go to church; and all have parents, who, no doubt, give them religious instruction at home; and I do all that I can *here* to aid in the all-important work.

Mrs. Covenant: This will not do, Miss Carlton. The religious part of education must supersede every thing else.

Child: Mother, does that lady put her scholars down cellar, and slap 'em when they don't say "Now I lay me" right, as you did ——

Mrs. Covenant: Hush! hush!

Child: Why, mother! you know you *did*, and how you scolded me, when I told you I didn't like to go to meeting without you. You know, mother, you shook me, and made me cry.

Mrs. Covenant: Hush! hold your tongue, Susan! If *I* can't make you pious, it does not follow that I should not require it of one who professes to make teaching her business. I wish you good morning, Miss Carlton. A school without set religious exercises must be very imperfect. It will never do for my children.

[Exit.]

[Enter *Mrs. Lovegood* and daughter.]

Mrs. Lovegood: Miss Carlton, I suppose.

Miss Carlton: Yes, madam. Will you take that chair?

Mrs. Lovegood: No, I am obliged to you. I called, Miss Carlton, to make some inquiries about your school. I understand that you use rewards, and encourage emulation in your school.

Miss Carlton: I do, madam. I can not get on without some encouragement myself, and I know not how I can reasonably expect my pupils to do so.

Mrs. Lovegood: Excuse me, my dear, if I say that you are behind the age. No teacher can expect the patronage of intelligent parents, if she can not lure children to knowledge and virtue for knowledge and virtue's sake. I think the spirit of emulation the very spirit of mischief, and I can never allow my child to be placed where she is exposed to such danger. My children obey me because they love me; and they yield a ready and cheerful obedience, because they know that I only require what is right, evidently right, and best for them. Maria, my dear, don't go so near that window — you may break it. Don't *strike* the glass, my dear — you will surely break it. Come here, my dear.

Maria: I won't!

Mrs. Lovegood: Why, Maria! my dear! You don't say you won't to your mother?

Maria: Yes, I do, though.

Mrs. Lovegood: My daughter, I am surprised to hear such unbecoming remarks from you, when you know I love you so.

Maria: Who cares for your love?

> [She breaks the glass, and *Mrs.*
> *Lovegood* seizes and shakes
> her.]

Mrs. Lovegood: Why, you little, disobedient hussy! what do you mean? [Slapping her.] There! take that! and that! and that! — and now see whether you will disobey me again.

Miss Carlton: Is this drawing by the cords of love?

Mrs. Lovegood: I am aware that you have the advantage of me; but I will shut her up for a month but what I will make her obey me. There! go home! Good morning, Miss Carlton. I do not often get into such a passion. Good morning.

> [Enter *Mrs. Plainsay* and child.]

Mrs. Plainsay: Miss Carlton?

Miss Carlton: That is my name, madam.

Mrs. Plainsay: I have a dear child, that I am anxious to place under an affectionate teacher; and I have heard so much of your skill, that I am induced to ask what are the general principles upon which you conduct your school.

Miss Carlton: I endeavor to make my pupils understand what they learn, and I endeavor to teach them only what will be useful to them.

Mrs. Plainsay: Yes, but how is your government? is it parental?

Miss Carlton: I endeavor to exercise such an authority as a *judicious* parent would approve.

Mrs. Plainsay: A *judicious* parent! Yes, I understand the insinuation. I presume you are unmarried, miss.

Miss Carlton: I am obliged to plead guilty, madam.

Mrs. Plainsay: I thought so. I have always maintained that none but a parent can understand the feelings of a parent, and be prepared to treat children as they ought to be treated. Pray, how *old* are you, miss?

Miss Carlton: [smiling.] About twenty-eight, madam.

Mrs. Plainsay: You have not a moment to lose, then. It is high time that you were beginning to think upon a certain subject.

Miss Carlton: I had almost come to the conclusion that it was high time to leave *off* thinking of it; for, you know, madam, it is in vain for me to think of it *alone*.

Mrs. Plainsay: Then you had better give up teaching. You may rely upon it that you will never be good for any thing while you remain single. You can never enter into the feelings of children, and exercise a parent's forbearance towards their faults. My children are so used to my indulgent care, that they could never submit to any harsher authority. This little dear ——

Child: I wish, mother, you would not always *dear* me so *before* every body; for it makes them think I am a little baby. You called me a little devil, this morning, when I broke the glass vase, though you know I did not mean to do it.

Mrs. Plainsay: Hold your tongue, Mary! How can you tell, before a stranger, what, in a moment of surprise, I may have said to you!

Child: Why, mother, it is not the first time you have called me so; and I have not forgotten how you beat me for it. I don't believe this lady, or any other, would punish a little girl so, when she was sorry, and did not mean to do wrong.

Miss Carlton: My dear, you must be in an error. Your mother knows best how to feel for her children.

Mrs. Plainsay: I may not be all that a mother *should* be, Miss Carlton; but this does not weaken my position that none but *parents* are qualified to manage *children*. It is evident that we shall never agree. Good morning, miss. [She takes her child's hand, and twitches her along, saying to her,] Come along! you saucy little minx! I never begin a sentimental flourish, but what you contrive to upset my whole theory by your babbling.

Child: Well, mother, I thought you said you always did right; and I could not see any harm in telling of it if it *was* right.

Mrs. Plainsay: Hush, child! Let me never hear you speak in my presence again. I'll pay you for exposing me. Come along!

[Exit.]

Miss Carlton: Well, I must get *married*, too, whether or no! [Sighing.] I hope I shall be resigned, should the time come. But who is this?

[Enter *Mrs. Doublerefined* and daughter.]

Mrs. Doublerefined: Good Morning. Miss Carlton, I suppose. What an exquisitely beauchiful morning it is! With your permission, I will recline a moment. I have been walking more than an eighth of a mile — an utter impracticability, if I were not determined to get rid of the importunity of Mr. Doublerefined, who thinks your school so superlatively excellent, that our child must participate in its advantages.

Miss Carlton: I am happy to learn that he approves of my endeavors.

Mrs. Doublerefined: I see you have a stove in the room.

Miss Carlton: Yes, madam. We could not warm so large a room with a grate.

Mrs. Doublerefined: A stove would present an inshuperable objection. It so increases the caloric, and diminishes the hydrogenic proportions of the circumambient atmosphere, that I should be inconsiderate to risk my offspring's health. I consider a stove an incontrovertible disqualification.

Miss Carlton: I have heard no complaint of its injurious effects upon any pupil.

Mrs. Doublerefined: You have no nerves, my dear. I would not inhabit Paradise, if it was heated by a stove. You have no carpet, I see, on your floor.

Miss Carlton: No, madam. I think a carpet in a work-shop would be out of place.

Mrs. Doublerefined: You are under a serious misapprehension, my dear. Perfect neatness is not incompatible with any employment intrinsically accommodated to our sex. A carpet prevents the introgression of vulgar footsteps. I carpet every thing.

Daughter: Ma, I wish you'd carpet my chamber, my feet get so cold on the bare floor.

Mrs. Doublerefined: My dear, when your elders are engaged in conversation, you should not interrupt them. Miss Carlton, you are aware, no doubt, that where ideology, as the phrenologists call that sublime aspiration of the mind which stretches after transcendental beauty, — you are aware that, when this ethereal imagination characterizes the individual, the mortal approximates to the immortal, and happiness is perennial.

Miss Carlton: I should think such delicacy of temperament would be an inlet to pain rather than pleasure. I have hitherto taken the world as my reason, and not as my imagination, paints it.

Mrs. Doublerefined: You are altogether too unimaginative, my dear. I should be happy to patronize your school, but, really, a stove will be an inshuperable objection. Good morning, my dear. My head already begins to swim.

Miss Carlton: There has been no fire in the stove to-day, madam; but you probably feel the effects of the fire that is to be made in it one of these days. [*Mrs. Doublerefined* goes out.] Well, I must be patient, although it seems as if I was tried a little above what I am able to bear. Here comes another patron.

[Enter *Mrs. Lofty* and daughter.]

Mrs. Lofty: Do I address Miss Carlton?

Miss Carlton: [courtesies.]

Mrs. Lofty: I have heard of your school, miss, and am inclined to send you one or two of my children.

Miss Carlton: I shall be happy to receive them, madam.

Mrs. Lofty: What number of pupils do you intend to receive?

Miss Carlton: Forty, madam.

Mrs. Lofty: Too many! too many by half! You can never get on with so many. I could never venture a child of mine in such a mob.

Miss Carlton: I hope there will be no reason to complain of their number, madam, or their conduct.

Mrs. Lofty: Who *are* they? Who *send* children to your school? Do any come from Topknot Street? Have you any *respectable* people among your patrons?

Miss Carlton: I have none other, madam.

Mrs. Lofty: Does Mrs. Inflate send to you?

Miss Carlton: No, Madam.

Mrs. Lofty: Does Mrs. Puffton, Mrs. Upstart, Mrs. Fineton?

Miss Carlton: No, madam, none of them.

Mrs. Lofty: Second rate then! [tossing her head] I suspect. My dear, I will make you a proposition. If you will limit your number to twenty, and charge three times what you do, so as to make your scholars *select*, I will try your school one quarter. Nothing but an *exclusive* school can expect to have respectable scholars.

Miss Carlton: I am satisfied with my pupils, madam, and not at all disposed to part with one of them — not even to have their places filled with what you call exclusively respectable pupils. Madam, you may insult *me*, but I can not hear you insult those who have protected and encouraged me. I will neither give up my present pupils, nor take your children, should you be disposed to send them. I am the daughter of a mechanic, madam, and not ashamed of my origin.

Daughter: Mother, was her father an oyster-man, as grandfather was?

Mrs. Lofty: Hold your tongue, child!

Daughter: Why, mother, grandfather told me he used to cry "Oys, buy oys?" about the streets before you were married, and then you wouldn't let him.

Mrs. Lofty: Hold your tongue! Your grandfather was a fool!

Daughter: He told me he was, mother, to give up selling oysters.

Mrs. Lofty: Come along. I will go and inquire after Mrs. Suitall's school, which I am told is the only respectable one in the city. [To her daughter.] Did not I tell you never to own that you had a grandfather?

> [She goes out, with a toss of her head.]

Miss Carlton: I fear I have been rude; but when I see such an assumption of superiority, I can not forget that I am a human being, equal to her who would trample on me. O dear! I am quite tired.

[Enter *Mrs. Grumpy* and daughter.]

Mrs. Grumpy: Are you Miss Carlton, the school-ma'am?

Miss Carlton: My name is Carlton, madam.

Mrs. Grumpy: I've *heerd* a great deal about your school, and I've determined to send you one of my *gals*, if you can only satisfy me on one *pint*. They tell me you have some new-fangled notions on the subject of grammar; and I never will have *nothing* to do with *no* one that does not know Murray's Grammar. I *larnt* that *myself*, and I never had no trouble in getting along, and I want my children to have the same advantages.

Miss Carlton: My pupils are taught Murray's Grammar, madam, as thoroughly as that system is taught elsewhere; but we do not stop at that system — we endeavor to go farther, and look deeper.

Mrs. Grumpy: That's deep enough. I've no *idee* that any good comes of trying to be too grammatical. In my day, we *was* all taught alike, and *them* new-fangled notions of *yourn wasn't* thought *on*. Murray's Grammar is enough for any *gal*. Hepsy, daughter, do you want to *larn that-air* grammar the lady tells *on*?

Hepsy: I don't want to study *no* grammar, mother.

Mrs. Grumpy: O, my dear, you must study some grammar, or how will you be able to pass through the world? for the only object of grammar is *passing*.

Miss Carlton: Madam, your child will not be required to study any *better* Grammar than Murray's, if you prefer his alone.

Hepsy: Mother, I don't want to study *no* grammar. I can *pass* well enough without.

Mrs. Grumpy: Well, dear, you shan't, then. I'll *larn* you myself, for I have often *heerd* that there is no need of any one's *larning* grammar, when *they* never hear *no* bad language used at home. Good morning, Miss Carlton. Hepsy prefers to be under my care; and I never use *no* violence when a child has any choice. Good Morning. Come, Hepsy, dear, come.
[Exit.]

[Enter *Mrs. Wilder* and two daughers with hoops.]

Mrs. Wilder: Are you Miss Carlton?

Miss Carlton: I am, madam. Will you take a seat?

Mrs. Wilder: I will, for I have just had a race after Emma, who was driving her hoop around a carriage. They are full of spirits, my girls, full of innocent fun. I understand you let your pupils play, Miss Carlton.

Miss Carlton: I do, madam, but not in study hours.
[*Mrs. Wilder* goes to sit down, and one of her children removes the chair. *Miss Carlton* saves her from falling.]

Mrs. Wilder: My dear, you are naughty to do so. They are full of spirits, Miss Carlton, as I was before them. I can not bear to repress the generous enthusiasm of youth, though it may sometimes overstep the bounds of propriety.

Miss Carlton: Is it not better to check it when it first appears? I like play, as much as I dislike and punish mischief. Respect to parents and teachers lies at the foundation of the youthful character.

Mrs. Wilder: Ah, that is too sentimental for me. Human nature is human nature, and it will act itself out, and must not be restrained because it perpetrates a little innocent mischief.

[While the mother is talking,
the daughter twists up a piece
of paper, and puts it for a
foolscap on her mother's
bonnet.]

Miss Carlton: [throws away the cap, and says,] I could not overlook any insult offered by a child to an indulgent parent. If you expect me to do so, madam, I must decline receiving your children.

[One of the children picks up
the cap, and pins it to *Miss
Carlton's* dress.]

Mrs. Wilder: Come, Emma and Hitty, dears, come. I will not place you in the hands of an old maid, who can not bear a little innocent play. Good morning, Miss Carlton. I hope you will have some children of your own, one of these days; and then we shall see how you will manage them.

[As she goes out, the girls drive
their hoops against her.]

Miss Carlton: Well, now I have done! I will die before I will undergo such torture any longer.

[She moves to go out, as *Mrs. Kindly* enters, with two children.]

Mrs. Kindly: My dear, have you any room for two of my children? Mrs. Prudent recommends you so highly, that I shall be pleased to have you take these two. Do with them as you would with your own, and I shall be satisfied.

Miss Carlton: I feel grateful for the confidence you repose in me, madam, and shall be anxious to deserve it.

[Enter *Mrs. Fairplay* with three children.]

Mrs. Fairplay: I have come, Miss Carlton, to place three of my children under your care, if you can oblige me by receiving them.

Miss Carlton: I shall be happy to receive them, madam.

Mrs. Fairplay: You will see what they know, and, of course, will put them to whatever study you think most useful to them.

Miss Carlton: I thank you, madam, for your kindness.

[Enter *Mrs. Goodheart* and four children.]

Mrs. Goodheart: Is this Miss Carlton?

[*Miss Carlton* courtesies.]

My dear, I have a large family of children, and wish to place four of them where they will be well instructed and kindly treated. I see you are engaged, and if you say you can take them, I will leave them with you.

[Enter *Mrs. Welcome* and five children.]

Mrs. Welcome: There — come all in! Don't be alarmed, Miss Carlton. They are all good girls, and wish to come to your school. They are acquainted with some of your scholars, I believe; and if you have room for them, they shall all come; for their late teacher has been married, and has relinquished her school.

Miss Carlton: I can take them, madam, and the more cherfully, because the conduct of my other pupils has recommended my school to you.

Mrs. Welcome: Well, there they are. Now, girls, don't let it be your fault if you don't learn.

[Enter *Mrs. Lovely* and six children.]

Mrs. Lovely: Excuse me, Miss Carlton — you seem to be engaged.

Miss Carlton: Not so that I can not attend to you, madam. These ladies have just honored me by placing their daughters under my care.

Mrs. Lovely: I came for the same purpose. My six children are anxious to enter your school, and if you can accommodate such a host, it will gratify them not to be separated, and I shall feel that they are safe.

Miss Carlton: I will do my best to accommodate them, and to justify your trust in me, madam.

[Enter *Mrs. Bountiful* with seven children.]

Mrs. Bountiful: I must apologize, Miss Carlton, for this intrusion; but I was coming to ask if you could receive my seven daughters, and they all insisted upon coming with me. I beg you to excuse their curiosity. They were afraid you might not be able to take so many, and no one was willing to be the rejected one. You will take them all, I hope.

Miss Carlton: I certainly will endeavor to, madam. If you, ladies, will be good enough to walk into the hall, I will make what further arrangements may be necessary.

[The ladies and children go out.]

Well, it seems that patient waiters are not likely to be losers in the school line, whatever they may be in the line matrimonial.

[She follows them into the hall.]

The End

BEAUTY AND THE BEAST

1854

Julia Corner

Julia Corner was born in London in 1798, the daughter of John Corner, an engraver. She wrote over sixty books for children and adolescents in her long life, including fourteen volumes of history, written between 1840 and 1848. Her *History of France*, written in 1840, had sold 31,000 copies by 1889. She was highly respected as well as highly successful, praised for her intelligible, fluent, and graceful prose as well as for her soundness. "She may," one eulogist wrote, "be styled one of the most useful writers of the age."[1] She died in London on August 16, 1875.

BEAUTY AND THE BEAST

Julia Corner wrote ten *Little Plays for Little Actors*, chiefly dramatizations of well-known fairy tales, between 1854 and 1867.[2] *Beauty and the Beast* is the first of these *Little Plays* and apparently is the first play she ever wrote.

It is an extraordinary effort for a first play. It is, of course, full of echoes, particularly echoes of Shakespeare — *A Midsummer Night's Dream, The Tempest,* and even *King Lear* — and echoes of the Christmas Pantomime, in the rhymed couplets and in the transformation scenes. It is also full of original touches: the ingenious, seemingly natural complications of the action, which extend the play to fourteen scenes;

the judicious use of music; and, line by line, the skillful variation of the verse, which retains the regularity of formal poetry while allowing the dialogue to sound like actual human speech.

Miss Corner had a good ear and a fine eye. Her writing is often really funny and, what is particularly rare in Victorian children's writers, truly touching rather than pathetic. But where Miss Corner unexpectedly excels is in her understanding of the practicalities of the theatre. Her parenthetical asides tell her actors and their parents, in the most practical terms, how easily the most apparently lavish scenes can be built and how the most apparently complicated effects can be achieved. Her stage directions support her inexperienced actors in every way. For example, "Zimri is sitting at a table in deep thought, leaning his head on his hand, with a book open before him. His soliloquy might be written in the book, which would save the trouble of learning it." And, again, in this direction for Beauty's first entrance, "Beauty may carry a little basket, as anything in the hand assists the action, when there are rather long speeches to make."

Beauty and the Beast has been dramatized for children many times since Miss Corner's version was written. Nevertheless, Miss Corner's play still holds its own in comparison with more recent versions and is as touching and charming today as it was when it was written.[3]

NOTES

1. S. Austin Allibone, *A Critical Dictionary of English Literature and British and American Authors* (Philadelphia: J. B. Lippincott and Co., 1858), 430.

2. The *Little Plays* had run to sixteen editions by 1901. For a brief account of the first fairy-tale plays in England, see William Sloane, *Children's Books in England and America in the Seventeenth Century* (New York: King's Crown Press, 1955), 70–71.

3. Mrs. Corner's *Beauty and the Beast* was produced in Orono, Maine, in the summer of 1989, by the Theatre of the Enchanted Forest. It was, by all reports, the hit of the season.

BEAUTY AND THE BEAST

AN ENTERTAINMENT FOR YOUNG PEOPLE

Preface

It happened, during the last Christmas holidays, that I was present on several occasions, when a party of young people, from about eight to twelve years of age, contrived to amuse themselves, as well as the elder portion of the company, very agreeably, for the greater part of an evening, by acting charades. The clever and spirited manner in which they represented a variety of characters, confirmed me in an idea I had previously entertained, of arranging some of the most popular and favourite stories of our childhood for similar performances. It struck me, that, in personating our old friends Whittington, Mr. Fitzwarren and the cross Cook, or Cinderella, her proud Sisters, and her fairy Godmother — the younger branches of many a family, especially in the country, might, during the winter season, find an innocent and lively recreation. Their memories would be improved by the necessity of learning perfectly the parts assigned them; and their ingenuity would be exercised in adapting their resources to the arrangement of the scenes to be represented.

I am aware that some persons object to juvenile amusements that bear any affinity to theatricals; but this appears to me an objection that favours the present purpose, since most children of talent and lively disposition are fond of assuming imaginary characters, inventing incidents, and framing dialogue suited to the illusion. Acting, among children, is therefore no novelty; and if proper subjects be selected, and care taken that they convey some useful or moral lesson, I am convinced, from experience as well as reflection, that such performances would be calculated to do good rather than harm. Children want to be amused; and I believe that amusement is beneficial to them, provided it has no bad tendency. I also believe that a very important part of education consists in promoting innocent and agreeable occupation for leisure hours, in order to prevent any disposition to indolence, either of mind or body. With these views and opinions, I offer my little plays as a pastime for the approaching holidays; and I sincerely hope they may prove the means of furnishing entertainment for many of my young friends in the long evenings.

Julia Corner

Characters

ZIMRI, A Merchant.
AZOR, The Beast.
ANNA,
LOLO,   } The Merchant's Daughters.
BEAUTY,
SILVERSTAR, A beneficent Fairy.
Four Attendant Fairies.

Costume

ZIMRI — A long flowing dress of some dark colour, fastened round the waist with a wide red or yellow sash or scarf. A turban, or a cap of black cloth or velvet.

AZOR — He must wear a mask, and be made to look as rough and as much like a monster as possible. A covering for the head might be made of shaggy fur, and he should have coarse brown woollen gloves. His disguise must be so contrived that he may be able to throw it off easily in the last scene, when he is restored to his natural form, and becomes a Prince; in which character he should wear a short tunic of some gay colour, with a tight vest, which might be made of white calico, slashed with the same colour as the tunic. A border of gold paper cut in vandykes would look very well round the bottom of the dress; and some gold paper bordering might be tastefully arranged on the vest, so as to make a brilliant appearance. A velvet cap with a white ostrich feather might also be put on in the last scene under the fur head-dress.

The Three Daughters may dress according to fancy; only keeping in mind that BEAUTY should be plainer and neater in her attire than her sisters.

SILVERSTAR — Her fairy dress should be two or three very full skirts, each shorter than the other, of white tarleton edged with light blue, and a blue scarf of the same light material, passed over one shoulder and tied under the arm on the other side; a wreath of white roses on her head, and a white wand twisted with silver paper in her hand. Any glittering ornaments may be worn, and the upper skirt should be ornamented with stars of silver paper; or a row of silver stars might be put on the blue edges of the skirts with gum. To personate the old beggar-woman, she must wrap herself in a large dark-coloured cloak, and wear a black hood over her head. The wand can easily be concealed in a pasteboard sheath painted black, which will serve for a stick to lean on; and when she throws off her disguise, she can draw the wand from the sheath and unbend it, as it should be made twice the length of the stick, and doubled to go into it. There will be no difficulty in this if the wand is made of several thicknesses of pasteboard pasted together, so as to be quite stiff; and when undoubled it can be held firmly at the place where it was bent.

The Attendant Fairies should all be dressed alike, in white, ornamented with artificial flowers and ribbons. They should hold between them chains of flowers, which might easily be made, as roses of coloured paper with some ivy leaves tacked on tape would form very showy wreaths.

Scene the First

A room in a cottage, meanly furnished.

Anna and *Lolo*, sitting idly, one on each side of a table.

Anna: Really, it is a shame and a disgrace
To make us live in such a wretched place.
What furniture! and then, a sanded floor!
I never shall be happy any more.

Lolo: Depend upon it, this is Beauty's malice;
She likes a cottage better than a palace;
I heard her say to father yesterday,
It was a charming place —

Anna: Yes, that's her way,
An artful puss! to make him think that she
Is so much better, I suppose, than we.

Lolo: Then only fancy this: he says we must
Do all the housework; sweep, and clean, and dust,
And cook the dinner too —

Anna: I'd rather die!
I, cook the dinner! no, indeed, not I.

                    [Enter *Beauty* (singing)]

Beauty: "Home, home; sweet, sweet home:
"There's no place like home — there's no place like
        home."

                    [*Beauty* may carry a little
                    basket, as anything in the hand
                    assists the action, when there
                    are rather long speeches to
                    make.]

Anna: Oh! pr'ythee, child, cease that eternal song;
I cannot bear to hear you all day long.
The house is never quiet for a minute;
Sweet home, indeed! there's not much sweetness in it.

Beauty: Oh, yes, it has a thousand charms for me;
I should be happy, if I could but see

My dearest father cheerful and content:
'Tis only for his sake that I lament,
Our loss of fortune. As for wealth or station
I care but little —
Lolo: Lor, what affectation!
Beauty: We do not tread on velvet, it is true; —
But there's the soft grass spangled with the dew;
The sun, too, looks as bright upon these walls,
As when it shone on our grand marble halls;
And though we can't wear jewels, silks, or lace,
We do not need them in this quiet place.
Anna: Oh, pray, miss, don't annoy us with your folly,
It is enough to make one melancholy
To hear you prating in that silly manner.
Lolo: I'm glad you've spoken to her, sister Anna;
For I've no patience with such airs and graces,
And younger sisters ought to know their places.
                    [Enter *Zimri*. The sisters rise
                    and come forward.]
Beauty: Your supper's ready, father; it is laid
In the green arbour, where you'll find the shade
Extremely pleasant —
Zimri: Thank you, Beauty, dear;
You always try your father's heart to cheer.
And, for my other daughters, how have they
Employed themselves this lovely summer's day?
Anna: Oh, really, sir, this cottage is so dreary,
It makes us feel extremely dull and weary.
Lolo: I'm sure I have been crying all day long.
Zimri: My children, you are acting very wrong:
We ought to bear misfortune patiently;
And, since my vessels have been lost at sea,
And I'm a poor man now, it is your duty
To take a lesson from your sister Beauty,
And cheerfully to bear this great reverse;
For discontent will only make it worse.
                    [Exit *Zimri*, with *Beauty* on his
                    arm.]

Anna: A lesson from that minx! upon my word,
            What next, I wonder —
Lolo: It is quite absurd:
            He'll make her so exceeding pert and vain,
            There'll be no bearing with her, that is plain.

                            [Enter Fairy *Silverstar*,
                            disguised as an old beggar
                            woman, leaning on a stick, and
                            bending almost double.]

Fairy: Ladies, bestow your charity, I pray:
            I have not tasted any food to-day;
            And I am very old, as you may see;
            Full ninety winters have passed over me.
            So I'm too feeble now to earn my bread.
            Nay, lady, do not turn away your head:
            It is but very little that I need;
            If I could work, I would not beg, indeed.
Anna: Pray, my good woman, don't stand chattering there,
            I'm sure we have not anything to spare.
Fairy: Yet surely you might give me, ere I go,
            A little bit of bread —
Anna [sharply]:   I tell you no.

                            [The *Fairy* still lingers at the
                            door.]

Lolo: What are you staying for, when you are told
            To go? You beggars are exceeding bold.
Fairy: Well, I am going. It is a monstrous pity
            When girls are not so good as they are pretty.
                            [Exit.]
Anna: Girls, too! I think she might have had the grace
            To say "young ladies," speaking to one's face.
Lolo: And taking us to task in that way, too.
            I hate the sight of beggars, that I do.

                            [While speaking the last line,
                            Lolo walks towards the door
                            followed by *Anna*, and they go
                            off the stage.]

Scene the Second

An arbour.

Zimri and *Beauty* at supper.

[The arbour might be easily constructed by covering two ladders or long boards with branches of trees, and large red and white roses, and setting them up against the wall some distance apart. A string from one to the other, with branches and flowers tied thickly upon it, would form the top. This could also be used in the garden scene of the *Beast*'s palace.]

Zimri: And so, my child, you can be quite content,
You say, to live in this retirement,
With all the household drudgery to do?
Beauty: I'm happy, father, anywhere with you;
And as to household work, I really find it
So easy, that, indeed, I do not mind it.
[Enter *Fairy.*]
Fairy: Kind gentlefolks, if you've a crust of bread
To spare, I'd thank you, for I'm almost dead
With hunger and fatigue; for I am old,
You see, or else I would not make so bold.
Beauty: You do seem very old, good dame, indeed;
Sit down and rest, and take what food you need.
[Places a stool for her.]
You are quite welcome to some bread and meat.
Zimri: Yes, that you are, good woman, so pray eat
As much as you desire. Meantime, I'll walk,
And leave you with my daughter here to talk. [Exit.]
Fairy: Maiden, your father has of late, I'm told,
Lost, by his ships being wrecked, a store of gold,
Besides two gallant vessels; is this true?
Beauty: Alas! it is, indeed; but who told you?
Fairy: It little matters, child, who told me so;
Bad news is sure to travel fast, we know.

But I have heard too, that all is not lost,
And that the ships, after being tempest tossed
For many days, were safely brought to shore,
Distant from hence a hundred miles or more.
Beauty: My father ought to know, without delay;
I'll go and seek him — [rises]
Fairy [rises also]:   Stay, dear Beauty, stay!
[She throws off her cloak and
hood, and drawing the wand
from the sheath, appears in
her fairy costume. *Beauty* gazes
in astonishment for a few
moments, then bends gracefully
on one knee.]
Fairy: Rise, gentle maiden; you've no cause to fear me;
I am the Fairy Silverstar; now hear me.
The news that I have told you is quite true,
But it may bring much trouble upon you.
Should you be willing, do you think, to make
Great sacrifices for your father's sake?
Beauty: I would indeed; even my life I'd give,
That he might once again in comfort live.
Fairy: That's well: I now am satisfied that you,
Whatever happens, will your duty do.
But I have yet another word to say:
Tell no one what you've heard and seen this day —
Not ev'n your father —
Beauty: Nay, then, how will he
Be told this happy news?
Fairy: Leave that to me.
A single word from you would break the spell;
Be silent and discreet. So, fare ye well. [Exit.]
[*Beauty* stands for a short time
gazing intently at the place
where the Fairy made her
exit; then rubs her eyes, as if
trying to awaken herself.]

Beauty: I hope it is not all a dream! Oh, no —
  I'm certainly awake; it must be so.
  And if this charming Fairy should befriend us,
  No doubt good fortune will again attend us.
  She said it would bring troubles upon me:
  I wonder what those troubles are to be?
  Well, never mind; no selfish thoughts shall make
  Me fear to suffer for my father's sake. [Exit.]

Scene the Third

The Room in the Cottage.

> [Enter *Zimri*, with a letter open
> in his hand.]

Zimri [reads]:   "Zimri, your ships are lying on the strand
  Of the Black Island; 'tis enchanted land:
  But if you've courage for the enterprise,
  The road to fortune now before you lies.
  You must depart before the dawn of day,
  And through the great Pine Forest take your way;
  Follow the path where purple flowers you'll find,
  But do not pluck them, if you have a mind
  The dangers of that forest to escape;
  For dangers hover there in many a shape.
  Then go, and prosper. Ere twelve months are o'er,
  You may be richer than you were before."

> [Having read the letter aloud,
> he folds it and puts it in his
> bosom.]

This is surprising, and perhaps may be
All false; but that I am resolved to see:
For, true or false, I'll go, at any rate,
And take the chance of what may be my fate.

> [Enter *Lolo, Anna*, and *Beauty*.]

Zimri: Children, I've news, and if it should prove true,
            It will be happy news indeed for you.
Lolo: Oh! pray, sir, let us hear it quickly, do!
Anna: What is it, sir? I'm all impatience too.
Zimri: My ships are safely come to land, I'm told;
            And what is more they are well stored with gold.
Anna: Lor! that is nice. What lovely gowns I'll wear!
            And I must have some jewels for my hair.
Lolo: I will have feathers, and a train of lace
            Full three yards long, that I may walk with grace.
                        [Walks about affectedly, as if
                        holding a train.]
Zimri: Hold! not so fast — there's much yet to be done;
            And I shall have, I fear, great risks to run.
            A long and dangerous journey I must make,
            To learn if this be true, or a mistake.
Beauty [in a tone of alarm]:   Dangerous! then, dear father,
            do not go.
Anna: How very silly, Beauty, to talk so.
            But surely, father, you will never miss
            So fine an opportunity as this.
Zimri: By no means, child; I shall set out to-night,
            And if I find the vessels are all right,
            I'll bring you each a present from the town.
            What would you like?
Anna: I'll have a velvet gown,
            Spangled with gold.
Lolo: My taste is simpler, far:
            A robe of violet, with a silver star
            Embroidered over, would be my delight,
            That I might represent the Queen of Night.
Zimri: And what for you, my Beauty, shall I bring?
            A rich pearl necklace, or a diamond ring?
Beauty: No, sir; it will be time enough for me
            When you come back to think of finery.
            Jewels and laces I can do without;
            To see you safe is all I care about.

Zimri: My dearest daughter, that is kindly spoken;
        Yet I should like to bring you some small token.
Beauty: Well, then, if I may choose what it shall be,
        I beg you'll bring a white moss rose for me.
Zimri: If I return, though fortune be denied,
        Your wish, my darling, shall be gratified.
        Now, children, come and help me to prepare
        For this long journey: there's no time to spare.
                    [Exit with *Beauty*.]
Lolo [in a contemptuous tone]:   A white moss rose! How
        utterly absurd!
Anna: A more affected thing I never heard!
                    [While speaking, they follow
                    Zimri, and go off the stage in
                    saying the last word.]

Scene the Fourth

[This may be the arbour scene, with as much green about as
possible. A polka should be played, and the four Attendant
Fairies come in dancing two-and-two, holding chains of flowers
between them. Having danced round the stage, two go to one
side and two to the other; then all bend one knee to the ground
as *Silverstar* enters.]

Silverstar: You've all obeyed my summons — that is right,
        For you will have some work to do to-night;
                    [They rise.]
        And it must be well done. At evening tide,
        A traveller will through the forest ride;
        The magic path to him you must disclose,
        Where the blue heath-bell in abundance blows:
        Tempt him to pluck the flowers, then you may raise
        A storm, and set the forest in a blaze;
        Lead him to turn his steed towards the east,
        And bring him to the castle of the Beast;

Take care to serve him with a splendid supper there,
And the best chamber for his use prepare.
But do it all in silence and unseen:
It is the order of our Fairy Queen.

1st Fairy: It shall be done; I'll hide within a flower,
And make it look so bright, he'll not have power
To pass it by.

2nd Fairy: And I will shout and scream,
So that the air shall full of noises seem.

3rd Fairy: And I will shake and bend the trees around,
Until their topmost branches touch the ground.

4th Fairy: I will a thousand flaming torches bear,
And flash them round and round him in the air,
West, north, and south, so that he needs must go
Towards the east, whether he will or no.

Silverstar: 'Tis well; I now am satisfied that you
Quite understand what you have got to do.
Then go; for look, the sun is on the wane:
At midnight I will see you all again. [Exit.]

> [The same polka played as
> before, and the Fairies go off
> dancing as they entered.]

Scene the Fifth

The interior of the Beast's Palace.

[This scene should be made as brilliant as possible, with as many lights as can conveniently be placed. Any gay looking coverings may be thrown over the chairs; and the table should be laid out for supper with some plates, vases of flowers, and lights. Some of the small coloured wax candles would have a pretty effect. It must be made apparent that the supper is only meant for one person.]

[Enter *Zimri*. He looks about
him in amaze.]

Zimri: It is a fearful night. The forest seemed
To be on fire, or else I must have dreamed;
And in this noble palace I have seen
No living creature yet. What can it mean?
My horse has found provision in the stable,
And here appears to be a sumptuous table
Spread for one guest. It cannot be for me;
Yet there is no one else that I can see.
                    [He goes to the table and takes
                    up a written paper.]
Hold! what is this? [Reads:] "Zimri, you need not fear
To take what fate has set before you here.
Sup freely, then; and when to rest inclined,
In the long gallery above you'll find
A chamber with a hundred tapers lighted;
It is the room for travellers benighted,
Who by some chance are to this castle led:
There you will find your couch already spread.
Repose in peace, until the morning light
Shall warn you to depart. And so, good night."
                    [Folding the paper and seating
                    himself at the table.]
Good night, kind host, whoever you may be;
I thank you for your hospitality,
And will enjoy it: though I know I stand
In peril now, upon enchanted land.

[While *Zimri* sups, a fairy song might be introduced with good
effect by some young lady, who should place herself so as not to
be seen. The accompaniment should be played very softly.
"Where the bee sucks," or "Oh, 'tis pleasant to float on the
sea," (from Oberon,) would be appropriate. If there are no
singers, some very soft airs might be played on the piano; or a
musical box would make good music for this scene. When the
music ceases, *Zimri* rises apparently much refreshed.]

I never heard a strain so truly sweet!
Thank you, kind fairies, for this charming treat.
Good night, once more. [He bows round.] I now will go to
    rest,
And hope that everything is for the best. [Exit.]

[A lively waltz or polka is now played, and the four Fairies appear. Each takes something from the table and carries it off, returning immediately for something more, till the table is cleared.]

Enter *Silverstar*. The Fairies kneel, and the music ceases.

Silverstar: Rise, my good sprites [they rise]; your task is
            bravely done,
        And you a merry holiday have won.
        But, ere you go, there is more work to do:
        The merchant takes his breakfast here, and you
        Must get it ready by the break of day;
        Then you're at liberty to go and play. [Exit.]
All the Fairies: Thanks! thanks!
1st fairy: Now, fairy sisters, let us haste
        In search of food to suit this mortal's taste,
        For day will soon appear —
1nd Fairy: Then we are free;
        Oh! what a merry holiday 'twill be!
                        [Music as before; the Fairies go
                        off dancing.]

Scene the Sixth

The Garden of the Palace

[As many flowers and shrubs should be brought into this scene as can conveniently be managed; — the arbour used in the second scene, and a large tree of white roses in the centre of the stage. This tree may easily be made by setting up some branches of laurel, or any evergreen, in a flower-pot, and tying a number of artificial white roses upon it, which could be made of tissue paper.]

Zimri: So far all's well — my breakfast might have graced
      A monarch's table — fairies have good taste.
      But what a splendid garden! — trees and flowers
      Like these are worthy of Arcadian bowers;
      And here's a white moss rose — the very thing
      Beauty requested me for her to bring.
                  [He gathers a rose, and a loud
                  roaring is immediately heard
                  — the *Beast* enters, and *Zimri*,
                  affrighted, retreats to the
                  farthest corner of the stage.]
Beast: Presumptuous mortal! Have I not bestowed
      Enough upon you here, in my abode,
      That now, with base ingratitude, you try
      To rob me of my treasures? — you must die!
Zimri: Indeed, my lord, I've robbed you of no treasure,
      Nor do I know what causes your displeasure.
Beast: Is it a trifle, then, do you suppose,
      To rob my garden of its fairest rose?
Zimri: Why, here are more than fifty on the tree,
      All quite as beautiful —
Beast: Don't talk to me,
      Oh, wretched man! But this is my reward
      For entertaining you —

Zimri: Really, my Lord —
Beast [interrupting him]:   My title is not Lord — 'tis
simply Beast;
    And so you'll call me, if you're wise at least.
Zimri: Well, then, good Beast, I hope you will forgive
    The wrong I've done, and suffer me to live.
    How could I guess that it was any harm
    To pluck one rose?
Beast: It bears a fatal charm,
    And he who gathers it is doomed to die.
Zimri: Ah! what a miserable man am I!
    Poor Beauty, too! her tender heart will break,
    If she should learn I've perished for her sake.
Beast: How so? And who is Beauty, merchant, say?
Zimri: She is my youngest daughter: yesterday,
    When I set forth upon this fatal track,
    The dear child begged that I would bring her back
    A white moss rose —
Beast: Then be it understood,
    If you've a daughter who is fair and good
    And dutiful withal, so that, to save
    Her father, she would come to be my slave
    I'll take her in your stead —
Zimri: No! I will die
    Rather than doom my child to slavery —
    That would be worse than death. — Yet, I implore
    You, Beast, to let me see her face once more.
Beast: Go then — ten days I give you — and take heed
    How you attempt that limit to exceed;
    It would be useless, for I have the power
    To bring you here again at any hour;
    So, if the maiden comes not in your room,
    On the tenth day from this, you meet your doom.
                  [Exit *Beast.*]
Zimri: Ten days! alas! then every chance is over
    My ships and missing treasures to discover,
    For it would take a hundred days or more

The coast of the Black Island to explore;
And then I might not find them: for I fear
That letter was a bait to lure me here;
And yet, I recollect, it warned me not
To touch the purple flowers — but I forgot
That warning to regard — Ah, cruel fate!
I see my error now it is too late.
                    [Exit.]

Scene the Seventh

The Merchant's Cottage

[*Anna* is sitting at the table reading. — *Lolo* enters, and *Anna* throws her book on the table and rises.]

Anna: Well, is it settled whether she's to go?
Lolo: It is: for she is bent upon it, so
          He has consented; and I heard him say
          Their journey must commence at break of day.
Anna: If that is certain, Lolo, it is plain
          That we shall never see her back again.
Lolo: So much the better; yet, how she can go
          To face that horrid monster, I don't know.
          I'm glad it was not me he fixed upon,
          For I am sure I never could have gone.
Anna: Nor I: my nerves are far too delicate,
          And so my father must have borne his fate.
                    [Enter *Zimri* and *Beauty*.]
Beauty: Take courage, father, this will all end well;
          For I know something more than I may tell;
          So do not fear for me —
Zimri: I wish, my dear,
          That I could see so little cause to fear;

Believe me, child, you will not feel so bold,
When this terrific monster you behold.

Lolo: Ah! poor dear sister Beauty: it will grieve us,
For you in such a shocking way to leave us;
I hope you will come back again some day.

Beauty: I thank you, sister; possibly I may.
Come, my dear father, let us take a walk
Through the green meadows, and then we can talk
About this Beast, and his fine fairy bowers;
I'm very gald that he is fond of flowers.

> [She takes her father's arm and
> they walk out together.]
> [Enter *Fairy* as the Beggar
> Woman.]

Anna: Why, here's that beggar woman, I declare;
[sharply] What do you want?

Fairy: I come, my ladies fair,
To offer you my services.

Anna: In what?

Fairy: To save your sister from a wretched lot;
But you will have to lend me your assistance,
Or else it can't be done.

> [She draws near to them.]

Anna: Pray keep your distance —
You save her! How excessively absurd!
Begone at once, without another word.

Lolo: You are a vile impostor, that is plain;
So never let us see your face again.

Fairy: I did it but to try you; and, I find
You both are truly selfish and unkind;
The time may come, when you will rue the day
You treated me with scorn.

Lolo: Begone, I say!

> [They push the Fairy out, and
> follow her.]

Scene the Eighth

The Hall in the Palace, and the table laid for supper as before,
but for two persons.

[Enter *Beauty*.]

Beauty: Alas! I fear my courage is all gone
Now I am left in this large place alone;
And yet, if I may judge from all I see,
Surely no harm can be intended me.
There's one apartment decked with flowers in bloom,
And over it is written, "Beauty's room;"
With many costly ornaments 'tis graced;
And books and music too are in it placed —
Ah! what is that?

[A loud roar is heard outside.]
[Enter *Beast*.]

Beast [in a gruff tone]: Beauty, how do you do?
I've come, my pretty maid, to sup with you.

Beauty [retreating in alarm]: My Lord — I'm very happy
— I am sure —

Beast: That is not true. I see you can't endure
This ugly form of mine; but I entreat you
Not to be frightened — I'm not going to eat you.

Beauty [timidly approaching]: Thank you, my Lord,
you're very good I know.

Beast: My name is Beast, and you must call me so.

Beauty: If such be your commands, I shall obey.

Beast: Nay — do not talk about commands, I pray;
It is your place to give commands to me,
For you are mistress here of all you see.

Beauty: Am I the mistress of this noble place?

Beast: Yes, Beauty, since you condescend to grace
It with your presence, and I hope you find
That every thing is ordered to your mind.

Beauty: All I have seen is very beautiful;
But I confess I find it rather dull

To be alone all day; if you could send
Some damsel hither, who would be my friend —
Beast: I cannot do it, I have not the power,
Even, to stay myself, beyond one hour;
So let us go to supper, time flies fast,
And that bright hour will very soon be past.

[They sit down to supper, and the *Beast* is very attentive in helping *Beauty* to the nicest things, and pours out wine for her. While they sup, some light lively music should be played, and another fairy song might be introduced. "Oh, bid your faithful Ariel fly," "Deep in a Forest Dell," or "Through the Wood," are good songs for the purpose; but the singer should not be seen, unless she is one of the fairies; then it must be supposed that *Beauty* does not see her.]

[When the music ceases, they
both rise from the table.]
Beast: It now is time for me to say adieu;
To-morrow I shall sup again with you.
Beauty: I'm glad of that, and shall feel much delight
If you will come to supper every night.
Beast: At nine o'clock the Beast you'll always see.
Beauty: Good night.
[The *Beast*, who is going
towards the door, turns back.]
Beast: Dear Beauty, will you marry me?
Beauty [in terror]:   No, Beast! I can't , indeed —
Beast: Ah! cruel fate!
I'm destined still to be unfortunate.
[Exit, making a dismal moaning
noise.]
Beauty [as if recovering from her fright]:   Oh, dear! I hope
he'll not ask that again!
The very thought has almost turned my brain.
Yet he's more gentle than I thought to find him,
And, but for this, I think I should not mind him.

Well, after all, I could but lose my life;
And I would rather die than be his wife. [Exit]

Scene the Ninth

The Merchant's Cottage

[*Zimri* is sitting at a table in deep thought, leaning his head on his hand, with a book open before him. His soliloquy might be written in the book, which would save the trouble of learning it.]

Zirmi: My poor dear child! could I but hope to see
           Her face once more, how happy I should be.
           It is a twelvemonth now, this very day,
           A joyless twelvemonth since she went away;
           And though I've tried to find the path again
           That led me to the castle, 'tis in vain;
           No trace of it remains. The forest wild
           Separates me for ever from my child.
           There's nothing now but misery in store!
                          [Enter *Silverstar*. *Zimri* rises,
                          and gazes on her with
                          astonishment.]
Fairy: You are mistaken, merchant; grieve no more;
           Beauty is safe, and you will soon behold
           A daughter who is worth her weight in gold.
           No evil has befall'n the charming maid,
           Whose duteous conduct will be well repaid,
           So, sleep in peace to-night, and banish sorrow:
           You will embrace your long lost child to-morrow.
Zimri: What happy words are these! and who art thou,
           Bright vision?
Fairy: I'm a fairy, you must know;
           My name is Silverstar.

Zimri [kneeling]:   Then let me kneel,
     To thank you with the gratitude I feel.
Fairy: Nay, rise; we fairies no such homage crave;
     'Tis our delight to help the good and brave,
     And break the spells that wicked spirits weave,
     Unwary mortals to torment and grieve.
Zimri [rising]:   My child is safe, you say? —
Fairy: You need not doubt it;
     From her own lips you'll soon hear all about it.
     Farewell! [Exit.]
Zimri [following]:   One moment, gentle fairy, stay!
                    [He returns, looking amazed.]
     Sure she has melted into air away.
     I fear I did not thank her as I ought,
     But joy has banished every other thought:
     This can be no delusion of the brain,
     And I shall be a happy man again. [Exit.]

Scene the Tenth

Beauty and the *Beast* at supper.

[They rise from table as if they had finished their repast, and
come to the front of the stage.]

Beast: The hour is nearly past, and I must go.
Beauty: Nay, stay a little longer. Do you know,
     I'm going to ask a boon which you must grant.
Beast: Speak, dearest Beauty, what is it you want?
Beauty: It is to go and see my father —
                    [*Beast* turns away from her
                    slowly, and goes towards the
                    door: she follows, and lays her
                    hand on his arm to detain him.
                    He comes back, and after

looking at her for a little while
in silence, shakes his head, and
says:]

Beast: No!
   Beauty, indeed, I cannot let you go.
   Ask anything but that, and I'll comply;
   But if you were to leave me, I should die.
Beauty: Surely a few days you might live, at least,
   Without me, then I would return, good Beast.
Beast: I am afraid that, if you once depart,
   You'll not come back, and that would break my heart.
Beauty: Indeed, I will, you are so kind to me,
   I would not, for world, ungrateful be.
   I'm sure you will consent —
Beast: Well, be it so;
   I can deny you nothing, therefore go;
   And, if you like, you may depart to night.
Beauty: Surely I do not understand you right!
   How can I go to night, at this late hour?
Beast: I'm going to place the means within your power.
                 [He gives her a ring.]
   Beneath your pillow lay this golden ring,
   'Twas given to me by the fairy King,
   And will convey you, with the greatest ease,
   The while you sleep, to any place you please.
Beauty: Thank you, that is delightful!
Beast: Now, adieu —
   Remember, three days hence, I look for you!
   And if you come not, it will cost my life.
             [He is going, but turns back
             when at the door.]
   Beauty, will you consent to be my wife?
Beauty: No, Beast; I've told you many times before!
   Pray, do not ask that question any more.
Beast: Ah, wretched Beast, when will thy sorrows end?
Beauty: I love you very dearly, as a friend,
   And do not like to cause you any pain;

So never speak of marrying, again.
                    [They go off different ways, the
                    Beast moaning.]

Scene the Eleventh

The Cottage

                    [Enter *Lolo*, talking to herself.]
Lolo: I wish that I had seen the Fairy, she
           Might have bestowed some gift, perhaps, on me.
           I hope she'll come again — then I would try
           To win her favour; and who knows but I
           May come to be a princess, or a queen;
           I'm sure I've heard such things have sometimes been.
           And why I should not have good luck, as well
           As any body else, I cannot tell.
                    [Enter *Anna*, running and out of
                    breath.]
Lolo: Good gracious me! what is the matter, child?
           Really you look as if you had gone wild.
Anna: Beauty is come, and brought us such fine things;
           Such caps and dresses, necklaces and rings —
Lolo: Brought them for us?
Anna: Yes, there's a box below;
           How it came there I'm sure I do not know,
           Unless it dropped down from the skies; for, see,
           The gate is locked and I have got the key;
           So that I'm certain no one has been here;
           Is it not very wonderful, my dear?
Lolo: It is indeed; but, sister, without joking,
           This girl's good fortune really is provoking.
           How handsomely the monster seems to treat her!
Anna: Yes, when we both believed that he would eat her;
           But since she has a Fairy for her friend,
           We must make much of her —

Lolo: So I intend.
                        [Exeunt *Anna* and *Lolo*.]

                        [Enter *Zimri* and *Beauty*.]
Beauty: I am so glad to be at home again —
        But, sir, you must not ask me to remain
        More than three days —
Zimri: Dear daughter, say not so,
        I cannot part with you so soon: oh, no!
        You must stay longer with us; your good Beast
        May spare you for a fortnight at the least.
Beauty: Well, let us now rejoice that we have met,
        And not begin to think of parting yet.
        Besides, I think you must be glad to hear
        I am so kindly treated, father, dear,
        That I am not afraid of going again.
Zimri: Indeed I am; still, it would give me pain
        To find this monster, with his luxury,
        Has made you think the less of home and me.
Beauty: Oh! sir, how can you fancy such a thing!
        That could not be, even were he a king.
Zimri: I hope not; yet if it be really so,
        You will not be in so much haste to go.
Beauty: I would not go, if I could have my will;
        But, though he's kind, I am his captive still;
        Nor do I know how long I must remain,
        Or if I ever shall be free again.
        Now let us go to breakfast, sir, and pray
        Don't talk of parting any more to day.
                        [She takes his arm and they go
                        off the stage together.]

Scene the Twelfth

The Palace, with the table laid for supper.

> [Enter *Beast*. He looks
> mournfully at the table.]

Beast: She is not here, and now ten days are past,
Ten weary days, since I beheld her last.
Ah! cruel Beauty — who would have believed
Those charming lips could ever have deceived?
Now, there is nothing more to hope, so I
May bid adieu to all my cares, and die.

> [He seats himself at the table
> but does not touch the supper,
> and remains there in an
> attitude of melancholy and
> profound meditation, while
> some very plaintive music is
> performed; after which he rises
> and comes forward.]

Beast: Thank you, good Fairies, but it is in vain;
I ne'er shall listen to those sounds again.
A victim to enchantment, Azor dies;
And she who might have saved, unpitying flies.

> [Exit.]

Scene the Thirteenth

The Cottage. *Beauty* asleep on a couch.

> [Enter *Fairy Silverstar*. She
> approaches the couch and
> waves her wand over it.]

Fairy: Dream, Beauty, dream the noble Beast is dying;
Under the fatal rose, behold him lying.
Dream, that while you are here in peace reposing,

His eyes in death are fast for ever closing.
Dream of the words that you have falsely spoken;
Dream of the promise so unkindly broken;
Repair the fatal error while you have the power,
For it will be too late if you delay one hour.
                    [Exit.]
                    [*Beauty* wakes and starts up as
                    if in terror.]
Beauty: Ah! what is this? surely I must have dreamed!
And yet, how like reality it seemed!
I thought I saw him dying, and I felt
So sad, as weeping by his side I knelt:
I hope it is not true. What can it mean?
How selfish and ungrateful I have been!
I will return this night, and he shall see
His kindness has not been quite lost on me.
He must not die: this dream is not in vain;
This magic ring shall take me back again.
                    [She takes the ring from her
                    finger, places it under the
                    pillow, and lies down again.
                    The scene then closes.]

[If the performance should happen to be in a room where there
is neither curtain nor folding doors, two of the Attendant
Fairies might appear, and raising *Beauty* from the couch, lead
her off the stage in her sleep.]

The Last Scene [14]

The Garden of the Palace

                    [The *Beast* is discovered lying
                    under the white rose tree,
                    apparently lifeless. *Beauty* is
                    kneeling by his side.]

Beauty: I fear it is all over. Oh! how wrong
        It was to break my word, and stay so long.
        Yet, hark! I hear him breathe — he is not dead! —
        He may revive. Dear Beast, lift up your head,
        And speak to me —
Beast [faintly, and without moving]:   Ah! Beauty, is it you,
        Come back to bid the Beast a last adieu?
Beauty: Oh! do not say the last — it must not be;
        Forgive me, dearest Beast, and live for me.
Beast [raising himself a little]:   One word might save me yet: say but that you
        Consent to be my wife —
Beauty: I do — I do!
                        [The *Beast* starts up, and,
                        throwing off his disguise,
                        appears in his proper form as
                        Prince Azor. He kneels at the
                        feet of *Beauty*, who has risen,
                        and regards him with
                        astonishment.]
Azor: A thousand thanks, sweet maid; once more I'm free
        From the Enchanter's power: and thus, you see,
        To no rude monster have you given your hand;
        But unto Azor, Prince of Silverland.
Beauty: Rise, noble prince. It is, indeed, most strange;
        But what has brought about this happy change?
Azor: I was condemned that hideous form to bear,
        Until I found a maiden, good and fair,
        Willing to be my bride. Thus, you've released
        From vile enchantment your most grateful Beast.
                        [Enter *Zimri, Lolo,* and *Anna*.
                        They all look bewildered.]
Lolo::   Where are we now, I wonder? —
Anna: Gracious me!
        Why, Lolo, here is Beauty! only see!
Zimri: The friendly Fairy, then, has kept her word.

[Enter *Silverstar*.]

Fairy: Yes, merchant, all your fortune is restored:
    The same Enchanter who is Azor's foe
    Waylaid your ships, so that they could not go
    Beyond his island: but they now are free,
    And, richly laden, soon in port will be.

Lolo [advancing pertly towards the Fairy]: Oh, charming
Fairy! —

Fairy [in a loud stern tone]: Silence, girl!
                  [A short pause, during which
                  all stand gazing on the *Fairy*,
                  who, after looking at the two
                  sisters in silence for a few
                  moments, speaks again in her
                  usual manner.]
                                  Behold
    In me the beggar you called rude and bold;
    When you believed that I was old and poor,
    Unpitying you turned me from the door.
    Now, hear your doom —

Beauty [interposing]: Nay, gentle Fairy, stay;
    For my sake pity and forgive them, pray.

Fairy: Since you plead for them, though they have
offended,
    I will not punish them as I intended;
    But they must wait on you, and humbly stand
    Beside your throne, when Queen of Silverland;
    For Azor now is King.

Azor: My thanks are due,
    Most kind and gracious Fairy, unto you;
    For I am sure, without your generous aid,
    I never should have won this lovely maid.
                        [He takes *Beauty's* hand.]

Silverstar: True, Prince, and now you've gained your
liberty,
    Long may you live, and happy may you be.
    It was my mission to dissolve this spell:

My task is ended; and so, fare ye well.

> [She retires slowly towards the back of the stage, while *Azor*, *Beauty*, and *Zimri*, bend gracefully, partly to her, and partly to the audience. The two sisters stand aside, as if ashamed, hiding their faces with their handkerchiefs; and thus the scene closes.]

The End

MRS. PECK'S PUDDING

1859

Eliza Follen

Eliza Lee Cabot was born in Boston on August 15, 1787, the daughter of Samuel Cabot and Sarah Barrett Cabot. In 1796, Cabot went to England to become Secretary to the U.S. commission negotiating American claims against England growing out of the Revolution. When the family returned to the United States, Cabot's poor health and financial difficulties forced the family to move frequently. Sarah Cabot died in 1809. When Samuel Cabot died ten years later, Eliza and two of her sisters established a home of their own.

Eliza had always had a deep religious impulse. She taught Sunday school at the Federal Street Unitarian Church of William Ellery Channing, in whose circle, in 1826, she met Charles Theodore Christian Follen, a political refugee from Germany. He and Eliza married in 1829, when she was forty-one and he thirty-two. Charles Christopher, their only child, was born in 1830.

In 1830, Follen ws made Harvard's first instructor in German. His appointment was not renewed, probably because of his strong, outspoken position against slavery, which his wife passionately shared. Thereafter, Follen earned his living as a teacher, lecturer, and Unitarian minister. He died at sea in 1840, returning from lecturing on German literature in New York.

Eliza then moved to Roxbury, where she prepared her son and other boys for Harvard and wrote to supplement her income. Her books inlcude many works for children and a memoir of her husband's life. She served as editor of the magazine *The Children's Friend* for seven years and for many years on the executive committees of Massachusetts and American antislavery societies. James Russell Lowell, writing of the women who ran antislavery bazaars in Faneuil Hall, wrote touchingly of her:

> And there, too, was Eliza Follen,
> Who scatters fruit-creating pollen ...
> Each several point of all her face
> Trembling bright with inward grace,
> As if all motion gave it light
> Like phosphorescent seas at night.

She died in Brookline of typhoid fever on January 26, 1860.

MRS. PECK'S PUDDING

Mrs Peck's Pudding is simply a little story dramatised, that was published in Hood's Magazine many years ago. The wit and fun were already at hand, and have received little addition. The plot, if a conclusion so simple may be called a plot, is nearly all that is original in the little comedy.[1]

In her New England way, Mrs. Follen is much too modest. A plot is not a play. It is, as the mathematicians say, necessary but not sufficient. Mrs. Follen changed the story from which she took her play considerably, improving it with virtually every change. She changed the venue of the story and she changed its tone. She collapsed a number of scenes into one and, as she said, changed the story's ending. But what makes *Mrs. Peck's Pudding* is its characterizations, which are virtually all Mrs. Follen's invention, and, most especially, its dialogue, which she edited and altered and sometimes invented: not the vaudeville mispronunciations and the malapropisms, but the language of the poor and the language of cold charity.

"This," says Billy, showing off his uniform to Peter, "is all the go in furren parts; all the men-helps wear a delivery other side of the water; don't be scared, little Peter."

Peter: I've lived too long in the woods to be scared at an owl, Bill. But you are awful smart. Can you work in them things?
Billy: La! Pete I'm as loose in 'em as a rotten nut in the shell.

And here is little Jackey, returning to his mother:

Mrs. Peck: Well, little fellow, what have you got, and where's the night-cap I gave you for a bag?
Jackey: Here. [Taking it out of his pocket] She wouldn't give me any flour without money, and gave me only this bundle, and called it everlasting manna, — it's everlasting heavy — and said you must feed us all on it.
Mrs. Peck: [Opening the bundle] It's a bundle of horrid tracts! Cruel woman.
Jackey: 'Taint my fault; she called it right good spiritual food. She's a wicked old girl.

Misery has an even darker side. Who would imagine that this speech of Mrs. Peck's could ever have appeared in a comedy for children?

Mrs. Peck: Don't touch me, don't comfort me, I won't be comforted. Don't help me, if you see me sinking to the floor, I'm like an over-driv beast. I don't know what I may do. . . . I've hoped as long as hoping was any good. [She rises excitedly.] I won't hope any longer, that I won't. I give up — blow upon blow. Luck sets all one way. This last is the drop too much. . . . We're a starving family, and if it wasn't wicked, I'd tie you all round my neck and jump into the frogpond with you, and die like our poor cat and kittens.

For the fact, of course, is that the vaudeville humor of *Mrs. Peck's Pudding*, like the stylized sentimentality of Victorian children's deathbed scenes, is style, not substance. It is, in fact, a defense against the substance, which would otherwise be intolerable. It is a way of blurring the image of true misery, that particularly heartless, faceless, and inescapable misery of the poor in the mid-nineteenth century.

NOTE

1. Eliza Lee Follen, *Home Dramas for Young People* (Boston and Cambridge: James Munroe and Company, 1859), vi. The play is taken from an anonymous story in *Hood's Magazine* 2 (12) (December 1844): [521]–35.

MRS. PECK'S PUDDING

A DRAMA IN TWO ACTS

Dramatis Personae

MRS. PECK, a poor widow.
MRS. SAWKINS, Hen Fancier.
MR. HABAKUK SHUFFLETOE.
STRANGER.
SUSAN, called Careful Susan,
POLLY, called Dirty Polly,
DICK, called Whistling Dick,   } Children of
CHARLEY, called Greedy Charley,   Mrs. Peck.
PETER, called Ragged Peter,
LITTLE JACK,
BILLY, a servant boy in livery.

Act I

SCENE I

A small room meanly furnished. *Mrs. Peck, Susan*, a girl of about sixteen. *Polly*, younger. *Dicky*, with a jews'-harp. *Charley* and *Peter*, playing marbles. *Little Jack* leans on his mother's knee.

Mrs. Peck [looking anxious and thoughtful]: How to get it I don't see; but a Christmas pudden I must and will have, — that's settled. It's onreligious not to have a pudden, and a plum-pudding, on Christmas Day; and as sure as I'm the Widder Peck, a pudden I'll have. But how? that's the question. I havn't a brass farden in the world, and I have not a single perkisite for it. I'm a widder without a mite, but a pudden I must have, and I will, and so. It is too bad to be as poor as Job's cat, and to go without everything you want into the bargain. Here children, I'm goin to have a Christmas pudden to-morrow. [The children gather round her clapping their hands.]

Jackey: But, mammy, we've no plums.

Susan: And not a speck of flour.

Polly: Nor a scrap of suet.

Charley: Nor a sign of orange or lemon peel.

Peter: Nor a dust of sugar.

Susan: And not a single egg.

Dick: And never a sarsepan to bile it in; for you remember you swopped your's away for a lot of salt pork tother day.

Mrs. Peck: I know all that. I've got nothing. But that's neither here nor there. I'm going to borry and beg. I'm a widder, and maybe I'll get what I want; for I mean to have a Christmas pudden by hook or by crook, you'll see I will. So all of you get ready to go after the perkisites to make it.

Charley: I'll go for the plums.

Mrs. Peck: No, you'll eat them; you shall go for the suet.

Charley: That's a pretty way to treat a feller; I'll have more pudden for that.

Mrs. Peck: Polly, you go and see if you can't squeeze a few raisins and some sugar out of Mr. Perry, the grocer. Jackey, you try to coax some flour out of Mr. Stone; not Mrs. Stone, she's a hard character. Susan, do you go to Mrs. Sawkins'; you know she was your school ma'am once. Try to distract three eggs from her. Do your prettiest; speak good grammar, and your best dictionary words to her, that she may see you remember her instructions. As for you, Dicky, take your jews'-harp and see if you can't play it to the tune of a sarsepan to bile our pudden in. [The children show great delight. *Jack* puts on a hat without a crown. *Susan* tries to take the poke out of her bonnet; and *Polly* pins up a tear in her dress.]

[Exeunt.]

The widow *Peck* alone.

Mrs. Peck: I've heard tell of a poor widder who went to a lottery office and enquired if she had'nt drawn a prize, and when they asked her what was the number of her ticket, she replied, "I have never a ticket, but then I did not know what the Lord might do for me." I'm sure I havn't any ticket in any lottery, but neither do I know what the Lord may do for me. I mean to hope for the best.

[The curtain falls.]

SCENE II

A small room; on the wall hangs a large picture of a cock and hens for a sign; underneath is written, "Fresh eggs laid here at the shortest notice." *Mrs. Sawkins* discovered. *Susan* enters, ringing the shop bell as she opens the door.

Mrs. Sawkins: How de'do, Susan? [*Susan* stands in the door.] Come in and sit down, won't you?

Susan: No, thank'ee, ma'am; I only came for three eggs, if you have them to-day. Your eggs are *so* nice.

Mrs. Sawkins: Yes, indeed. My hens lay none but the very best; you can have as many as you want. But sit down and take off your bonnet, Susan, do.

Susan: No, thank'ee, ma'am, — I mus'nt stay; mother wants me at home. [After a pause.] It's a beautiful day, isn't it, Mrs. Sawkins?

Mrs. Sawkins [rising]: That it is, Susan, and my hens know it too, as well as you and I do. It's right fresh eggs you want?

Susan: Yes, ma'am, quite fresh if you please.

Mrs. Sawkins: You can have as many as you want. There's my Polly Phemus, now, lays the beautifullest fresh eggs you ever see. [Takes down a small basket.]

Susan: Polly who?

Mrs. Sawkins: Polly Phemus. You see, Susan, I give female names to all my hens, and I know every one by her voice, and every hen knows her name when I call her.

Susan: I never heard of such a thing.

Mrs. Sawkins: No? Then I'll tell you all about my henery, as I call it, after my husband Henery, who's always gone to sea.

You just sit down now, — your mother ain't in such a dreadful hurry, is she? and I'll tell you all about it. [*Mrs. Sawkins* forces *Susan* into a chair and sits down by her.] Well, you see I've Pollies, and Sallies, and Annies, — they're all remarkable hens, and so you see I gave them remarkable names.

Susan: Was Polly Phemus a queen?

Mrs. Sawkins: I don't know about that, but the sound, Susan, that's the thing. Then I have a Polly Glot, a Polly Anthus, and she's such a beauty.

Susan: Isn't it strange to name hens? Do they come when you call them?

Mrs. Sawkins: Like lightning. But you must hear about my Sallys and Annies. There's my Sally-Ratus and my Sally-Mander. She's a Shin high, and a master fine hen.

Susan: Yes, indeed, and I'd like to see her, ma'am; but can't you give me the eggs now, please?

Mrs. Sawkins: Presently, Susan; don't be impatient, I must tell you about my Annies, and then you shall have the eggs. First, there's my Annie Condy, she is named after a wonderful creature that comes from foreign parts, a great curiosity; they had one in the managery.

Susan: What sort of a creature is she, ma'am?

Mrs. Sawkins: All I know for certain about her is, that she is a tremend-i-ous quadruped that swallows down live human beings just as my hens do worms.

Susan: Oh, my!

Mrs. Sawkins: Captain Sawkins told me all about her; he saw one. Then I have an Annie Liza, named after my two daughters that I lost; was not that a good thought? And then, last of all, my Annie Tommy, my only name of the masculine gender, or as Dickens says, of the opposite sex. You read Dickens, Susan?

Susan: Yes, ma'am; don't he tell of little Oliver's asking for more? I often think of that story at home. Can I have the eggs now, Mrs. Sawkins, if you please?

Mrs. Sawkins: Don't be so impatient, Susan; all in good time. You see Polly Phemus is on her nest in the candle-box at this blessed minute — she's an everlasting layer. She's awful black, with a white tuft on her head, and perfect beauty. Did you say only three?

Susan: Yes, ma'am; only three.

Mrs. Sawkins: Four cents apiece, Susan, and you shall have them warm.

Susan: Mother can't pay for them now, if you please, ma'am; but she will out of the first money she earns.

Mrs. Sawkins: Dear, dear me! that alters the case; I'm sorry to refuse, but eggs is eggs, day before Christmas, Susan. It's not laying season now, and my hens never lay out of rule; they are very particular hens.

Susan: I thought you said, ma'am, they were all laying, and I could have as many as I wanted.

Mrs. Sawkins: Do be reasonable, Susan. You see, since my hens have suffered from bad debts, they've grown desperate particular. It is not possible for you to have eggs without money. I should not dare to look Polly Phemus in the face; her comb would turn pale if I were to let you have her eggs without money, and she'd stop laying right off.

Susan: What shall we do for our Christmas pudding? [She looks very sorrowful.]

Mrs. Sawkins: Don't be downcast. Susan, I'll do some mangling for you and your mother, and won't charge anything.

Susan: We've no clothes to mangle, thank'ee ma'am.

Mrs. Sawkins: Be patient, Susan. You see my poultry is so very particular; they would dissolve partnership right away if I was not particular too. They expect four cents for every egg they lay. To a friend who took three, I'd throw in that speckled one in the moss basket in the window; it's as good as need be. Twelve cents, Susan, that's all, and I'll give you all Shin highs.

Susan: We havn't twelve cents in the world, and mother has set her heart so upon having a Christmas pudding, and we've nothing to make it of.

Mrs. Sawkins: The more's the pity; but my hens are preemptory. Polly Phemus won't take promises, and Annie Liza knows pence from piecrust, and you might talk till doomsday before you could get an egg from Annie Condy, free gratis for nothing; but just show them the money, and they'd go off to their nests and lay like lambs.

Susan: Our pudding is gone; no pudding, poor, dear mother. [She looks very sorrowful.]

Mrs. Sawkins: I've a capital receipt for a Christmas pudding, I'll give you Susan.

Susan: Thank you for your generosity, ma'am. [She turns to go off, repeating the words, no pudding. Then returns, takes the receipt, and exit with her handkerchief to her eyes.]

[The curtain falls.]

SCENE III

A street

[Enter *Peter*, looking about on the ground as if seeking something.]

Peter: I can't find a scrap of orange peel anywhere. I guess some plaguey old fat man has slipped down on his back to-day, and so the nasty old police have had all the lemon and orange peel cleaned up. I wish he'd kept on his fat legs till after Christmas, and then the streets wouldn't be so thunderation clean. Mother's awful sot about her pudden, but I don't see that I can find anything good to flavor it with. [He looks around.] There comes big Billy, with his ridiklus delivery on, as he calls it. He's a great goose, but he's good-natured, and maybe he'll help me to something. [Enter *Billy*, dressed in an extravagant livery; he has a very pompous, patronising air.]

Billy: Ha! young un! How are you? Do you know who I am? Look at my new dress. [He struts about to show his finery.] This is all the go in furren parts; all the men-helps wear a delivery tother side the water; don't be scared, little Peter.

Peter: I've lived too long in the woods to be scared at an owl, Bill. But you are awful smart. Can you work in them things?

Billy: La! Pete, I'm as loose in 'em as a rotten nut in the shell; but what are you looking after, Peter?

Peter: My Ma' wants some orange or lemon peel to flavor a Christmas pudden with, and I'm just trying to find some in the street.

Billy: But, Peter, that would be dirty.

Peter: Oh, I can rub the mud off, and Ma' can wash it. But don't you remember once, before you had your new delivery on, you gave me a whole parcel of orange and lemon peel, and bits of preserves, and nice things?

Billy: Oh, yes, that was just after we had a dinner party. We've none to-day.

Peter: Hav'nt you any of the scrapings of the plates, a few raisins, or a rotten lemon, or something or other, Billy?

Billy [strutting about]: Nothing at all, Peter; all gone to the pigs, Peter.

Peter: I wish I was a pig, so I do. Mr. Billy, you might pity a poor boy and help him if he is'nt a pig. My poor Ma'; she won't have nothing for her pudden; you don't care for nothing but your new delivery. Deliver me from such friends. [He turns to go off, crying.]

Billy [aside]: I can't stand them rags. Don't cry, Peter. Some other day I'll have something for you; an orange perhaps.

Peter: That won't flavor our pudden to-morrow. Good-by, Billy, you are too fine to be a good friend.

Billy: Stay a minute, Peter, I'll see what I can find. [Goes off.]

Peter [rubbing his hands and jumping about]: I'll get it after all. It takes me, you'd better believe.

Billy [as he enters with a bundle]: Here, Peter, is something good. Tell you mother it is real good stuff; and to make the best of it.

Peter: Thank'ee, Billy. Hurra! Hurra! aint I a buster. [Exit, Hurraing.]

[Curtain falls.]

Act II

SCENE I

Mrs. Peck alone at the table as before.

Mrs. Peck: Why don't some of the children come back. Let's see, I'm pretty sure of the flour if only sharp-nosed Mrs. Stone should happen to be out. Her husband's kind o' soft-hearted. The suet I shall have to a dead certainty. The fruit I think I'm sure of. Peter, little ragged rogue, will bring me something certainly. The eggs I may count upon; and as for the sarsepan, who'd refuse that? Well, I'm e'en a'-most sure of my pudden. Can't I see it now, smoking hot, covered all over with plums looking like the back of Col. Fisher's coach dog. Here comes Charley, with suet. [*Charley* enters with the suet.]

Charley: There, Ma', is the suet; the butcher was proper good-natured; I should think he was made of suet. He gave it to me right off in a minute.

Mrs. Peck: And did'nt he ask you anything for it?

Charley: No, for I told him before hand, I'd no money, and he must give it; and so says he, "There, you rogue, carry that to your mother, and tell her I send her the — the botherments (that was the word I think), the botherments of the season," or something like that anyhow. Aint he a trump, and a good fat one too; but I'm plaguey hungry.

Mrs. Peck: Never mind, Charley, take a drink of water. Here comes Polly. [Enter *Polly*.] Oh, she's got a paper in her hand. Well, Polly, what have you got?

Polly: Nothing but that [gives a brown paper parcel to *Mrs. Peck*], and I don't believe it's anything good, for when the grocer gave it to me, he didn't look good; he looked a sort of impudent.

Mrs. Peck [she tears off the paper]: A pretty perkisite for a Christmas pudden. It's a piece of brown soap. A villian!

All: A piece of brown soap for a Christmas pudden!

Polly: I knew it was'nt anything good. He's a bad man, mother, with his white apron always clean. I hate him.

Mrs. Peck: And did you tell him you wanted sugar and raisins for a Christmas pudden?

Polly: I did, and when I told him I had'nt anything but thanks to pay for them, he said, "fiddle-sticks."

Mrs. Peck: Hard-hearted man.

Polly: Then he said he'd take pity on me and give me just what I wanted most. And when I thanked him again, he laughed and looked so sarsily into my face; I knew he meant something impudent, a nasty old cheat. I wish I had the washing of his ugly mug, I guess I would'nt spare the soap.

Mrs. Peck: And did'nt he tell you what he gave you?

Polly: No; when I asked him what it was, he said I mus'nt look at it till I got home, and that I must beg you to use it freely; and then he sort o' laughed all over, and said, "this is doing good in secret." Ain't he wicked?

Enter Jack.

Mrs. Peck: Here's Jackey. Well, little fellow, what have you got, and where's the night-cap I gave you for a bag?

Jack: Here. [Taking it out of his pocket.] She would'nt give me any flour without money, and gave me only this bundle, and called it everlasting manna, — it's everlasting heavy, — and said you must feed us all on it.

Mrs. Peck [opening the bundle]: It's a bundle of horrid tracts! Cruel woman.

Jack: 'Taint my fault; she called it right good spiritual food. She's a wicked old gal. I begged hard for the flour, and the more I said it was for charity, the more she would'nt give it; and she called us all carnal-minded sinners, and said we were greedy. And I'm sure we've nothing to be greedy with; and then to give a feller these nasty thunderation old tracts. I wish she'd nothing else to eat herself, I do.

Mrs. Peck: You told her it was for a Christmas pudding.

Jack: Yes, and that the bag was made out of poor daddy's night-cap; and that I wanted the very best flour. And first she filled it; but when she found I'd no money, she emptied it right out, and threw the bag in my face, she did.

Mrs. Peck: My poor Jackey.

Jack [sobbing]: And when she said she could'nt book it, and I told her she need'nt, she laughed, and called me a little scamp.

Mrs. Peck: Too bad, Jackey.

Jack: And then I cried, for I couldn't help it. And I told her last year we had only a little teenty-taunty pudden, and now we should'nt have any. She called me a lubber, and told me she'd give me some spiritual manna; and when I just asked if it was vittles or drink, she called me greedy, and said a Christmas birch-rod would be good for me.

Mrs. Peck: I'd like to see anybody dare to touch a rod to my little Jackey.

Jack: And then she gave me the tracts and told me to bring them to you, and said I was a greedy little heathen; and I think she was an old cross patch with her everlasting manna. I suppose it's physic or pizen, and I won't touch it. I hope she'll get her beans yet, some day.

Mrs. Peck: Never mind, Jackey, dear, don't cry any more; she's a hard-hearted woman. Here comes Susan, perhaps she's got something good. [Enter *Susan*. She walks up to the table feeling in her pocket as she walks.] Have you got the eggs in your pocket, Susan? In the name of mercy, how long you are. Have you broken them?

Susan: I have no eggs, mother. [She looks sorrowful and still feels in her pocket.]

Mrs. Peck: For goodness sake what have you got there?

Susan: An excellent receipt for a Christmas pudding.

Mrs. Peck [screaming]: The only thing in the world I don't want for a pudden. Haven't I made Christmas puddens ever since I was born into this wicked unfeeling world? and to send me a receipt for one is downright aggravating. [Enter *Peter*, with a bundle, and throws it on the table.]

Peter: There, mother, you have the perkisites for a Christmas pudden, and a whopping lot of em, too.

Mrs. Peck: Well, after all, we are in luck. [*She tries to untie the bundle. After a while it bursts open, and she takes out a pair of red plush breeches.*] Oh, mercy on me! A pair of old red breeches for a Christmas pudden. [*Holds them up with a look of horror.*] I shall go off my reason. I can't stand it. A pair of red breeches for a pudden, and a Christmas pudden, too. Take em off out of my sight. [*The children throw them under the table. Peter puts his hat on them, and Polly her bonnet, and Susan spreds a bit of paper over them.*]

Peter: There, Ma', you can't see them now. That's what comes of showing my ragged back to Bill. I wish I was all front, I do. I wish he had his ugly head in them. To give me a pair of old breeches to make a Christmas pudden of. I should like to hide him with his thunderation delivery on as he calls it, old fool. [*Here Dick is heard playing on his jews'-harp.*]

Susan: I suppose Dickey has got the sarsepan.

Mrs. Peck: Of course he has got the sarsepan now there's nothing to put in it. [*Enter Dick. He goes up to the table and gives his mother a teetotum, and then goes on playing his harp.*] As I live, an ivory teetotum. Is that for a pudden, too? [*Laughs hysterically.*]

Dick: You see, Ma, first I went to Mrs. Smith's to borrow a sarsepan, and she said you was welcome, but that the sarsepan had a hole in the bottom; "but" said she, "you might stick some dough into the place." Well! I thought that wouldn't do, so I went to Mrs. Quigley's, and she said her sarsepan had gone a visiting aleady. Then I went to Mrs. Green's, and she snarled out — "My sarsepan's full of sarse, so get out with your tarnel jews'-harp." Then I went to Mrs. O'Heran's, and says she, "Oh yes, dear, and you're welcome, only I have but one, and that's a frying-pan, and I'm using it."

Mrs. Peck: That's the way with all my friends.

Dick: So I was coming home playing my jews'-harp to keep up my spirits, when Tom Jones call'd me from the window to come in there and play a tune.

Mrs. Peck: They are as mean as the dirt, — you got nothing there of course.

Dick: I went in, and I told the boys I wanted to ask their cook to lend mother a sarsepan. "You'll get it over your ears if you ask her for anything, " they said; but I'm not easily scared. So down I went into the kitchen playing Yankee Doodle. "Will you be so kind as to lend mother a sarsepan," says I. You should have seen her. "Get out, you little sarpent," says she; "make tracks about the quickest, or I'll put you in the ash hole." So I ran stamping like thunder all the way up into the parlor.

Mrs. Peck: And did not the boys give you anything for Christmas?

Dick: They asked me to play to them, and I did; and then I told them about the pudding, and that we had no sarsepan to cook it in. And then the biggest boy seem'd sorry, and said if we had no pudding we should want something to divert us, and so he gave me that beautiful teetotum.

[The *Dick* begins again to play.]

Mrs. Peck: Divert a fool's head [throws herself back in her chair]; the world's gone mad, and I am mad too. The more you want a thing, the more you can't get it. The more you don't want a thing, the more they give it to you. Here I just want to make a pudden for Christmas, and what have they given me to make it of?

Charley: A nice large bit of suet and the botherments of season; I don't know what they are.

Mrs. Peck: Yes, the suet is one thing, and the botherments, as you call them, I have too. Well the suet, a square of brown soap, a bundle of tracts, a pair of old red breeches, a receipt for a pudden, and a teetotum, children, that's for our Christmas pudden. [She laughs hysterically; the children laugh, too, till they see their mother begins to weep.] I give up; Christmas must go over, and no plum pudden. Who knows what will come of that? There was your poor father and I, always on our wedding day, as sure as it came, had pickled streaky pork and peas-pudden for dinner, till once we miss'd it, and in less than a week after he was call'd away. Yes, he died after that.

Jack: And why didn't you die, too, Mammy?

Mrs. Peck: Oh, Jackey, I couldn't, and I would not leave you all to the alms-house; and here I am now with six fatherless children and not a dollar, and no pudden. No merry Christmas for us — its all over. [A knocking at the door. *Susan* smooths up the things in the room. *Mrs. P.* tries to recover herself.] Some one knocks; open the door, Susan.

> [*Susan* opens the door. A stiff, perpendicular looking man enters. He has on a black coat, a white cravat, and green spectacles, and carries a blue cotton umbrella in one hand, and a red book in the other; an ink horn with a pen in it, dangles from a buttonhole.]

Mrs. Peck [looking fiercely at him]: Is it taxes you're come for? If it is, seize at once. I han't got a brass farden in the world. Here are six starving orphan children; that's the schedrule of my property.

> [She laughs again hysterically. The man looks round slowly and stiffly without speaking; at last sees *Dick.*]

Man in black [in a strong nasal tone]: Boy, didn't I see you peeping in at a cake shop, and didn't you say you was hungry?

Dick: Yes, sir, and you asked me if my mother wasn't in distress.

Man in black: Very good, very good; and you replied yes, you were in very great distress.

Dick: Yes, that's a fact, for a sarsepan to bile a pudden in, that we hain't got yet.

Man in black: Very good! very good!

Mrs. Peck: Yes, sir, you see very great distress; we've nothing to eat, and we want to have a pudden for Christmas, and I can't get any of the perkisites for a pudden. And see my six orphan children.

Man in black: Very good! very good! I'm a perambulating member of the district visitation and donation and consolation society. I am come to relieve your necessities.

Mrs. Peck [clasping her hands]: Blessings on you, sir. Then at last I shall have a Christmas pudden for my dear children. For years I have had one in a respectable way, and it would almost break my heart not to have one now.

Man in black: Very good! very good! [He takes his book and writes on one of the leaves; tears out the leaf and gives it to her.] There, good woman, is an order for what you are in want of. Providence provides.

Mrs. Peck [Starts up from her chair.]: Bless you! bless you, sir! I was near despair. You have saved us.

Man in black: Very good! very good! Always trust.

Mrs. Peck [Goes towards him as if she would take his hand; he motions her off.]: What is your name, generous stranger?

Man in black: 'Tis enough to know that I am an unworthy perambulating member of the district visitation, donation and consolation society.

Mrs. Peck: But, good sir, we can't remember all that; tell us your own particular Christian name, that we may remember it with gratitude.

Man in black: Very good! very good! My name is Habakuk Shuffletoe; but I'm nothing, nothing, but a fellow sinner, and a perambulating member of the district visitation, donation and consolation society.

Mrs. Peck: If the blessing of a poor widder and her six fatherless children is any reward to you, you have it.

[She and the children gather around him; he looks annoyed and motions them off.]

Man in black: Very good! very good! That's enough. [Takes away his hand from *Polly*.] That'll do, that'll do. Habakuk Shuffletoe, children, is my name. Widow, shall we sing a stave? [They sing.]

"See the wicked how they fly
From vani*tee* to vani*tye*,
And the unrighteous how they flee
From vani*tye* to vani*tee*"

[Exit *Man in Black.*]

Mrs. Peck: Now, children, you may be as merry as you please. So much for resolution. I said I would have a pudden, and here you see I've got it. [*Peter* sticks the breeches on a broom and marches round. *Polly* mimics *Shuffletoe's* "Very good!"] At last my pudden is sure. There, that'll do, children, it is time for one of you boys to go to the shop and get all the perkisites for our pudden. Of course its an order on the grocer for everything. Where did he put it, Susan?

Susan [at the table reading the paper: she looks troubled]: Mother, it's an order on Mr. Jones for six yards of flannel.

Mrs. Peck [screaming]: Six yards of flannel!

[She snatches the order from *Susan*; looks at it, drops it, and falls into a chair. Stares stupidly at the wall. The children gather round her and try to comfort her. She pushes them away.]

Mrs. Peck: Don't touch me, don't comfort me, I won't be comforted. Don't help me, if you see me sinking into the floor, I'm like an over-driv beast. I don't know what I may do.

[The children run away from her all but *Susan*, who is a little behind her. After a short silence she screams out —]

Wipe Jackey's nose.

[All the children run to wipe the little fellow's nose; *Polly* has no handkerchief; takes the tail of her gown; the boy

                              struggles, and *Susan* gently
                              leads him off.]

Tear up that horrid paper.

                              [*Susan* takes it up, and is
                              putting it in her pocket.]

   Susan: Six yards of flannel are much better than nothing.

   Polly [Flies at her, seizes it and tears it into atoms.]: We won't keep the nasty thing. "Very good," "Very good," — the scamp, we won't keep his nasty order.

   Mrs. Peck: I've hoped as long as hoping was any good. [She rises excitedly.] I won't hope any longer, that I won't. I give up — blow upon blow. Luck sets all one way. This last is the drop too much. We shall never prosper, never have another Christmas pudden, never, never, never. We're a starving family, and if it wasn't wicked, I'd tie you all round my neck and jump into the frog-pond with you, and die like our poor cat and kittens.

   Jack: I won't be tied round your neck and jump into the frog-pond.

   Dick: Nor I.

   Charley: Nor I.

   Peter: Nor none of us, nor you, mother, won't do so.

                              [She bends her head over the
                              table. *Susan* quietly puts her
                              arm round her. *Polly* kneels
                              down and puts her head in her
                              mother's lap. *Jack* creeps close
                              up to her, and takes her hand,
                              and the curtain falls.]

                           SCENE II

Mrs. Peck at the table, on which is a pitcher of water and two or three mugs. A plate with part of a loaf of bread on it. *Peter* is trying to pull on the red breeches. *Dick* is playing his jews'-harp. *Polly* tosses away the bit of soap which was lying on one of the chairs, the other boys are playing with the teetotum. *Susan* picks up the soap and tries to set the room in order. A small tallow candle on the table.

Mrs. Peck: Come, children, eat what supper I have for you — bread and water — your last as far as I can see. Poverty's a staring us all in the face, every one on you. I can't get work; I can't get nothing. I shall have to give up. No merry Christmas, no pudden, no nothing. Eat your bread and drink some water, and go to bed, and leave me to break my heart alone by myself.

Susan: Dear mother, don't despair; we can change the suet for a bit of lean meat to-morrow. You can sell the old breeches for something.

Polly: And I'll sell the soap, nasty stuff.

Peter: I know a great goney that perhaps will buy the breeches. He wears a delivery sometimes.

Charley: We can't sell the books, so let's make a fire of them.

Jack: And here, mother, here's a five cent piece a fat man gave me for picking up his cane for him.

Mrs. Peck: Don't talk, children, I can't bear it; I did hope to have a Christmas pudden for you to-morrow. I'd set my heart on it.

Susan: Mother, you've cut the bread into only six pieces, and taken none for yourself.

Mrs. Peck: I don't want any, Susan. Eat your dry bread, children; don't ask me to eat. I can't, when you have so little.

> [The children each break off a
> piece of their bread and put it
> before her.]

Dick: I won't eat, mother, if you don't.

Charley: Nor I.

Polly: Nor I.

Jack: Mammy, take a piece of little Jack's. I know you will.

Peter: I have more than I want.

Susan: Dear mother, eat a little to please us. Don't be down-hearted. Haven't I heard you say, "The darkest day, Live till to-morrow, will pass away." Come, mother, let us hope for brighter days to come.

Mrs. Peck: I shall never hope again. My poor children — I cannot bear to look at you. Rich people talk of poverty; what do they know about it? Could they feel for one moment the bitterness of a mother's heart when she looks upon her hungry children, and has nothing to give them but her tears, they would know what poverty is.

Susan: I know we shall have some help yet. At Christmas time mother, rich people do remember the poor.

Mrs. Peck: I can't hope; I'm like a pelican in the wilderness smiling at grief; I've nothing to give you all but my heart's blood.

Jack: I won't have that any how, so don't talk so, Mammy.

> [A knocking at the door. *Polly* opens it. A stranger enters; he has gray hair and a long beard, and a large cloak on. He looks earnestly at the whole family before he speaks; then addresses *Mrs. Peck*.]

Stranger: You have had, good woman, a visit to-day from a perambulating member of some charitable society?

Mrs. Peck: That we have, and be hanged to him, with his "Very good! very good!" and his "Visitation, donation and consolation society."

Stranger: And you told him you were in distress?

Mrs. Peck: Yes I did, in distress for something to make a Christmas pudden of for my hungry children.

Stranger: And he said he was come to relieve you, and he gave you something?

Mrs. Peck: Yes, indeed, six yards of flannel to make a pudden of. [The children repeat her words.]

Stranger: Hold your tongues, children. [He turns away to laugh.] And this man's name was, I think, Habakuk Shuffletoe?

Mrs. Peck: The very man, sir, with his long face and his psalm singing, and his "Very good! very good!"

Stranger [laughing]: But let's to business. Pol— [He stops, turns away, and recovers his first voice, which he had lost when he nearly said Polly.] You have seen better days, Mrs. Peck; that is your name, I think?

Mrs. Peck: That I have, sir. My father lived in a house with a buffalo on the top, and a pizarro all round it, and a beautiful front door with a turpentine walk up to it, and he made soap and candles to report to furren parts, and folks said Mr. Peck had a good ketch when he got me. But at last my father fail'd and lost everything, and if it hadn't been for that, and if Mr. Peck hadn't died five years ago and left nothing but debts, and me with six children, and my brother Jack hadn't a gone to Calliforny, and I never heard of him since, I should have been as respectable and well off a person as anybody, and good company for the smartest folks, instead of being nothing but the poor Widder Peck, with six starving children, and no soul to help me or them.

Stranger: You spoke of your brother Jack, where is he?

Mrs. Peck [Looks at him, he turns away, and pats little Jack's head.]: He went, as I told you, to Calliforny six years ago, and we han't heard a word from him; he was as generous as a prince, but I s'pose he's dead. Maybe the Kangaroo Indians have eaten him up. I loved him dearly. I named my youngest after him; I often tell my children about their uncle Jack.

Stranger [much moved]: Come, let's to business. Hearing that you had seen better days, and were a sufferer, and had six orphan children, I have come to help you. You want at present a Christmas pudding. I like old customs too. I must do something for this pudding.

Mrs. Peck: Are you a perambulating member of the visitation, donation and consolation society?

Stranger: No; I go on my own hook. Here's a purse; use it freely, and have a good pudding, and send one of your boys at 9 o'clock to-morrow to this place on this card. We'll see if we can't find a new dress for Christmas Day for them and the girls, and we'll have some evergreens to dressup your room with, and you'll let me come and dine with you, and we'll have a merry Christmas after all, as sure as my name is [he stops].

Mrs. Peck: What is your name [much agitated]; what is your name? Tell me.

Stranger [in an old cracked voice]: Never mind an old man's name; a friend, that's enough.

Mrs. Peck [she tries to look in his eye]: He's too old; it can't be; angel of mercy tell me your name; I feel so kind of all overish every now and then when you speak.

Stranger: I'll tell you my name to-morrow when I come to dinner. [The children gather round him; he kisses them all.] You dine at 2; send the children at 9. Good bye Pol— oh, poor Widow Peck, I mean.

Mrs. Peck: What did you say? [Looks earnestly at him.]

Stranger: Nothing. Good bye, good bye; that's all.

Mrs. Peck: What can all this mean? I never felt so in my life. I feel so I don't know howish; so a sort of all goneish. What an anonimous day it has been. Is this a real purse with money in it? He almost call'd me Polly. He's an angel without wings. Children, all of you run off to bed after you have eaten your bread and water, and think of to-morrow. I'll go after the perkisites for our Christmas pudden myself. After all I shall have it.

[Curtain falls.]

The End

BIBLIOGRAPHY

It is not my intention that this bibliography be comprehensive. What I hope it will do is give readers a list of the chief sources I used in compiling this anthology and, more importantly, give researchers in the field a place to begin their work. It is chiefly for the convenience of future researchers that the bibliography is arranged in the categories it is.

BIBLIOGRAPHIES

Bibliographie de la Littérature Française du dix-huitième siècle. 3 vols. Edited by Alexendre Cioranescu. Paris: Éditions du Centre National de la Recherche Scientifique, 1969.

Blanck, Jacob. *Bibliography of American Literature*. Edited by Virginia L. Smyers and Michael Winship. New Haven and London: Yale University Press, 1983.

Bond, Donald F., comp. *The Eighteenth Century*. Northbrook, Illinois: AHM Publishing Corp., [1975].

British Library. Department of Printed Books. *Eighteenth-Century British Books: A Subject Catalogue Extracted from the British Museum General Catalogue of Printed Books by G. Averley [et al.]*. Folkestone, Eng.: Dawson, 1979.

Cambridge Bibliography of English Literature. Cambridge: Cambridge University Press, 1969.

Faxon, Frederick W. *Literary Annuals and Gift Books: A Bibliography, 1823–1903.* Reprinted with supplementary essays by Eleanore Jamieson and Ian Bain. [Pinner, Middlesex]: Private Libraries Association, 1973.

Hixon, Don L., and Don A. Hennessee. *Nineteenth-Century American Drama: A Finding Guide.* Metuchen, N.J. and London: Scarecrow Press, 1977.

Levy, Jonathan, and Martha Mahard. "Preliminary Checklist of Early Printed Children's Plays in English, 1780–1855." In *Performing Arts Resources,* edited by Barbara Naomi Cohen-Stratyner, vol. 12, 1–97. New York: Theatre Library Association, 1987.

Stratman, Carl J. *Britain's Theatrical Periodicals, 1720–1967: A Bibliography.* New York: New York Public Library, 1972.

Stratman, Carl J., David G. Spencer, and Mary Elizabeth Devine, eds. *Restoration and Eighteenth Century Theatre Research: A Bibliographical Guide.* Carbondale, Ill.: Southern Illinois University Press, 1971.

Tanselle, G. Thomas. *Guide to the Study of United States Imprints.* 2 vols. Cambridge: Harvard University Press, Belknap Press, 1971.

COLLECTIVE BIOGRAPHY

Allibone, S. Austin. *A Critical Dictionary of English Literature and British and American Authors living and deceased from the earliest accounts to the latter half of the nineteenth century.* Philadelphia: J. B. Lippincott and Co., 1858; Detroit: Gale Research Company, 1965.

Appleton's Cyclopedia of American Biography. New York: D. Appleton and Company, 1889.

Baker, David Erskine, et al. *Biographica Dramatica, or, A Companion to the playhouse, containing Historical and critical Memoirs, and original Anecdotes, of British and Irish Dramatic Writers [. . .].* 3 vols. London: Longman,

Hurst, Rees, Orme et al., 1812; New York: AMS Press, Inc., 1966.

Biographie générale depuis les temps les plus reculés jusqu'à nos jours, avec les renseignements bibliographiques et l'indication des sources à consulter. Paris: Firmin Didot Frères, 1861.

[Boase, Frederic]. *Modern English Biography.* 3 vols. London: Frank Cass and Co., Ltd., 1965. [Originally published 1892–1921 in 6 vols.]

Dictionary of American Biography. 2d ed. New York: Charles Scribner's Sons, 1928.

Dictionary of National Biography. Edited by Sir Leslie Stephen and Sir Sidney Lee. London: Oxford University Press, 1901.

Dictionnaire de Biographie Française. Paris: Letouzey et Ané, 1956.

National Cyclopedia of American Biography. New York: James T. White, 1898.

Nouvelle Biographie Générale. Paris: Firmin Didot Frères, Fils et Cie, 1858.

GENERAL REFERENCE

Andreae, Gesiena. *The Dawn of Juvenile Literature in England.* Amsterdam: H. J. Paris, 1925.

Annals of the American Pulpit. Edited by William B. Sprague. New York: Robert Carter and Brothers, 1865.

Auerbach, Nina. *Private Theatricals: The Lives of the Victorians.* Cambridge and London: Harvard University Press, 1990.

Barish, Jonas. *The Antitheatrical Prejudice.* Berkeley and Los Angeles, and London: University of California Press, 1981.

Barnes, Eric. *Anna Cora: The Life and Theatre of Anna Cora Mowatt.* London: Secker and Warburg, 1954.

Barnett, Dene. *The Art of Gesture: The Practice and Principles of 18th Century Acting.* Heidelberg: Carl Winter Universitätsverlag, 1987.

Barry, Florence V. *A Century of Children's Books*. London: Methuen & Co., Ltd., [1922].

Bate, Walter Jackson. *Samuel Johnson*. New York and London: Harcourt Brace Jovanovich, 1977.

Bernbaum, Ernest. *The Drama of Sensibility: A Sketch of the History of English Sentimental Comedy and Domestic Tragedy, 1696–1780*. Harvard Studies in English, vol. 3. Gloucester, Mass.: Peter Smith, 1958.

Booth, Michael, ed. *Prefaces to English Nineteenth Century Theatre*. Manchester: Manchester University Press, [1980].

Brenner, Clarence D. *Le développement du proverbe dramatique en France et sa vogue au XVIIIe siècle, avec un proverbe inédit de Carmontelle*. Berkeley: University of California Press, 1937.

Brenner, Clarence D., and Nolan A. Goodyear, eds. *Eighteenth-Century French Plays*. New York: Appleton-Century-Crofts, Inc., 1927.

Campbell, Lily B. *Divine Poetry and Drama in Sixteenth-Century England*. Cambridge: Cambridge University Press; Berkeley and Los Angeles: University of California Press, 1961.

Caron de Chanset, J.-B.-P. "Essai sur l'art dramatico proverbial." In *Le Courrier d'Henri IV*. La Haye and Paris: Rue Saint-Jean-de-Beauvais, 1775.

Carpenter, Humphrey, and Mari Prichard, eds. *The Oxford Companion to Children's Literature*. 4th ed. New York: Oxford University Press, 1984.

Clark, Barrett. *European Theories of the Drama with a Supplement on the American Drama*. Revised by Henry Popkin. New York: Crown Publishers, 1965.

Cushing, William. *Anonyms: A Dictionary of Revealed Authorship*. Cambridge, Mass.: William Cushing, 1889.

____. *Initials and Pseudonyms: A Dictionary of Literary Disguises*. Waltham, Mass.: Mark Press, Inc., 1963.

Darton, F. J. Harvey. *Children's Books in England: Five Centuries of Social Life*. 3d ed., revised by Brian Alderson. Cambridge: Cambridge University Press, 1982.

Davis, James Herbert, Jr. *The Happy Island: Images of Childhood in the Eighteenth-Century French Théâtre d'Education*. New York/Bern/Frankfurt am Mein/Paris: Peter Lang, 1987.

Davis, Tracy G. "The Actress in Victorian Pornography." *Theatre Journal*, 41 (October 1989): 292–315.

Dictionnaire des Lettres Françaises. Publié sous la direction de Georges Grente [et al.]. Paris: Librarie Arthème Fayard, 1951–.

Enciclopedia dello Spettacolo. 9 vols. Roma: Casa Editrice Le Maschere, 1954–1962.

Encyclopaedia Britannica; or, A Dictionary of Arts and Sciences. 3 vols. Edinburgh: A Bell and C. Mcfarquhar, 1771.

European Theories of the Drama, with a Supplement on the American Drama. Edited by Barrett Clark, revised by Henry Popkin. New York: Crown Publishers, 1965.

Field, Louise Frances (Story). *The Child and His Book. Some Account of the History and Progress of Children's Literature in England*. 2d ed. London: Wells, Gardner, Darton and Co., [1892].

Frye, Northrop. "Towards defining an Age of Sensibility." In *Eighteenth Century English Literature. Modern Essays in Criticism*, edited by James Clifford, 311–18. New York: Oxford University Press, 1959.

Fülöp-Miller, René. *The Jesuits: A History of the Society of Jesus*. New York: Capricorn Books, 1963.

[Genest, John]. *Some Account of the English Stage, from the Restoration in 1660 to 1830*. 10 vols. Bath: H. E. Carrington, 1832.

Gignilliat, George Warren, Jr. *The Author of Sandford and Merton: A Life of Thomas Day, Esq*. New York: Columbia University Press, 1932.

Gofflot, L. V. *Le Théâtre au College du Moyen Age à nos Jours*. Paris: H. Champion, 1907.

Griffin, Nigel. *Jesuit School Drama: A Checklist of Critical Literature*. London: Grant and Cutler, 1976.

Halsey, Rosalie V. *Forgotten Books of the American Nursery: A*

History of the Development of the American Story-book.
Boston: C. E. Goodspeed, 1911.

Hart, James D., ed. *The Oxford Companion to American Literature.* 4th ed. New York: Oxford University Press, 1980.

Hartnoll, Phyllis, ed. *The Oxford Companion to the Theatre.* 3rd ed. London: Oxford University Press, 1967.

Hawkins, Frederick. *The French Stage in the Eighteenth Century.* 2 vols. London: Chapman and Hall, 1888.

Hearne, Betsy. *Beauty and the Beast: Visions and Revisions of an Old Tale.* Chicago and London: University of Chicago Press, 1989.

Herold, Christopher. *Mistress to an Age: A Life of Madame de Staël.* Indianapolis and New York: Bobbs-Merrill Company, [1958].

Hewins, Caroline M. *A Mid-Century Child and Her Books.* New York: Macmillan Company, 1926.

Hogan, Charles Beecher, ed. *The London Stage, 1660–1800: A Calendar of Plays, Entertainments & Afterpieces,* 5 vols. Carbondale: Southern Illinois University Press, 1968.

Journal Encyclopédique, 1756–1793. France: A Lenardan; Genève: Slatkine Reprints, 1976.

Jourdain, Eleanor F. *Dramatic Theory and Practice in France, 1690–1808.* London: Longmans, Reed, and Co, 1921.

Kelly, Katherine. "The Queen's Two Bodies: Shakespeare's Boy Actresses in Breeches." *Theatre Journal,* 42(1) (March 1990): 81–93.

Kemble, Frances Ann. *Records of a Girlhood.* 2 vols. New York: Henry Holt and Company, 1878.

____. *Records of Later Life.* New York: Henry Holt and Company, 1882.

Kiefer, Monica. *American Children through Their Books, 1700–1835.* Philadelphia: University of Pennsylvania Press, 1948.

Kinne, Willard Austin. *Revivals and Importations of French Comedies in England, 1749–1800.* New York: Columbia University Press, 1939.

Kurz, Harry. *European Characters in French Drama of the Eighteenth Century.* New York: Columbia University

Press, 1916.

La Tour du Pin Gouvernet, Henriette Lucie Dillon, marquise de. *Memoirs of Madame de La Tour du Pin.* Edited and translated by Felice Harcourt. Introduction by Peter Gay. New York: McCall Publishing Company; London: Harville P., 1969.

Lamb, Charles. *The Letters of Charles Lamb to which are added those of his sister Mary Lamb.* 3 vols. Edited by E. V. Lucas. London: J. M. Dent and Sons, and Methuen and Co., Ltd., 1935.

____. *The Works of Charles and Mary Lamb.* London: Methuen and Co., 1903; New York: AMS Press, 1968.

Leathers, Victor. *British Entertainers in France.* Toronto: University of Toronto Press, 1959.

Levy, Jonathan. *A Theatre of the Imagination.* Rowayton, Conn.: New Plays Incorporated, 1987.

Lynch, James J. *Box, Pit and Gallery: Stage and Society in Johnson's London.* Berkeley and Los Angeles: University of California Press, 1953.

McCabe, William H. *An Introduction to the Jesuit Theater. A Posthumous Work.* Edited by Louis J. Oldani. St. Louis: Institute of Jesuit Sources, 1983.

McCaslin, Nellie. *Theatre for Children in the United States: A History.* Norman: University of Oklahoma Press, 1971.

MacLeod, Anne Scott. *A Moral Tale: Children's Fiction and American Culture, 1820–1860.* Hamden, Conn.: Shoestring Press, 1975.

Meigs, Cornelia Lynde, ed. *A Critical History of Children's Literature. A Survey of Children's Books in English, Prepared in Four Parts by Cornelia Meigs [et al.].* Rev. ed. New York: Macmillan Publishing Co., 1969.

Meserve, Walter. *An Emerging Entertainment: The Drama of the American People to 1828.* Bloomingon: University of Indiana Press, 1977.

Mowatt, Anna Cora. *Autobiography of an Actress: or, Eight Years on the Stage.* Boston: Ticknor, Reed, and Fields, 1854.

The New England Primer improved for the more easy of true reading of English. To which is added the Assembly and

Mr. Cotton Mather's Catechism. Boston: Edward Draper, 1777.

A New theatrical dictionary, containing an account of all the dramatic pieces that have appeared from the commencement of theatrical exhibitions to the present time. London: S. Bladon, 1792.

Nicoll, Allardyce. *A History of English Drama, 1660–1900.* 6 vols. Cambridge: Cambridge University Press, 1967.

The Oxford Book of Light Verse. Chosen by W. H. Auden. Oxford: Clarendon Press, 1938.

Pickering, Samuel F., Jr. *John Locke and Children's Books in Eighteenth Century England.* Knoxville: University of Tennessee Press, 1981.

Proceedings in observance of the one hundred and fiftieth anniversary of the First Church in Lincoln, Massachusetts, August 21 and September 4, 1898. Cambridge: Cambridge University Press, 1899.

The Reader's Encyclopedia of World Drama. John Gassner and Edward Quinn, eds. New York: Thomas Y. Crowell Company, 1969.

Receuil général des proverbes dramatiques en vers et en prose, tant imprimés que manuscrits. 16 vols. London [i.e. Paris?]: Chez les libraires qui vendent les nouvautés, 1785.

Robert Merry's Museum. Edited by S. G. Goodrich. Boston: Bradbury and Soden, 1841.

Roe, Gordon F. *The Victorian Child.* London: Phoenix House Ltd., 1959.

Roston, Murray. *Biblical Drama in England from the Middle Ages to the Present Day.* Evanston, Ill.: Northwestern University Press, 1968.

Seneca, Lucius Annaeus. *Letters from a Stoic. Epistulae Morales ad Lucilium.* Selected and translated with an Introduction by Robin Campbell. London and New York: Penguin Books, 1969.

Shapiro, Michael. *Children of the Revels: The Boy Companies of Shakespeare's Time and Their Plays.* New York: Columbia University Press, 1977.

Sherbo, Arthur. *English Sentimental Drama*. East Lansing, Mich.: Michigan State University Press, 1977.

Simons, Joseph. *Jesuit Theater Englished: Five Tragedies of Joseph Simons*. Translated from the Latin by Ricahrd E. Arnold [et al.], edited by Louis J. Oldani and Philip C. Fischer. St. Louis: Institute of Jesuit Sources, 1989.

Sloane, William. *Children's Books in England and America in the Seventeenth Century*. New York: King's Crown Press, 1955.

Smith, Sydney. *The Works of Sydney Smith*. 3 vols. Philadelphia: Casey and Holt, 1844.

Vail Motter, Thomas Hubbard. *The School Drama in England*. Port Washington [N.Y.]: Kennikat Press, [1968].

Waldo, Lewis P. *The French Drama in America in the Eighteenth Century and Its Influence on the American Drama of That Period, 1701–1800*. Baltimore: Johns Hopkins Press, 1942.

Wordsworth, William, and Samuel Taylor Coleridge. *Lyrical Ballads*. W. J. B. Owen, ed. London: Oxford University Press, 1967.

Wray, Edith. "English Adaptations of French Drama between 1780 and 1815." *Modern Language Notes*, 43 (1928): 87–90.

WORKS ABOUT INDIVIDUAL PLAYWRIGHTS

Butler, Marilyn. *Maria Edgeworth: A Literary Biography*. Oxford: Clarendon Press, 1972.

Carrière, J. M. "Berquin's Adaptations from German Dramatic Literature." *Studies in Philology*, 32 (1935): 608–17.

Forster, E. M. "Hannah More." In *Abinger Harvest*, 229–35. New York: Meridian Books, 1955.

Foster, Edward Halsey. *Catharine Maria Sedgwick*. New York: Twayne, 1974.

Hare, Augustus J. C. *Maria Edgeworth: Life and Letters*. 2 vols. Boston: Houghton Mifflin, 1895.

Harmond, Jean. *A Keeper of Royal Secrets: Being the Private and Political Life of Madame de Genlis*. Preface by Émile

Faguet. New York: Brentano's, 1913.

Jauffret, Louis-François. *Oeuvres de Berquin, mises en ordre.* Paris: Chez Le Clerc, 1802.

Jones, M. G. *Hannah More.* Cambridge: Cambridge University Press, 1952.

Krakeur, Lester Gilbert. "Le Théâtre de Madame de Genlis." *Modern Language Reivew*, 35 (1940): 185–93.

Levy, Jonathan. "The Dramatic Dialogues of Charles Stearns: An Appreciation." In *Spotlight on the Child: Studies in the History of American Children's Theatre.* Edited by Roger L. Bedard and John Tolch. Westport, Conn.: Greenwood Press, 1989.

Longfellow, Henry Wadsworth. *The Letters of Henry Wadsworth Longfellow.* Edited by Andrew Hilen. 2 vols. Cambridge: Harvard University Press, Belknap Press, 1966.

Macpherson, Geraldine Bate. *Memoirs of the Life of Anna Jameson, Author of "Sacred and Legendary Art," etc. by her niece.* Edited by Margaret O. (Wilson) Oliphant. Boston: Roberts Brothers, 1878.

Morin, Paul. *Les source de l'oeuvre de Henry Wadsworth Longfellow.* Paris: Emile Larose, 1913.

Murch, Jerom. *Mrs. Barbauld and Her Contemporaries: Sketches of Some Eminent Literary and Scientific English Women.* London: Longman, Green and Co., 1878.

Newby, P. H. *Maria Edgeworth.* London: Arthur Barker, Ltd., 1950.

Newcomer, James. *Maria Edgeworth.* Lewisburg, Pa.: Bucknell University Press, 1973.

Oliver, Grace A. *A Study of Maria Edgeworth, with Notices of her Father and Friends.* Boston: A. Williams and Company, 1882.

"[Review of Hannah More.]" *The Critical Review; or, Annals of Literature*, 199–204. London: A. Hamilton, 1782.

"[Review of Hannah More.]" *The Monthly Review; or, Literary Journal*, 75 (1786): 31–35.

"[Review of] *Théâtre à l'usage des jeunes personnes, vol. 1.*" Lettre VI. *L'Année littéraire* (1779): 104–32.

"[Review of] *Théâtre à l'usage des jeunes personnes.*" *Journal encyclopédique ou universel.* (1780): 103–14.

"[Review of] *Théâtre de Societé.*" Lettre XI. *l'Année littéraire* (1781): 217–48.

Schmidt-Clausen, Uta. *Michel-Theodore Leclercq und das Proverbe dramatique der Restauration.* Braunsschweig: G. Westerman, 1971.

Sedgwick, Catharine Maria. *Life and Letters of Catharine M. Sedgwick.* Edited by mary E. Dewey. New York: Harper and Brothers, 1871.

Slade, Bertha Coolidge. *Maria Edgeworth, 1769–1849: A Bibliographical Tribute.* London: Constable Publishers, [1937].

"[Summary of a performance at Covent Garden of Mme de Genlis's] *The Child of Nature,*" *The London Stage* (November 28, 1788), Carbondale, Ill.: Southern Illinois University Press, 1960–1968.

Thomas, Clara. *Love and Work Enough: The Life of Anna Jameson.* Toronto: University of Toronto Press, 1966.

Wahba, Magdi. "'Madame de Genlis in England.'" *Comparative Literature,* 13 (1961): 221–38.

Welsh, Mary Michael, sister. *Catharine Maria Sedgwick: Her Position in the Literature and Thought of Her Time up to 1860.* Washington: Catholic University of America, 1937.

Yonge, Charlotte. *Hannah More.* Boston: Roberts Brothers, 1888.

WORKS BY INDIVIDUAL PLAYWRIGHTS

Amalie, Princess of Saxony. *Social Life in Germany, Illustrated in the Acted Dramas of Her Royal Highness, the Princess Amelia of Saxony.* London: Saunders and Otley, 1840.

Barbauld, Anna. *The Works of Anna Laetitia Barbauld.* 2 vols. London: Longman, Hurst, Rees, Orme, Brown, and Green, 1825.

Berquin, Arnaud. *The Children's Friend.* Boston: Folsom, [1790?]; reprinted Newburyport, [1794].

____. *The Looking-Glass for the Mind: or, Intellectual Mirror.* London: E. Newbery, 1792.

Brackenridge, Hugh Henry. *The Battle of Bunker's Hill: A Dramatic Piece of Five Acts, in Heroic Measure.* Philadelphia: Robert Bell, 1776.

Collett, John. *Sacred Dramas: Intended chiefly for young Persons.* Evesham: [Longman and Co.?], 1805.

The Common School Journal. Vol. 1, no. 1 (Nov. 1838) — v. 13, no. 24 (Dec. 15, 1851). Boston: [Marsh, Capen, Lyon, and Webb], 1839–1851. [Edited first by Horace Mann, then by William B. Fowle. Various publishers. Continued under the title: *The Common School Journal and Educational Reformer.*]

Corner, Julia. *Beauty and the Beast: An Entertainment for Young People.* Series 1, no. 1, of *Little Plays for Little Actors.* London: Dean and Son, 1854.

"Cyrus: A Drama." in *Education at Home: or, A Father's Instructions.* London: Baldwin, Cradock and Joy, 1824.

Dramatic Pieces calculated to exemplify the mode of conduct which render young ladies both amiable and happy, when their school education is completed. 3 vols. London: John Marshall, [c. 1786]. [Preface signed "P.I."]

Edgeworth, Maria. *Comic Dramas, in Three Acts, by Maria Edgeworth.* Boston: Wells and Lilly, 1817.

____. *Little Plays for Children. The Grinding Organ, Dumb Andy, The Dame School Holiday. Parent's Assistant.* vol. 8. London: R. Hunter and Baldwin, Cradock, and Joy, 1827.

____. *Maria Edgeworth: Chosen Letters. With an Introduction by F. V. Barry.* Boston and New York: Houghton Mifflin Company, [1931].

Evenings in New England. Intended for Juvenile Amusement and Instruction. (By an American Lady) Boston: Cummings, Hilliard and Co., 1824.

Follen, Eliza Lee (Cabot), comp. *Home Dramas for Young People.* Boston and Cambridge: James Munroe and Company, 1859.

_____. "Mrs. Peck's Pudding." In *Hood's Magazine*, 2(12) (December 1844): [521]–35.

Fowle, William Bentley. *Familiar Dialogues and Popular Discussions, for Exhibition in Schools and Academies of Either Sex, and for the Amusement of Social Parties.* Boston: Tappan and Dennet; New York: Mark H. Newman; Philadelphia: Thomas Copperthwait & Co., 1844.

_____. *The Hundred Dialogues, New and Original; designed for Reading and Exhibition in Schools, Academies, and Private Circles.* Boston: Morris Cotton, 1856.

_____. *Parlour Dramas; or, Dramatic Scenes for Home Amusement.* Boston: Morris Cotton; New York: J. M. Fairchild, 1857.

Garnier, Charles Georges Thomas. *Nouveaux proverbes dramatiques [ou] receuil de comédies de societé pour servir de suite aux théâtres de societé et d'education.* Paris: Chez Cailleau, 1784.

Genlis, Stéphanie de. *The Juvenile Theatre. Containing the Best Dramatic Productions of the Celebrated Madam de Genlis.* New York: D. and G. Bruce, 1807.

[_____]. *Lessons of a governess to her pupils; or, Journal of the method adapted by Madame de Sillery-Brulart in the education of the children of M. d'Orléans.* 3 vols. London: G. G. J. and J. Robinson, 1792.

_____. *Memoirs of the Countess de Genlis.* 8 vols. London: Henry Colburn, 1825.

_____. *The Theatre of Education. A New Translation from the French of Madame la Marquise de Sillery, late Madame la Contesse de Genlis.* London: J. Walter, 1787.

_____. *Theatre of Education. Translated from the French of the Countess de Genlis. . . . In four volumes.* London: T. Cadell and P. Elmsley, and T. Durham, 1781.

Godwin, William. *Dramas for Children, Imitated from the French of L. F. Jauffret.* London: M. J. Godwin, 1808.

Hare, Augustus J. C. *The Life and Letters of Maria Edgeworth.* Boston and New York: Houghton Mifflin Company, n.d.

Hoole, Barbara Hofland (Wreaks). *Little Dramas for Young People.* London: Longman, Hurst, Rees, and Orme, 1810.

Howitt, Mary. "The Grandmother." In *Christmas Blossoms and New Year's Wreath for 1852*. Boston: Phillips and Sampson, 1852.

Jameson, Anna. *A Commonplace Book of Thoughts, Memories, and Fancies*. New York: D. Appleton and Company, 1855.

____. "Much Coin, Much Care." In *Home Dramas for Young People*. Compiled by Eliza Follen, [125]–50. Boston and Cambridge: James Munroe and Company, 1859.

Jauffret, Louis-François. *Théâtre de Famille*. 2 vols. Paris: Impr. de Guilmet, an VIII, [1800].

Leclercq, Théodore. *Proverbes dramatiques*. Paris: Aimé André/Ladrange, 1835.

Longfellow, Henry Wadsworth. *Manuel de Proverbes Dramatiques . . .* Portland, [Maine]: Samuel Colman, 1830; 2d ed., 1832.

More, Hannah. *Sacred Dramas: Chiefly Intended for Young Persons: The Subjects Taken from the Bible. To Which Is Added, Sensibility, A Poem*. London: T. Cadell, 1782.

____. *The Works of Hannah More*. 2 vols. New York: Harper and Brothers, 1835.

Morney, Charles Auguste Louis Joseph, duc de. *La manie des proverbes, proverbe en un acte, arrangé par M. de Saint-Rémy [pseud.]*. Paris: Michel Lévy, 1862.

Pierce, Sarah. "Ruth." [1811?]. [From an unfinished manuscript in the possession of the Litchfield (Connecticut) Historical Society].

Sedgwick, Catharine Maria. *The Deformed Boy*. Brookfield: E. and G. Merriam, 1826.

Stearns, Charles. *Dramatic dialogues for the use of schools*. Leominster, Mass.: John Prentiss and Co., 1798.

Storrs, Richard Salter. *A Dialogue Exhibiting Some of the Principles and Practical Consequences of Modern Infidelity*. Sag Harbor, N.Y.: Alden Spooner, 1806; Tarrytown, N.Y.: William Abbatt, 1932.

Weisse, Christian Felix. *Die beiden Huethe*. Prague und Leipsig: Bey Joseph Groebe, 1778.

INDEX